WERTHEIM FELLOWSHIP PUBLICATIONS

LONDON : HUMPHREY MILFORD
OXFORD UNIVERSITY PRESS

THE SWEDISH COLLECTIVE BARGAINING SYSTEM

BY

PAUL H. NORGREN

ASSISTANT PROFESSOR OF ECONOMICS
WORCESTER POLYTECHNIC INSTITUTE

CAMBRIDGE · MASSACHUSETTS
HARVARD UNIVERSITY PRESS
1941

PRINTED AT THE HARVARD UNIVERSITY PRESS
CAMBRIDGE, MASSACHUSETTS, U.S.A.

FOREWORD

Mr. Norgren's study of collective bargaining in Sweden is important because in that country one finds rapid economic progress combined with a high degree of labor organization and with powerful trade unions. Sweden has raised its per capita income as rapidly since 1900 as the United States, and its recovery from the depression beginning in 1929 has been far more complete than that of the United States. Mr. Norgren does not argue that the rapid economic progress of Sweden has been the result of the strength of organized labor there, but he points out that Sweden's experience demonstrates that highly developed collective bargaining is quite reconcilable with rapid economic progress.

Sweden obtains about one-third of her standard of living by sending goods abroad and by importing other goods. The necessity that she compete effectively in the export trade has influenced the policies of both unions and employers. What Mr. Norgren calls the Swedish "system" of collective bargaining has several features which should be of particular interest to American unions and employers. One is the high degree of organization on the part of employers. Not only are the larger employers organized into powerful national organizations, but these in turn belong to a federation which exercises a great influence over labor policies. Likewise, on the union side the federation of national unions exercises great influence over its members. Another feature is the prevalence of national agreements and the absence in these agreements of detailed restrictions which interfere with production. In part, the absence of such restrictions is the result of the national scope of the agreements, because it is not easy to write detailed shop rules into an agreement which covers an industry. Still another feature is the prevalence of the piece work system of payment which even extends on a considerable scale into the building trades.

Both unions and employers jealously guard the right to strike or to lockout. Mr. Norgren notes that collective bargaining in Sweden has not been unaccompanied by the loss of a considerable amount of time from industrial disputes and that there have been widespread and prolonged lockouts as well as strikes. Stoppages, however, have always been characterizd by a high degree of restraint on both sides. Collective bargaining in Sweden is more bilateral than it has yet become in most American industries because Swedish employers do not share the timidity of most American employers in resisting demands of trade unions. The reason for this probably is that negotiations in Sweden are usually industry-wide. Consequently, a shutdown does not mean that one employer loses his business to other domestic competitors — although it may mean losses to foreign competitors.

Of unusual interest is the emergence of long-range and national (as distinguished from industry-wide) wage bargaining as represented by the depression-recovery compromise between the leaders of the union and employer federations which Mr. Norgren describes. This compromise suggests that collective bargaining in Sweden may be reaching the point where it may be able to make a truly national wage policy which takes account of the effect of wage changes upon the entire economy. Plainly the setting of wages by thousands of local bargains or even by industry-wide bargains cannot be expected to take account of the total effect of wage changes, and one cannot avoid doubting whether near-universal setting of wages by collective bargaining will work satisfactorily, except in periods of rapid technological change, unless it is done by methods which take account of the effects upon the general level of employment.

Mr. Norgren has informed himself concerning his subject by extensive field work in Sweden. His study is notable for the clarity of its analysis and for balanced judgment. It should be of great interest to both employers and trade unionists in this country.

Sumner H. Slichter

AUTHOR'S PREFACE

THIS IS PRIMARILY a field work study. The original version was submitted to the Department of Economics at Harvard University as a doctoral dissertation in 1939. The analysis and most of the descriptive subject matter contained in Part Five have been added subsequently.

The data on which the study is based were gathered in Sweden during the summer vacations of 1937 and 1938, principally through interviews with labor leaders, employers, government officials and others intimately acquainted with the country's collective bargaining institution. These people were all very generous and coöperative, and supplied me with a great deal of information from their own experience and personal knowledge. They also made available to me — as gifts or loans, and often at considerable sacrifice — many of the publications which have been used in preparing the monograph.

Among those who gave most unsparingly of their time and resources were: Herr Albin Lind, editor of *Fackföreningsrörelsen*, official journal of the Swedish Federation of Trade Unions; Herr Knut Larsson, secretary of the Wood Products Union; Dr. Tage Lindbom, director, and Herr Ivar Dahlberg, librarian, of the Labor Movement Archives; Herr Gustaf Vahlberg, vice-chairman of the Metal Workers' Union; Herr Gustaf Söderlund, administrative director of the Swedish Employers' Federation; Herr Frithiof Söderback, director of the S. E. F.'s "General Branch"; Herr Georg Styrman, director of the Machine Industry Association; Herr Torsten Andersson, director of the Sawmill Industry Association; Herr Olle Ekblom, governor of Jönköping County and former state mediator in the Second District; Herr Carl Christian Schmidt, secretary of the State Mediation Service; Herr Gunnar Huss, general director, and Herr Gustaf Cederwall, staff member, of the State

Unemployment Commission. Two of those who were particularly generous are no longer living: Dr. Oskar Borge, director of the Labor Movement Archives, and Dr. Sigfrid Hansson, general director of the Royal Social Board.

I am especially indebted to the committee in charge of the Jacob Wertheim Fellowship on Industrial Relations of Harvard University, composed of Professors John D. Black, Richard S. Meriam, and Sumner H. Slichter, for a grant to defray the expenses of my second visit to Sweden, and for making it possible to have the monograph published. Professor Slichter has guided the course of the work throughout. It is chiefly owing to his counsel and encouragement that I have been able to persevere in this first attempt at field research. Professor Meriam, Professor Gunnar Myrdal, and Mr. Richard Sterner have read the manuscript, and have made many helpful suggestions.

I owe the greatest debt of all to my wife. Without her cheerful and wholly unstinting assumption of the incident burden of pecuniary and domestic cares it would have been impossible even to begin the task, much less carry it through to completion.

P. H. N.

March 17, 1941

CONTENTS

PART FOUR

BARGAINING WITHIN THE AGREEMENT FRAMEWORK

PART FIVE

CONCLUSION

TABLES

INTRODUCTION

Bargaining between organizations of workers and employers occupies an important place in the economic life of Sweden. It is the chief, one might almost say the only, means by which the wages and working conditions of the country's industrial wage earners are determined. It is, moreover, an old and established institution. In certain branches of economic activity it has been widely used for nearly half a century, and its present well-nigh universal application extends back over approximately two decades.

By contrast, collective bargaining in the United States has as yet scarcely progressed beyond the infant stage. Until very recently, established and (more or less) continuous dealings between employers and trade unions have been confined mainly to nonmanufacturing lines: coal mining, railroad transportation, printing, the building trades, and a few others. The managers of American factories have always been opposed to any other kind of labor contract than that with the individual worker; and, largely because of their unrelenting hostility toward wage earner organization in any form, unionism in the sphere of mass manufacturing has remained weak and ineffective — where it has existed at all.

During the past three or four years, to be sure, this situation has been considerably altered. Powerful unions have sprung up in a number of important fabrication industries and have gained recognition and bargaining rights. As a result, employers' and workers' representatives in hundreds of workplaces over the entire country have for the first time been faced with the problem of attempting to settle the terms of the labor bargain on a joint basis. Many of these attempts have been only partly successful, while others have failed altogether. And it is scarcely necessary to point out that lack of experience in bargaining has been one of the major factors militating against their success.

This difference in the relative maturity of worker organization and collective bargaining in the two countries suggests that if the lesson of Sweden's long experience in the field could be made available to American workers and employers, it would be of assistance to them in ironing out some of their difficulties. They should be able to profit not only from the positive attainments of the Swedish bargainers, but also from the mistakes they have made.

It was with this thought in mind that the writer undertook the investigation of which the present monograph is the outcome. The primary object has been to present an expository picture of the Swedish industrial-relations system and its functioning — i.e., to describe the principal terms of employment agreed upon between the parties to the collective labor contract, the methods and procedures by which these terms are arrived at, and the practices followed in applying them. In addition, an effort has been made to ascertain the policies adhered to by the organized workers and employers in their dealings with each other and to discover, where possible, the motives behind these policies.

As to scope, the aim has been to cover the whole, or at any rate the major part, of the country's productive activity. This has not been unduly difficult, for the interindustrial pattern of the Swedish bargaining setup is unusually homogeneous. Many of the principal agreement provisions and procedural methods are either identical or closely similar in all the principal industries — a fact which is attributable chiefly to the unifying influence of the workers' and employers' central federations. Because of the wide purview of the study, it has been necessary to place the heavier emphasis on these "overall" features; by the same token, the rules and practices which are peculiar to certain industries or occupations have received only minor attention.

This does not mean that studies of individual industries would not be worth while. On the contrary, a detailed exposition of how bargaining is carried on in such lines as iron and steel, textiles, and wood products would undoubtedly be of considerable value to the bargaining parties in the corresponding American industries. But the broader survey has seemed logically to come first, in that it provides a better vantage point from which to approach particular branches of production. The writer hopes to be able to make a thorough examination of some of the leading Swedish industries in the not-far-distant future. The chapters on wage bargaining in the building and machinery trades, included in the latter part of the present study, may be regarded as a first step in this direction.

The main body of the study falls naturally into three parts, dealing respectively with the contents of the collective agreements, the agreement-making process, and the bargaining which takes place during the operable life of the agreements. The sequence of the treatment is to some extent arbitrary, but not entirely so, for the contracts themselves contain the basic specifications from which the bargaining apparatus is built up. Moreover, both agreement making and intra-agreement-period bargaining are concerned primarily with the revision or adjustment of existing provisions.

In the section preceding the study proper an attempt has been made to trace the development of the unions and employers' associations and to show how the present scheme of relations between these organizations has evolved. It is hoped that this brief historical survey will provide the American reader with sufficient background to make the subsequent exposition clear.

PART ONE

THE DEVELOPMENT OF WORKERS' AND EMPLOYERS' ORGANIZATIONS

CHAPTER I

THE RISE AND GROWTH OF TRADE UNIONS IN SWEDEN

BEGINNINGS: FROM MASS PROTESTS TO LOCAL UNIONS

THE SWEDISH labor movement, using the term in its historical sense, may be said to have started in the late seventies and early eighties of the last century. Its earliest manifestations took the form of strikes among unorganized workers. Most of these strikes were of the nature of spontaneous protests against the low wages and bad working conditions prevalent in the country at that time.

The industrialization of Sweden had not begun until after 1850, but the codevelopments of this process — the establishment of factories and workshops in the larger centers of population by individualist entrepreneurs and the concentration in these centers of a mass of propertyless wage earners competing with each other for the available jobs — were already well under way. Along with industrialization had also come increased commercial contact with the outside world and its inevitable concomitant, increased sensitivity to economic crises and depressions.

It was during these depressions, when the competition-harassed factory owners sought to reduce wages, that most of the afore-mentioned spontaneous strikes took place. A number of uprisings of this sort had occurred during the 1860's, when Swedish industry was still in its infancy and the impact of the business cycle had not yet reached the proportions of a major shock. But in the main these were small, half-hearted and of brief duration. After a few days or weeks the workers' resources would give out, forcing them to return to work.

It was not until the next major slump, which began in 1879, that these "natural" strikes became a matter of serious concern. In May of that year the sawmill owners in and around Sundsvall cut the wages of their workers 15 to 20 per cent (from a level of about 50 cents a day). A plea for reconsideration of the cut by a workers' committee was turned down, whereupon some four or five thousand wage earners, mostly unskilled and all unorganized, left their jobs.

This strike was soon broken — although not until a regiment of infantry, despatched by order of the king, had surrounded the strikers and cowed them into submission. But the very magnitude of the walkout (it was by far the largest thing of its kind that had ever happened in Sweden) made the employers appreciate for the first time the potentialities latent in collective worker action. What is perhaps more important, it provided the workers with a significant example of the futility of unplanned, spontaneous attempts to defend themselves against arbitrary treatment by the employers. This aspect of the Sundsvall strike was undoubtedly one of the chief factors contributing to the growth of union sentiment in Sweden during the immediately ensuing years.

Trade unionism proper — i.e., the banding together of workers into formal associations for the purpose of improving their terms of employment — first began to make significant progress in 1882. Its rise at this time was due in no small measure to the efforts of an organization of woodworkers in Stockholm. This organization — one of the first trade unions (in the modern sense) to be established in Sweden [1] — had been formed in 1880 by a group of workers in a local joinery factory.[2]

In the summer of 1881 a strike of major proportions had broken out in the Stockholm building industry. Like its precursors, this strike was primarily a semi-instinctive mass

[1] In 1846 the craft journeymen's gilds (*skrågesällskap*), which had been in existence in Sweden since the twelfth century, were dissolved by law. With the advent of legal proscription, the gilds in certain trades were "converted" into sick and death benefit societies; but apart from this there was practically no organization among Swedish workers for more than thirty years thereafter. S. Hansson, *Den Svenska Fackföreningsrörelsen*, fifth edition (Stockholm, 1937), pp. 10–11.

[2] S. Hansson, *Svenska Träarbetareförbundets Historia, 1889–1923* (Stockholm, 1925), p. 36.

protest against low wages, and practically all of the participants were unorganized. Within a few weeks it too had ended in failure.

But while its immediate results were negative, the Stockholm conflict had important positive repercussions — thanks to the presence in the community of an active union organization. Realizing that the lack of united worker action had been the chief cause of the strike's collapse, the organized woodworkers began to spread the doctrine of unionism among the building craftsmen, and even among factory workers in other industries in the city. In December, 1881, they arranged a mass meeting in a local theater, to which wage earners in all lines of work were invited. The meeting was well attended, and resulted in the setting up of a committee to work out "a program and statutes for trade unions." This committee included — in addition to several members of the woodworkers' union — two painters, two shoemakers, a metal worker, a paper hanger and a stone cutter. Dr. Anton Nyström, a young physician who had acted as the workers' spokesman in the building strike, was chosen to lead the committee's deliberations.[3]

In March of the following year the committee presented the results of its efforts. Among other things it proposed that the projected unions should seek "to unite all workers in the trade, for the purpose of bettering their condition, both economically and socially, through the medium of discussions and through collective practical measures; to obtain for the workers a better income than the majority of them now have; to further the workers' skill in their trade; to set up pension funds and 'support funds'; if possible to prevent, through its intervention, scarcity of employment and strikes."[4] It also proposed the collection of 50 öre a month dues and the payment of strike benefits. Twenty thousand copies of this program were printed and distributed among the workers in Stockholm and in other cities and towns throughout the country.

[3] Hansson, *Den Svenska Fackföreningsrörelsen*, fifth edition, p. 17.

[4] Hansson, *Svenska Träarbetareförbundets Historia*, p. 39.

Although the actual results of this first definitive agitation, initiated by the Stockholm carpenters, cannot be accurately gauged, it appears to have done a good deal toward starting the Swedish trade union movement on its way. In the years immediately following many unions were formed, not only in the capital but in a number of other cities as well.[5] By 1886 organization among the workers had attained sufficient proportions to permit the convening, in Gothenburg, of a Scandinavian trade union congress, at which some fifty Swedish worker groups were represented.[6]

It is significant that this first substantial growth of the labor movement occurred not among the lowest and most miserable classes of workers but in the relatively well-paid craft occupations — chiefly the building, printing, and other "hand" trades.[7] The unskilled workers, despite their greater need of economic betterment, lacked the necessary background and capacity for getting together. In the first place, they constituted the lowest group in the community in point of native intelligence. The great bulk of them probably did not even realize that they were keeping one another's wages down through competition, much less appreciate that combination offered a means of overcoming the evil. Moreover, the very fact of their low economic state tended to make them listless and apathetic toward any suggestions for bettering themselves.

The craft workers, on the other hand, were not only inherently more intelligent and aggressive, but they also had within each trade a tradition of unity — carried over from the days of the gilds — and a mutual pride in their common stock of skill and knowledge which made it comparatively easy for them to build up compact and cohesive bodies for the purpose of furthering their common pecuniary interests.

[5] At least two of these, the Malmö woodworkers' union and the Lund bricklayers' union, are known to have incorporated the entire 1882 program in their original statutes.

[6] T. Lindbom, *Den Svenska Fackföreningsrörelsens Uppkomst* (Stockholm, 1938), pp. 95–101.

[7] The craft workers have, indeed, been the first to organize in practically all countries where unionism has gained a foothold.

Perhaps the most important *positive incentive* to organization among the skilled workers was the desire to keep their terms of employment from being undermined by "outsiders." The formation of unions in the early and middle eighties was confined mainly to urban communities. During this period a major migration from the rural districts to the cities was under way, and in consequence the competition for the available job opportunities in the latter was very keen. This movement affected the craftsmen more seriously than other occupations, for the "immigrants" with some knowledge of a skilled trade would offer to work at considerable reductions from the prevailing rate of pay, and the "native" workers would have to follow suit or lose their jobs. There is no doubt that the concern over this "progressive undercutting" was one of the major factors which led the skilled workers in the cities to band together.[8]

The next groups of wage earners to organize were those within the metal products and machinery trades — machinists, molders, blacksmiths, and other "iron workers" (*järnarbetare*). These workers were also above the average in intelligence and had a basis of solidarity in the skill and trade knowledge which they held in common. But unlike the craftsmen they had few traditions, for the manufacture of machinery and similar highly fabricated metal products in Sweden was scarcely more than two decades old. Another point of difference was that the metal workers' unions held less strictly to craft lines than those in the printing, woodworking, and other handwork occupations. For example, the Stockholm Ironworkers' Union, formed in 1884, included among its members at least four classes of

[8] Cf. Lindbom, *op. cit.*, pp. 37–44. It should be noted, however, that the principal means adopted by the skilled workers for keeping their wages up was group action rather than deliberate limitation of membership. Instances of unions excluding applicants on grounds of insufficient skill are not, indeed, entirely rare, but the available evidence indicates that it was far from being a widespread practice. Undoubtedly many of the city workers would have liked to draw a dividing line between competent and incompetent craftsmen, so as to shut out the "immigrants," but the possibility of successfully carrying out such a scheme was probably quite small.

workmen: filers, lathemen, smiths and "general mechanics." [9]

However, there was one large category of relatively highly skilled metal workers who did not come in at this time, nor indeed until many years later — those employed in the *järnbruk* or bulk iron and steel producing plants. The manufacture of iron and steel occupied a peculiar position in the Swedish industrial setup, and still does, to some extent. It was by far the oldest of the fabrication industries, some of the *järnbruk* having been in existence for over two hundred years. Moreover these plants — practically all located in rural villages in central Sweden — were owned by individual families, which had held possession of them for generations.

The worker staff at the typical *bruk* was also practically a fixed institution. Particular jobs and occupations in the steel-making process were handed down from father to son, and families of workers rarely moved into or out of the community. Under such conditions, it was only natural that there should exist a strong mutual feeling of loyalty and sympathy between the *brukspatron* and his millhands, a feeling which was strengthened by the fact that the latter were rated considerably higher in the social scale than the agricultural laborers who tilled the millowner's fields. The steel mill workers therefore, were bound to be poor union material. They had little incentive to form organizations among themselves, and union agitators from the cities found the wall of tradition and sentiment practically impossible to surmount. The marked differences in organizability between these people and the urban metal workers is evidenced by the fact that while a majority of the latter were union members by the middle nineties, the *bruksarbetare* did not come into the movement in any appreciable numbers until 1905, and even then only after a strong organizing campaign had been inaugurated by the central union in Stockholm.

[9] The molders, however, kept to themselves — and do to this day.

THE MOVEMENT WIDENS; NATIONAL UNIONS FORMED

At about the time when the metal workers in the larger cities were banding together, some of the older local organizations began to unite into central associations (*förbund*) covering whole geographical sections or even the entire country. The metal workers themselves founded such a national union in 1888. The locals had already begun to be involved in strikes and lockouts, and the desire for better financial support and greater bargaining power during these workless periods appears to have been the main causal factor in bringing them together.

The consolidation movement gathered headway during the succeeding decade, and by the turn of the century thirty-two national unions had been established. These were by no means all purely craft organizations. At least six of them — the "Laborers' and Factory Workers' Union" (*Grov- och fabriksarbetareförbundet*), and those of the transport, sawmill, leather, textile, and brewery workers — were, in fact, composed predominantly of people outside of the "skilled trades," in the narrow sense of the term.

It was during the early nineties that the first groups of unskilled workers overcame the natural handicaps that had been holding them back and began to form unions of their own. In this they received little direct aid from the craft unionists, who refused to admit them into their own organizations and only rarely took the trouble to help them band together into separate bodies.

However, the skilled workers did play an important *passive* role in getting their less fortunately situated fellows started along the road of collective self-help. Through their organizations they had already achieved substantial gains in wages and better working conditions, and it was only natural that the unskilled workers, whose terms of employment had improved little if at all, should sooner or later observe this and begin to emulate them. It would be more accurate, perhaps, to say that they had it called to their attention, for in almost every case the unskilled unions were built up through the efforts of zealous and energetic individuals, who succeeded in breaking down the workers' inertia only after years of persistent agitation.[10]

But unlike the craftsman the semiskilled and unskilled workers did not confine their organizations within narrow occupational lines. Indeed in one case — that of the aforementioned Laborers' and Factory Workers' Union — they went almost to the opposite extreme. The local organizations which united to form this body included such diverse elements as building laborers, longshoremen, teamsters, unskilled metal workers, and brickyard, sugar factory, wood pulp, and paper mill employees. It became what might be termed a "multi-industrial union," and such it remains (though with somewhat narrower scope) to this day. The available evidence indicates that it was the advantage of superior numbers more than anything else which induced these widely separated groups of workers to make common cause. Since they had no special skill to give them bargaining power, they had to pin their hopes on the only alternative — numerical strength.

Strange as it may seem, the Laborers' and Factory Workers' Union proved to be a quite outstandingly successful organization. What is more, it became a sort of "organizational nursery," from which several important national unions covering single industries later emerged. The first instance of this occurred in 1897, when a group of longshoremen broke away from the L. F. W. U. and formed the Transport Workers' Union. Like the parent organization, it became a conglomerate of occupations, including — besides longshoremen and other dock workers — teamsters, cab drivers, and even (nowadays) gasoline station attendants.[11]

[10] Prominent among these were: N. O. Vester, who organized the building laborers in Skåne; Charles Lindley, who performed a similar service for the dockworkers in Stockholm, and who later became the head of the Transport Workers' Union; and Janne Jönsson, the pioneer agitator among the paper mill workers. *Förbundskamraten* (Journal of the Laborers' and Factory Workers' Union), 1931, No. 4, pp. 12–18.

[11] More recently the L. F. W. U. has given birth to the Paper Workers' Union and the Road and Watercourse Workers' Union. See Chapter III, p. 55.

Of the remaining "unskilled" *förbund* founded during the nineties, special interest attaches to the sawmill workers' and the textile workers' unions, since these were the only two national organizations of major importance which took on a more or less purely industrial union character from the outset. In the lumber industry this was the most logical if not indeed the only workable form to adopt, for most of the jobs in the sawmills represented operations rather than trades, and the number of workers in each mill following the same occupation was usually small. Moreover, the difference in the skill required to perform the most difficult and least difficult tasks was not so great as to make this a crucial factor. Similarly with textiles, except that this industry harbored a special group of "aristocrats," the loom fixers, who considered themselves on a plane above the other workers. Shortly after the union's formation the loom fixers broke away and started an organization of their own, and they have continued in this *särställning* ever since. Of the other national unions the great majority were exclusively craft or unioccupational at the start. But the sawmill and textile unions formed a nucleus of industrial unionism which was later expanded by the addition of other similar bodies, until it encompassed by far the greater part of the country's organized labor force.[12]

COALITION: THE SWEDISH FEDERATION OF TRADE UNIONS

In 1897, the year when the transport and sawmill workers were consolidating their local unions into *förbund*, plans for a central organization of all the national unions began to materialize. The principal initiators of this scheme were Herman Lindqvist, chairman of the Woodworkers' Union, Ernst Blomberg, head of the Metal Workers' Union, and two or three other prominent unionists.

In August of the following year this group succeeded in assembling a congress of union representatives for the express purpose of forming such a central body. Some twenty-four national unions and a number of "local cen-

[12] See Chapter III.

trals" (*lokala centralorganisationer*) [13] were represented at this gathering.

The assembled delegates were practically unanimous in favoring a confederation, but when it came to deciding the basis on which it should be set up, sharp differences of opinion arose. Lindqvist and Blomberg wanted to give the central body considerable power and to make it a reinsurance agency for extending financial aid to the national unions in both strikes and lockouts. However, the majority sentiment was against such strong centralization, and the congress finally voted that the functions of the new organization should be limited to gathering statistics for the constituent unions and to providing financial support in "defense conflicts" (*försvarsstrider*) [14] alone. The provision of benefits for aggression conflicts — i.e., strikes for better wages or conditions — was to be left to the individual national unions. The fathers of the federation idea were forced to console themselves by asserting that "it was only a question of time before the scope of the central organization's powers would be widened." [15] In this, however, they were mistaken. Decentralization has remained the principal functional characteristic of the Swedish trade union movement ever since and, as we shall have occasion to emphasize repeatedly in the ensuing pages, has militated considerably against its effectiveness in upholding the workers' end in the struggle over the terms of employment.

Another difference of opinion arose over the question of deciding on and conducting strikes. One faction held that the local centrals, which were to be represented in the federation on a par with the *förbund*, should have some say in

[13] The local centrals, of which there was one in practically all the larger cities, had grown up along with the national unions. These bodies, representing unions of all kinds within the particular locality, had gradually assumed such functions as conducting organizing campaigns and taking charge of local strikes.

[14] Lockouts, strikes for rights to organize or bargain, strikes called on account of employers' attempts to reduce wages, etc.

[15] Landsorganisationen, *Minnesskrift, 1898–1923* (Stockholm, 1923), p. 37.

this regard. Here again the national unions won the day; neither the locality groups nor the central body were given any voice in the matter of strikes.

The most troublesome question of all was that of the official connection between the federation and the Social-Democratic Party. Many of the leading unionists had been prominent members of the party since its formation in 1889. At first it appeared as though this problem would be disposed of rather easily for the congress itself decided, by a two to one majority, that each constituent association "must, within three years after its admission to the federation, also affiliate itself with the Social-Democratic Party." But when the question was later referred to the rank and file, powerful opposition arose in a number of national unions. The Metal Workers' Union refused to join at all under these conditions, and six years were to elapse before this large and powerful *förbund* finally came into the federation's fold. In the meantime the strong sentiment against an obligatory political tie-up had forced the second congress (held in 1900) to substitute for the "must" clause a stipulation to the effect that the federation "should work for" the member unions' affiliation with the party.

The new "union of unions" was given the name of *Landsorganisationen i Sverige* (which we shall translate as the Swedish Federation of Trade Unions or S. F. T. U.) and its administration was delegated to a *sekretariat* or executive board of five persons, one of whom — the chairman — was to be a paid, full-time official. This group was to be responsible to a *representantskap* or council, composed of one delegate from each national union, and in the final analysis to the *kongress*, a larger representative body which was to meet at intervals of several years.

The basic organizational structure of the S. F. T. U. like its formal, functional setup, has remained practically unchanged ever since. In recent years the policy-making powers of the central organization, as exercised by the executive board, have been expanded considerably, but this has been achieved mainly through the channels of personal influence.

To this aspect of the union movement's development we shall return at a later stage of our study.[16]

THE ADVENT OF LARGE-SCALE BARGAINING AND CONFLICT

In contrast to the decade 1890–1900, which was primarily a period of union consolidation and extension of the movement into new fields, the first eight years of the new century were characterized chiefly by *internal* expansion — i.e., the formation within the existing national unions of new locals and the numerical strengthening of old ones. The membership of the *förbund* affiliated with the S. F. T. U., which in 1899 totaled about 37,000 had risen by the end of 1907 to 186,000 — a fivefold increase. This remarkable growth was, no doubt, partly due to a more or less "natural" spread of the idea of unionism, but it was more particularly the result of the vigorous organizing campaigns which the national unions carried on during this period. The metal workers' foray into the iron and steel district, which brought a majority of the *bruksarbetare* into their union within two years, is a case in point.

It was during this time, also, that the collective agreement was first introduced on an appreciable scale into Swedish labor relations. To be sure agreements had not been uncommon in the nineties. But most of the employers were then still openly opposed not only to signing contracts with the workers' organizations but even to the idea that any such organizations should exist. The unions were therefore obliged to devote most of their efforts to securing recognition and the right to bargain. In this struggle they were eventually the winners, but up to the turn of the century they had not succeeded in incorporating the results of the bargaining process in a written document. Before the new century was far advanced, however, the employers had formed organizations of their own, corresponding in objectives if not in scope to those of the workers. This episode marked a distinct modification in the general employer attitude toward the written agreement, and in the immediately

[16] See Chapter XVIII.

ensuing years its use became widespread in a number of the major Swedish industries. These two vitally important occurrences — the development of employers' organizations and the introduction of collective agreements — will be described in greater detail in subsequent chapters.

Most of all, perhaps, the new decade was a period of open conflicts between the unions and the employers — and this despite the advances made in peaceful bargaining. Work stoppages of more than local proportions were by no means unknown in the nineties. For example, one might mention the country-wide lockout of the cigar and tobacco workers in 1896, and the strike in the northern sawmill districts three years later.[17] The first stoppage of major significance, however, was the so-called political strike of 1902. This was in reality not a strike in the ordinary sense but rather a political demonstration. It was initiated by the leaders of the unions and the Social-Democratic Party (frequently the same persons) as a public protest against the government's failure to extend the franchise to the working classes. Workers in all parts of Sweden, totaling some 84,000, took part in this strike, which lasted two days. It was so well organized and the plans kept so well under cover that it took the country completely by surprise. The employers indignantly protested that they were being made to suffer for a grievance which was none of their doing. The unionists might have replied by pointing out that a number of prominent large-scale employers were also conservative members of the Riksdag, in which capacity they had been instrumental in preventing the very legislation which the workers were seeking.[18]

[17] Kungliga Kommerskollegium, *Arbetsstatistik, E: 1* (*Arbetsinställelser under Åren 1903–1907*) (Stockholm, 1909), pp. 327–335; also T. Lindbom, *Tobaksarbetarnas Stockholmsavdelning* (Stockholm, 1934), pp. 34–60.

[18] It is difficult to say what part this particular incident played in enabling the workers finally to attain the right to vote, but it is certain that the increase in union strength and influence during the first two decades of the century had a good deal to do with it. A "partial franchise" was granted to wage earners in 1906; and virtually universal suffrage was established in 1919. H. R. G. Greaves and C. P. Mayhew, "Constitution," in

However the balance of justice lay in this regard, the event "opened the employers' eyes," as Sydow observes, and "showed them how powerless they were vis-à-vis the unions." [19] What is more important, it crystallized the vague and inarticulate sentiment for organization, already fairly prevalent among them, and led directly to the founding, a few months later, of the three associations which were to determine the future course of the "Swedish employer movement." [20]

The first major economic test of strength took place in the machinery industry during the years 1903–1905. This conflict is important in the annals of Swedish industrial relations chiefly because of two innovations which accompanied it: the introduction by the organized employers of the large-scale lockout and the concluding (after the struggle had dragged itself out to a virtual stalemate) of the first national agreement in a major industry. The latter event is especially significant for the present study, since it laid the foundations for the Swedish bargaining system as it exists today, and we shall have occasion to refer to it repeatedly in the course of the subsequent discussion.[21]

The years 1906–1908 were also prolific breeders of strikes and lockouts. The employers' organizations were expanding rapidly during this period, and in most cases it was through these organizations, rather than as individuals, that the employers took the field against the equally fast-growing unions. The climax came in 1909, when the so-called general strike kept practically the whole of the country's manufacturing industry shut down for nearly three months.

The details of the causes and events leading to this bitter and (for the workers) ill-fated struggle will not be gone into. However it may be said without too great inaccuracy that

---

Democratic Sweden (M. Cole and C. Smith, editors, New York, 1939), pp. 13–14.

[19] Hjalmar von Sydow, *Om Den Svenska Arbetsgivareorganisationen, dess Verksamhet och Betydelse* (Stockholm, 1932), p. 5.

[20] See Chapter II.

[21] See especially Chapter IV, pp. 68–69.

it came about principally because the leaders of the employers' organizations — particularly of the Swedish Employers' Federation, which had come to occupy a dominating position in the field — were convinced that the time had arrived for a major test of strength with the unions. The essentials of the situation which led them to this decision may be set forth in fairly brief terms.

For nearly a decade, the workers' efforts to improve their terms of employment had met with practically uninterrupted success. The rapid growth in the numerical and organizational strength of the unions was, no doubt, one of the main factors accounting for this success. Equally important was the fact that business conditions had been prosperous and the country's industries expanding almost continuously, which made it possible for the employers to grant repeated wage increases without undue difficulty. At all events, the long-continued uptrend gave rise to a widespread notion in union circles that a rising pay scale was the natural order of the day and that the proper subject of discussion at wage negotiations was not *whether* but by *how much* wages should be increased.

But with the advent, early in 1908, of an economic downswing of major proportions, business managers in Sweden were forced to retrench. Accordingly, as the depression deepened during the ensuing summer and fall, one after another of the employers' organizations took a definite stand against granting further wage increases as long as current conditions should continue. At the same time they held fast to their policy of seeking national agreements and its corollary, a leveling out of divergences in wage rates between different localities and sections. The carrying out of these policies would be course mean that wages in many workplaces would have to be lowered.

Under these circumstances it was inevitable that the feeling between the organized workers and employers should become very acute. On a number of occasions in 1908, widespread stoppages appeared imminent. In most cases these situations originated in disputes at particular workplaces, and were initiated by local unions intent on continuing their upward push. The leaders of the S. F. T. U. were well aware of the danger of pursuing an aggressive wage policy under such unfavorable economic conditions but, owing to the decentralized functional setup to which we have already referred, were unable to bring their influence to bear in the earlier stages of these disputes.[22]

The employers finally concluded that the only way to put an end to this situation, and dispel the notion of a permanently rising wage level, was through a large-scale open conflict. Accordingly, in July, 1909, the Employers' Federation — acting on the pretext of a number of local wage strikes then going on, chiefly in paper mills and clothing establishments — put into effect a lockout covering all its member firms in the sawmill, wood pulp, paper, textile, and iron and steel industries. The heads of the S. F. T. U. (in this instance taking the initiative, despite the statutory limitation of their powers) replied by calling out the entire membership of all the constituent unions. Many unorganized workers joined in the walkout and at the height of the conflict some 300,000 people were out.

However, the workers were ill prepared for a long siege, particularly from the all-important standpoint of economic resources. About a month after the opening of hostilities the first breach in their front appeared, when the S. F. T. U. made a settlement with the employer groups outside the S. E. F. — principally the machinery manufacturers and the master builders — whereby the workers in the plants belonging to these organizations were to return to work under status quo conditions.

The fight between the unions and the Employers' Federation continued for two or three months longer, but in the meantime many of the strikers themselves, organized as well as unorganized, drifted back to work. By December the

[22] This summary account of the causes underlying the general strike is based on data contained in the *Redogörelse för Lockouterna och Storstrejken* (*Arbetsstatistik A:9*), compiled by the Royal Board of Trade (Kungliga Kommerskollegium) in 1910. See especially Part I, pp. 27–28.

worker forces had completely "run out in the sand," as the Swedes put it, and the whole dismal affair was over.

RETREAT AND RALLY: THE LONG FORWARD PUSH

The failure of the general strike proved a severe setback for the Swedish labor movement, from which it did not entirely recover for nearly a decade. Union membership, which had been well over 200,000 in 1908, fell off 30 per cent during the following year, and by the end of 1910 was scarcely more than half the 1908 figure. The business depression which prevailed during the period undoubtedly played its part as a cause of the defection (as depressions always do), but there is every reason to believe that the disastrous outcome of the big strike was the major causal factor. The organizers sent out by the unions during the poststrike years observed "a certain discouragement" among the rank and file. The heads of the S. F. T. U. averred that the workers had become too accustomed to seeing the unions pushing ahead year after year; that they were consequently unable to understand it when "*konjunktur* conditions . . . shifted the balance of power to the employer side, and tended to believe instead that there was something the matter with the way their organizations were being run." [23] They might have added (what probably only a few workers knew) that the rapid growth and strengthening of the organizations on the other side had shifted the relative bargaining strength *permanently* in the direction favorable to the employers.

Apathy among the workers and uncertain business conditions kept the unions in backwater until well on into the war years. During 1916, however, there was a substantial influx of new members, attributable, in part at least, to the serious inroads on the level of real wages made by the accompanying monetary inflation.

The upswing in membership continued, with increased momentum, during the three ensuing years, and by the end of 1920 it had reached the 400,000 mark — more than 70

[23] *Landsorganisationens Verksamhetsberättelse* (Yearbook of the Swedish Federation of Trade Unions), 1910.

per cent above the prewar high point. The postwar depression brought a slight reversal, but in 1923 the forward push was resumed. For fifteen years thereafter the total of union members continued to mount steadily, reaching 500,000 in 1927, 600,000 in 1931, 700,000 in 1935, and 880,000 at the end of 1937. At the present writing it is still *en haussé*, although there is some indication that the upslope of the trend has begun to flatten.

The distribution of this remarkable growth (more than fivefold within a quarter century) is also of considerable interest. While nearly all the national unions founded during the "consolidation period" of the 1890's and early 1900's have shown substantial increases, the really outstanding rise in membership has occurred in the less skilled, and especially in the nonmanufacturing, occupations, in most of which unionism was practically unknown prior to 1920. The accompanying table will serve to throw some light on this aspect of the labor movement's development.

Of the later arrivals in the trade union family, the municipal workers were the first to get under way. By 1923 their union had attained the 15,000 mark, but by 1937 this figure had been more than doubled. The agricultural workers, responding to a vigorous organization campaign launched by the S. F. T. U., built up their organization from nothing to 16,000 in 1917–1920, but with the advent of the postwar depression many farm laborers dropped out, and it was not until 1929 that the membership of the agricultural union began to climb again. Since then it has increased more than fourfold; at the present time it comprises a substantial proportion of the country's "hired" agricultural working force.

Another intensive campaign was also started in the early twenties among the logging workers of central and northern Sweden, but this, too, gave only temporary results. The real upswing of the Logging Workers' Union did not begin until after 1933. In the past four years, thanks to the revival in the lumber trade and more especially to a new and intensified organizing campaign, its numerical strength has

GROWTH OF NATIONAL UNIONS IN SWEDEN, 1898–1937

Name of Union	Membership 1898	1908	1923	1930	1937
Painters' Union	2,530	2,560	4,110	8,810	13,800
Masons' Union	4,360	4,470	3,340	7,930	10,600
Electricians' Union	...	1,240	3,870	5,780	8,600
Wood Workers' Union	6,620	12,070	16,200	...	...
Wood Construction Workers' Union [a]	...	...	11,200*	20,100	31,600
Wood Products Union [a]	...	...	8,920*	16,400	23,300
Metal Workers' Union	8,870	33,900	55,300	101,600	146,800
Molders' Union	1,430	2,880	4,620	6,510	8,750
Mine Workers' Union	660	4,500	2,760	7,370	8,180
Stone Workers' Union	3,670	5,870	4,050	11,500	9,150
"The United Unions"	570	3,600	6,890	6,510	11,050
Laborers' & Factory Workers' Union	6,950	40,100	33,300	61,800	79,700
Paper Workers' Union [b]	...	...	20,200	35,300	36,900
Sawmill Workers' Union	4,430	11,000	28,300	38,800	27,200
Textile Workers' Union	500	5,980	17,300	27,200	35,000
Clothing Workers' Union	1,620	3,290	7,500	13,700	23,400
Shoe & Leather Workers' Union	2,000	4,320	9,060	10,800	11,100
The Printing Unions [c]	3,230	7,970	10,140	17,400	19,800
Food Industry Unions	1,500	3,060	9,380	19,900	24,400
Brewery Workers' Union	...	2,900	3,970	5,880	6,630
Tobacco Workers' Union	1,460	2,580	2,980	2,600	2,460
Railway Workers' Unions [d]	500	27,600	38,100	48,200	42,800
Transport Workers' Union	4,670	9,470	13,300	26,200	32,000
Unions in state enterprise [e]	1,060	5,560	15,110	18,100	25,600
Municipal Workers' Union	...	1,220†	15,500	23,300	37,500
Road and Watercourse Workers' Union	...	...	1,520	8,140	21,300
Seamen's Union(s)	...	2,800	6,370	14,700	15,800
Agricultural Workers' Union	..	4,800	5,860	10,200	34,100
Logging Workers' Union	...	...	12,400	10,600	39,800
Merchandising Workers' Union	...	1,590	6,210	18,200	32,100
Hotel & Restaurant Workers' Union	...	...	1,520	7,920	14,700
Miscellaneous Minor Unions	2,430	4,420	3,430	5,970	11,070
Syndicalist Unions	...	...	32,800	28,200	35,300‡
Total	58,600	210,000	400,300	639,400	880,500

Sources: Landsorganisationen, *Sifferuppgifter och Grafiska Framställningar*, 1888–1912, pp. 8–9; *Sifferuppgifter och Grafiska Framställningar*, 1913–1930, pp. 6–7; *Verksamhetsberättelse*, 1937, p. 7.

[a] Formed in 1923 by division of Wood Workers' Union into two separate unions. [b] Formed in 1920 from a segment of Laborers' and Factory Workers' Union. [c] Typographers', Bookbinders', and Lithographers' National Unions. [d] Railway Workers' Union and Locomotive-men's Union (the latter is not affiliated with the S. F. T. U.). [e] Postmen's, Telephone and Telegraph Workers', Asylum Workers', and Civilian Defense Workers' Unions.

* 1924 figures. † 1910 figures. ‡ 1935 figures.

risen from 12,000 to nearly 40,000 members. In wholesale and retail trade, a particularly difficult branch of business to unionize, energetic proselytizing has also been going on in recent years. Despite the widespread response, however, the greater proportion (probably between two thirds and three quarters) of the country's salespeople still remain unorganized. The best record of all, in point of percentage increase, is that of the Road and Watercourse Workers' Union, composed mainly of laborers, which has expanded more than tenfold in a decade and a half.

Of the older unions, the Laborers' and Factory Workers' and the Metal Workers' groups have been most successful, the former having more than doubled and the latter nearly trebled its membership since 1923. It is probable that the expansion of the affected industries has been the most important factor here, unionism having been already so well established as to make planned agitation almost unnecessary.

With nearly a million union members in a country of six million inhabitants, it must be apparent that the degree of organization among wage earners is unusually high.[24] No attempt at an accurate quantitative analysis of this question will be made here, but it will be worth our while to outline, in rough terms, the salient distributional features. The railroads and the several branches of government service and state-owned enterprise are, practically speaking, completely unionized. A coverage of well over 80 per cent obtains in all the major manufacturing lines except textiles and clothing, where a considerable proportion of the female

[24] It is difficult to arrive at an accurate estimate of the degree of organization, since there is no way of segregating definitely the part of the working population which is "organizable." However, a fairly indicative (and undoubtedly conservative) figure may be obtained if one takes as a basis the total of "workers" in the several industrial subdivisions, as given in the official census. These include agriculture, forestry, industry and handicraft, and trade and transportation; the aggregate number of workers as of 1937 may be taken as approximately 1,300,000 (1930 census figures, plus 2.5 per cent to allow for increase in population). The degree of organization according to this definition is, therefore, 68 per cent. (Statistics from *Statistisk Årsbok för Sverige, 1937*, pp. 36–40.)

workers still remain "on the outside." The only important occupations in which union members are still in the minority are agriculture (workers on the smaller farms), retail trade, and household service.

As for the policies and activities of the Swedish unions after 1909 (which we may for convenience designate as the close of the "organizational stage"), a brief summary will suffice for our present purposes. These later periods of the labor movement's development will be treated in greater detail at appropriate places in the subsequent chapters, since most of what has taken place during the past twenty-five years is intimately associated with the main subject of our study — the development and present functioning of the collective bargaining institution.

Shortly after the outbreak of the war, the government arranged a conference between the principal trade union and employer organization leaders. The result of this was an informal understanding "that stoppages should be avoided under these grave circumstances." [25] This truce was faithfully observed until about the middle of 1916. During the last two years of the war, however, strikes and lockouts — especially the former — occurred with increasing frequency, the main cause being, as one might surmise, the employers' reluctance or neglect to raise wage rates fast enough to keep pace with the rise in prices. Nor did the end of the inflation period bring any appreciable improvement. In fact, the labor market continued to be disrupted by numerous stoppages almost throughout the decade of the twenties.[26]

In 1929, a marked abatement occurred, the number of workers affected by strikes and lockouts falling by 80 per cent, as compared with the previous year. Since then, except for a brief upsurge in 1931–1932, the stoppage problem has been much less serious than previously.

Despite the prevalence of open conflicts during its earlier half, the period since the war of 1914–1918 has witnessed a

[25] Hansson, *Svenskt Fackföreningsliv under Fem Decennier*, p. 83.

[26] The principal stoppages during the period 1920–1934 are summarized in Chapter X.

steady growth in the use of collective bargaining. The handling of disputes through bilateral negotiations between employers and union representatives has become more and more common. Uniform methods of procedure, both for agreement making and grievance adjustment, have been worked out, and collective agreements have increased both in number and scope.

A third important episode in the history of Swedish labor relations since the war has been the gradual but by now practically completed change-over of the Swedish national unions from the craft to the industrial form of structure. To this effort in "planned evolution," which has had a profound effect on the development of the bargaining institution, we shall direct our attention in Chapter III.

CHAPTER II

THE EMPLOYERS' ASSOCIATIONS

THE FOREGOING account of the rise and development of the workers' organizations gives us part of the background needed for an understanding of the Swedish bargaining system. But it is equally necessary to tell how the employers' organizations have evolved — for in Sweden dealings between labor and management are to a very large extent "collective on both sides."

STATUS OF ORGANIZATION PRIOR TO 1902

The employers were a good deal slower than the workers in getting together. At the turn of the century, when national unions had already been established over practically the entire field of industry, combinations among employers were still almost unknown. The only coworking arrangements of any extended scope prior to this time were to be found in tobacco products and custom tailoring, both of which lines were composed mainly of small handicraft enterprises. Organization in industry proper was confined to a few highly localized "common interest groups," such as the association of foundry owners in Stockholm, which concluded a wage contract with the organized molders in 1890,[1] and the Norberg Mine Owners' Association, hastily formed to fight a miners' strike in 1891.[2]

Of these earlier employers' combines, only one appears to have had more than an indirect influence on the strong consolidation of whole industries which took place during the first decade of the new century. This was the *Verkstadsförening*, or Machine Industry Association, set up in Gothenburg in 1896 through the efforts of one James Keiller, the English owner of one of the city's largest machine shops.

[1] G. Styrman, *Verkstadsföreningen* (Stockholm, 1937), p. 56.

[2] H. Sundholm, *Järnbruksförbundet* (Stockholm, 1931), pp. 11–14.

This association, purely local at the start, later expanded until it covered practically the whole of the country's fabricated metal products industry.

The employers' slowness in following up the rapid spread of unionism in the nineties with organizations of their own is at least partly explainable. The only really well-established line of manufacturing in Sweden at that time was the iron and steel (*järnbruks*) industry. The ***brukspatroner*** (at any rate the majority of them) were individualists of the first water — self-sufficient, full of family pride, and suspicious of their competitors. It is scarcely to be wondered at that they did not readily take to the idea of organization.

The wood products industries, on the other hand, were still too new for organization. Lumber production did not begin to approach sizable proportions until about 1880; wood pulp, paper and fabricated wood products not until the middle nineties. All of the producers were new at the game and practically all were producing for the highly competitive export market. As a result, the atmosphere among the employers in these industries was scarcely any more conducive to *anschluss* than it was in iron and steel.

UNITED FRONT SENTIMENT CRYSTALLIZES

The time was not far distant, however, when the incentives to organize would become strong enough to cancel out even these powerful deterrents. As the unions continued to grow and consolidate, the pressure on the employers became ever more insistent. Even when the workers lost, as when the sawmill owners in Norrland succeeded in smashing the newly formed unions among their employees in 1899, the defeat was most often only a temporary setback. With the advent of an economic upswing the workers' organizations promptly sprang up again, and within a few years had more than regained their former strength.

The event which finally jarred the employers into realizing what was happening was the afore-mentioned "political strike" of 1902.[3] Almost overnight the sentiment toward organization in managerial circles, and especially in the

[3] Chapter I, p. 15.

sphere of manufacturing, underwent a drastic change. Many who had been apathetic, or even openly opposed to a united front, now became strong supporters of the idea. Nor did it take long for this new spirit to materialize into concrete results. Within two months after the strike the foundations had been laid for three important associations of employers: two nation-wide and one district-wide in scope. One of the former — the Swedish Employers' Federation — was later to become the parent body and rallying ground of employer combinations over practically the whole industrial field.

On June 7, less than a month after the strike, a large group of machine shop and foundry owners from all over the country met in Gothenburg, under the sponsorship of the above-mentioned local organization, and formed the Swedish Machine Industry Association (*Sveriges Verkstadsförening*).[4] On the same day another conference was held in Malmö, at which 150 employers, representing 227 different enterprises in southern Sweden, were present. The outcome of this meeting was the Malmö General Employers' Association (*Allmänna Arbetsgivareföreningen i Malmö*). Both these bodies were destined to play an important part in the organization movement among Swedish employers in the immediately ensuing years.

The most significant (from the standpoint of future developments) of these aftermaths of the political strike took place early in July, 1902. The leading instigator of this meeting was Robert Almström, a manufacturer of porcelain ware. In answer to an appeal made by him, a small group of employers — representing several different industries — met in Stockholm and decided to form an association or federation of employers, with the express intention of extending it to cover all manufacturing industries throughout the whole country. Although the decision to unite was made and the general outlines of the organization mapped out at this

[4] Although the formal launching of the Machine Industry Association did not take place until September of the same year, the decision to organize — for present purposes the most important event — was made at the June meeting. Styrman, *op. cit.*, p. 82.

meeting, it was not until September of the same year that the project was formally launched and the name *Svenska Arbetsgivareföreningen* (Swedish Employers' Federation) adopted. The September meeting was attended by thirty-three employers, representing some ten or twelve different lines of manufacturing, who accordingly became the charter members of the Federation.

The essential purposes of the S. E. F. as expressed in the original statutes, were "to assist (its members) in settling conflicts between them and their workers and to render them pecuniary aid for losses incurred through strikes and lockouts." [5] The "pecuniary aid" was to be financed partly through the payment of dues and partly through pledges of liability (guarantee bonds), both to be based on the number of workers employed by each member firm. The former was to constitute the ordinary source of payment; the guarantee bonds were to be used only after the ordinary means had been exhausted.

BUILDING AN EMPLOYERS' FEDERATION

During the first two years of its existence, the progress of the S. E. F. was rather slow. By the end of 1904 approximately one hundred new member firms had been added, but these were mostly small establishments. The larger employers, particularly those in the major fabrication industries, stayed outside. The main reason for their aloofness appears to have been their distrust of the Federation's insurance device, which many of them regarded as a weak and ineffective, and at the same time costly method of fighting the unions.[6]

[5] C. Hallendorff, *Svenska Arbetsgivareföreningen, 1902–1927* (Stockholm, 1927), p. 33. The author is indebted to this work for much of the historical material contained in the present chapter.

[6] By contrast, the Machine Industry Association had adopted a "strong" policy early in its career. In the spring of 1903 it declared a large-scale lockout against the national unions operating within the machinery industry — a measure which effectively halted the workers' forward push, at least for the time being. This apparently held more appeal for the average employer than did strike insurance, for the Association grew by leaps and

Another reason for the S. E. F.'s slow progress at the start was its practice of admitting firms to membership only as such — i.e., as individual enterprises, without regard to industrial affiliation or geographical location. This probably seemed sensible and logical enough to the original framers of the Federation, most of whom were engaged in branches of industry in which there were relatively few enterprises. However, for the employers in such industries as iron and steel, sawmills and wood pulp, there was a real incentive to organize by industries, because of the many problems — labor and others — which the firms in each line of production had in common.

About the beginning of 1904 the S. E. F. leaders began to investigate the possibilities of bringing the Machine Industry Association, a proposed Iron Masters' Association, and two or three other smaller combines, into the Federation. They soon discovered, however, that the organizations in question were only willing to come in on the condition that their identity be kept intact. A series of negotiations with these groups followed and, as a result, a change was made in the statutes of the S. E. F., allowing industry associations (*yrkesförbund*) to become members, and giving them a prominent place in its organizational setup. At the same time, the provisions stating the Federation's policy regarding strikes and lockouts (both as to positive action and insurance payments) were more definitely and explicitly formulated.

These two reformulations of policy appear to have had the intended effect, at least to some extent, for the rate of influx of new members showed a decided acceleration in the ensuing months. During 1905 the Federation's membership (in point of workers employed) increased by nearly 50 per cent. Industry associations accounted for a substantial portion of the increase, six such bodies (three local and three national — including the important Iron Masters' Association) being admitted during the afore-mentioned two years.[7]

bounds. Within a year, it could count among its members a substantial majority of the country's technical metal products establishments.

[7] A seventh group admitted was the Malmö General Employers' Associa-

It was at about this time, also, that the Federation first gave definite sanction to the idea of concluding written agreements with the workers' organizations. In 1905 the S. E. F. executive board sent out a circular, in which the member employers were advised that when they undertook to conclude agreements with a union, they should do so in coöperation with the board, "partly in order to obtain conformity in the general provisions, and partly to avoid the inclusion of provisions which might lead to misunderstandings within the Federation. . . ."[8] The circular further stated that in order to be approved by the Federation, every agreement must contain a provision affirming the employers' "full freedom to take on and discharge workers, to lead and allot the work, and to employ workers regardless of whether they belong to organizations or not."

For our present purpose the chief importance of this utterance lies in the fact that it connoted at least tacit approval of collective agreements from the employers' side. It was subsequently approved by the General Meeting (*Stämma*) — though not without considerable objection from certain employers who were opposed to having any collective agreements at all — and became the much-publicized Section 23 of the Federation's statutes.

It was in connection with the second half of this newly introduced by-law that the S. E. F., in 1906, first entered the industrial arena as a party in negotiations with the unions. Individual firms, and even one or two industrial groups belonging to the Federation, had been dealing with their workers in this way for some years, but never before had the head organization, as such, undertaken to bring about a collective conference to attain a desired end. The end de-

tion, to which reference has been made above (p. 27). This body, it will be remembered, was organized as a local (or rather district) combination of employers in a number of different industries. The setting up of such groups and their admission into the S. E. F. was provided for in the statutes from the very start, but the idea was apparently not a practicable one, as no other associations of this kind have been able to survive.

[8] Hallendorff, *op. cit.*, p. 58.

sired in this case was the acceptance by the *unions* of the clause stipulating "full freedom" for the employer to hire and fire both organized and unorganized workers. The immediate incentive was provided by a number of widespread strikes, in some of which — so the employers insisted — the workers were attempting to impose the closed shop (*organisationstvång*).

Instead of going to the individual national unions involved in these strikes, the Federation leaders approached the heads of the central workers' organization, the S. F. T. U., with a proposal for a parley on the subject of the employer's "right to run his business in his own way." The S. F. T. U. chiefs accepted this offer. With the aid of an impartial chairman, Count Hugo Hamilton, the parties had relatively little trouble in reaching a solution satisfactory to both sides. The unions were to allow the introduction of the "full freedom" clause, but by way of compensation the employers would permit the inclusion of a statement according the workers full freedom to organize, with the added stipulation that "if the worker believes that he has been discharged under circumstances which he interprets as a violation of the right to organize he may, through his organization, require that an investigation be made for the purpose of obtaining justice."

When this compromise was submitted to the subsidiary organizations, difficulties arose. For while the S. E. F. constituent associations and firms gave their unanimous approval, a number of the national unions refused to accept it. The Employers' Federation then announced its intention of declaring a federation-wide lockout if the pact were not accepted within a month. This, the first threat of its kind ever made by the central employers' organization, proved remarkably efficacious. The S. F. T. U. leaders, caught between two fires, were forced into applying pressure to the recalcitrant unions, and when the deadline date arrived all had been brought into line.

Although this "December Compromise," as it was called, was never submitted to writing as a formal agreement between the two central bodies, it has nevertheless been meticulously observed ever since. It is, moreover, incorporated almost verbatim in many of the written contracts between the individual national unions and the corresponding industry associations on the employer side.[9]

The rate of growth of the S. E. F. had improved in 1905 and 1906, as compared with the first three years of its existence. However, it was not until 1907 that the Federation began to expand in earnest. During that year its membership more than doubled, as regards both number of firms and total employees. No less than twelve industry associations of national or seminational scope were admitted, among which five — the Sawmill, Wood Pulp, Paper Mill, Textile, and Ready-made Clothing Associations — represented major industries. The rapid growth continued, though with some abatement, through 1908, when seven more associations were added. By the end of 1910 the scope of the Federation had been extended to include a part at least, and in some cases the major part, of all the principal fabrication industries except machinery and building construction. It had thus attained, less than a decade after its formation, practically its full maturity stature.

The rapid influx of new firms and associations during and after 1907 was due to a number of factors. Only the most important will be considered here. The statute revision admitting industrial groups, which probably did not gather full momentum as an incentive until about this time, undoubtedly had a good deal to do with it. A second factor was the intensification of its "organizing campaign" — both in the sphere of publicity and by direct agitation. This in turn was in no small measure a function of a significant change in the Federation's leadership. During the first four years of its existence, the S. E. F. had been at a distinct disadvantage for lack of a single strong personality equipped and empowered to guide its progress. The ten or twelve prominent employers who had taken the greatest interest in starting the organization were all either unable or unwilling

[9] Cf. Chapter V, pp. 88–89.

to give their entire efforts to building it up. And the first executive director, Gustav Falkenström, was by no means a strong man. Early in 1907, however, the Committee of Delegates appointed to the directorship a prominent government official named Hjalmar von Sydow. Simultaneously the executive board elected von Sydow as its chairman, thus placing in the hands of a single individual the administrative responsibility and executive authority which had previously been delegated to Director Falkenström and Chairman Robert Almström. Thanks to this concentration of power and to his own energy and resourcefulness, the new director played a prominent role both in expanding the Federation's membership and in building it up as a militant employers' organization during the immediately ensuing years — indeed, through the next quarter century.[10]

Finally, one may mention the spontaneous gravitation into the S. E. F. of many "hold-out" employers. Prior to 1907 there were many of these who had not yet felt the impact of unionism. But with the rapid growth of the union movement at this stage, an increasing number of employers found themselves confronted by powerful worker organizations demanding substantial concessions in the form of higher wages and improved working conditions. In their desire to avoid having to give in to such demands these enterprises quite naturally turned to the S. E. F., either directly or through industry groups — for the Federation had at least made a start in the direction of providing aid in situations of this sort, even though the results had so far been unimpressive.

The range and volume of the S. E. F.'s activities, both peaceful and otherwise, increased even faster than its size during these years. A number of the newly admitted industry groups — notably those in iron and steel, textiles, and pulp — concluded national agreements with the corresponding national unions, and many smaller groups and individual firms concluded local agreements. As for open conflicts, the Federation had ample opportunity to test both its policies of

[10] Hallendorff, *op. cit.*, pp. 87–89.

positive action and its insurance scheme, the biggest and most difficult test of all coming with the general stoppage of 1909. The last named event we have already accounted for, albeit very briefly. The development of the central agreements, which the Federation's policies influenced to a marked degree, will be described in Chapter IV.

COUNTER-ORGANIZATION IN THE MACHINERY AND BUILDING TRADES

The Machine Industry Association, although inaugurated on a national basis almost simultaneously with the Swedish Employers' Federation, made considerably faster progress in the immediately ensuing years. There were a number of reasons for this. In the first place the commodities produced, and more especially the occupations of the workers employed by the member firms of the M. I. A. fell within the same general class, whereas the S. E. F.'s more ambitious program included the most widely separated branches of industry. There was, therefore, a considerably greater community of interest among the machine makers than among the constituent firms of the S. E. F. Moreover, the M. I. A. had already adopted definite policies at a stage when the S. E. F. leaders were still fumbling and vacillating. As stated, the machinery manufacturers put the large-scale lockout into effect early in 1903. Two years later, after another big lockout, they signed the first national agreement in a major industry — again well ahead of the S. E. F.

Finally (and this may be the most significant of all) the Machine Industry Association was fortunate in having energetic and purposeful single individuals at its head during its infancy — James Keiller at first, later John Bernström, head of the big cream separator corporation. However, this factor had its drawbacks as well as its advantages. The failure of the S. E. F. and the M. I. A. to unite during these pioneering years was undoubtedly due in large measure to the recalcitrance and domineering disposition of Bernström, who apparently feared that he and his association would be relegated to a place of minor importance if the latter merged with the Federation. Even after the S. E. F. had revised its statutes, mainly with the express idea of attracting the machinery group, the merger was not forthcoming.

At about this time — the summer of 1905 — the machinery employers were in the midst of their second major lockout, and in connection with the merger question they made a request that the Federation come to the aid of the Machine Industry Association through sympathetic lockouts by S. E. F. members. The Federation employers were willing to extend financial aid, but did not fancy the idea of shutting down their plants. The M. I. A. later dropped the lockout request and asked instead for a loan of 500,000 kronor. But even this did not help much in effecting a settlement. A misunderstanding arose, the machine makers thinking they were getting a loan with no strings attached, whereas the S. E. F. intended that there *should* be strings enough to prevent misuse of the sum lent. It was on this rock that the merger proposal broke, leaving a breach between the two associations which required more than a decade to bridge over. To be sure, there was considerable coöperation between the two organizations during the big strike in 1909, but it was not until 1917 that the ice finally thawed and the Machine Industry Association found its place within the council of S. E. F. industry associations — thereby, incidentally, increasing the Federation's "worker coverage" by some 40 per cent at a single step. This organization was, and still remains, by far the largest of the S. E. F.'s subsidiary groups.

Another early employer combine, not mentioned hitherto, was the so-called Central Employers' Association (*Centrala Arbetsgivareförbundet*). This organization, expressly intended to cover only the building and "handicraft" trades, was formed in the summer of 1903 by a number of building contractors, together with entrepreneurs in such closely associated lines as sheet metal work, plumbing and house painting. On several occasions during the next few years, parleys were held between representatives of this group and the S. E. F., with the idea of fostering coöperative action and even of effecting a merger. But the coöperation appears never to have extended beyond certain exchanges of information (e.g., the names of striking workers) during conflicts. The C. E. A.'s dislike of the strike-lockout insurance method and the S. E. F. leaders' aversion to admitting small enterprises (of which there were many within the building trades associations) were the chief factors which kept these organizations from combining.

They finally did get together, but not until late in 1918. The fusion was accomplished through an agreement between the heads of the S. E. F. and the C. E. A., by which the latter body was dissolved and in its stead five occupational groups were formed — the building contractors (construction entrepreneurs), the pipe fitting firms, the master tinsmiths, the master painters and the trucking companies. These associations were admitted to the S. E. F. as industry groups soon afterwards. However, the three last-named subsequently withdrew, chiefly because the wage policies of their members (all small contractors) were incompatible with those of the central organization.

With the adhesion of the machinery manufacturers and the construction contractors, the external expansion of the S. E. F. was practically completed. Two or three new groups of minor importance have been added since then, but in the main the development during the past two decades has been internal — that is, more firms have been brought into the associations already affiliated with the Federation and many of those already in have grown larger.

"UNAFFILIATED" EMPLOYER GROUPS

Although the S. E. F. encompasses the principal part of organized employerdom in Sweden,[11] the portion remaining

[11] In view of the paucity of strong employers' associations in the United States, even within particular lines of business, it may seem strange that in Sweden the major portion of *all* businesses should have banded together into one cohesive organization. However, it must be remembered that the total number of enterprises in Sweden is, comparatively speaking, very small — both within each industry and over the economy as a whole. Hence the

outside is by no means negligible. There are at least twenty "unaffiliated" associations of national or seminational scope, each corresponding in its own sphere to the industry groups belonging to the employers' Federation. Together they comprise approximately 7,000 employers, with a total wage earner force of nearly 100,000.[12] Most of these operate in comparatively small industries or occupations, such as newspaper publishing, hotels and restaurants, bakeries, and the house painting and sheet metal trades. In many cases the firms which comprise them are small-scale hand trades or service enterprises, hence are not considered good shareholder (membership) material by the Federation. Nor are these small employers, as a rule, especially desirous of being in the S. E. F. Among other things, they object to its costliness.

However, there are three non-S. E. F. employers' organizations which not only operate in comparatively large industries but whose members are, on the average at least, establishments of substantial size — those covering ocean transportation, the private railway companies, and agriculture (the large landed estates). Each of these concludes one or more national agreements with worker groups, the two first named having such understandings even with the salaried "white collar" employees. But in none of them is the lockout a practicable weapon, and this is one of the prin-

physical possibilities of bringing a majority of all employers together in a single organizational entity and giving satisfactory representation to each are considerably better there than in this country, where the number of business units is nearly twenty times as great. Moreover, combinations by individual industries in as small and industrially diversified a country as Sweden could not provide adequate financial support in widespread strikes or lockouts, except by exacting unduly heavy membership fees. Indeed, it may be questioned whether the Swedish employers could ever have achieved anything approaching parity with the powerful union movement, either in coercive or bargaining strength, in any other way than through a "multi-industrial" united front. Cf. Chapter XVI, esp. pp. 278–281.

[12] O. Ekblom, "P.M. Beträffande Organisationsrörelsen på Arbetsmarknaden," in *Statens Offentliga Utredningar, 1935:66*, p. 499. A subsequent estimate made by the writer indicates that the figure of 100,000 is somewhat low. (See *infra*, p. 47.)

cipal factors which keeps them outside the S. E. F., in whose policies lockout strategy and finance occupy a prominent position. They are, therefore, more nearly "pure" defense organizations than the S. E. F. industry groups.

A fourth group, the Forest Work Association (*Föreningen skogsarbeten*), covering the large logging concerns in the northern part of the country, might also be included in this category. But this is a comparatively new combine and its status is still more or less embryonic. Since 1937 it has had a kind of district agreement with the "contractors" (farmers with horses for hauling logs) and the woodcutters jointly, consisting of a section defining the relationship between owners, contractors, and workers, and a normative contract form. (The setting of piece rates for hauling and cutting is left to the parties at each particular workplace.) In addition, the organization supplies its member firms with expert aid in negotiating wage agreements with the unions.

Even in the sphere of public enterprise we find what might be termed, without too great inaccuracy, an employers' association — the Swedish Cities' Negotiating Organization (*Svenska städernas förhandlingsorganisation*). Its membership is composed of the municipal works administrations of approximately forty of the largest communities in the country. Through the organization, these cities conclude a central agreement with the Municipal Workers' Union, its principal subject matter consisting of so-called general provisions (stipulations concerning vacations, overtime, machinery for settling disputes, etc.). In the matter of wages it serves only in an advisory capacity, the individual municipality being the actual contracting party in the wage contracts. However, this group is not in any sense a "fighting organization," since neither it nor the member localities make any use of the lockout weapon.

In the field of state-owned enterprise, the bargaining agent on the employer side is usually the administrative commission in charge of the particular undertaking. For example, the agreement for the state railway repair shops is concluded between the Royal Railway Commission (*Kungliga Järnvägsstyrelsen*) and representatives of the Railroad Workers' Union (*Svenska Järnvägsmannaförbundet*). Obviously there cannot be any employer organization, in the ordinary sense of the term, when the state is the only employer.

MAKEUP AND FUNCTIONING OF THE EMPLOYERS' FEDERATION

In order to round out our picture of organization on the management side, we must now describe briefly the organizational setup of the S. E. F. and its internal functioning. Its policies as regards relations with the unions and the practical application of these policies will be discussed under the headings "Negotiation" (Chapter IX) and "Collective Bargaining and Stoppages of Work" (Chapter X).

The individual firms, or shareholders as they are called, are considered as such only in their capacity as insurance risks — i.e., in matters pertaining to guarantee bonds, fees, and benefits.[13] Each shareholding firm pays dues or "insurance premiums," reckoned on the basis of 20 kronor per year for each adult male worker employed and 10 kronor for each female and minor male worker. The proceeds, after administration expenses have been paid, go into the strike-lockout insurance fund. Each firm must also post a guarantee bond amounting to 200 kronor per adult male worker and 100 kronor for females and minor males. In cases of unusually widespread or long-drawn-out conflicts, when the insurance fund becomes depleted, the S. E. F. may borrow against these bonds from the shareholders, in order to keep the insurance payments up. The usual benefit paid to employers involved in strikes or lockouts is one krona per worker per day, but the rate may be raised if the stoppage lasts more than a month. In recent years, higher than ordinary stoppage benefits have often been paid to individual

[13] Certain of the constituent associations — e.g., the Machine Industry Association — have their own strike-lockout insurance schemes, but these are entirely separate from, and in addition to, the S. E. F. institution.

employers as an alternative to giving them aid through sympathetic lockouts.[14]

For all other purposes the industry groups, together with the single "locality association" and the "General Branch," [15] are the significant entities. The final authority in the S. E. F. is the General Meeting, the members of which are elected by the constituent associations on the basis of one for each association, plus one for each thousand workers employed. This body decides such matters as revisions of the statutes, and elects the executive board. The members of the board, which exercises the decision-making power in all the ordinary and many extraordinary actions of the Federation, are at present fifteen in number. They include, in addition to the administrative director of the Federation (a full-time employee), at least one prominent industrial executive from each of the principal industries (iron ore, copper and steel products, machinery, sawmills, paper, pulp, wood products, building materials, building construction and textiles). The board ordinarily meets once a month. The executive committee, made up of the Federation's administrative director and two other board members, meets approximately once a week and decides on many current issues of lesser importance, for which the decision of the full board is not considered necessary or on which prompt action is desirable.

Above the board, but below the General Meeting in authority, stands the Committee of Delegates (*Fullmäktige*), with a membership of approximately fifty. The chief functions of this group (which, like the General Meeting, is chosen by the constituent associations) are to decide the question of compulsory effectuation of sympathy lockouts (when the association called on by the executive board to close down in sympathy with some other association refuses

[14] Cf. von Sydow, *op. cit.*, p. 17.

[15] This is a sort of catch-all group, embracing those industries and occupations in which only one or at most a few firms are S. E. F. members, and for which, consequently, it is not considered feasible to form separate industry associations. Among these lines of business the most prominent are rubber products, chemicals, quarrying, pottery, and food processing.

to comply) and the question of utilizing the guarantee bonds of the shareholding firms. However, since these questions arise only on rare occasions, in practice the executive board (or its constituent group, the executive committee) makes nearly all the important decisions. It plays an important role in terminating, drafting proposals for, and concluding agreements; in deciding on action regarding strikes; and in declaring and effectuating lockouts. To carry out the board's orders, the S. E. F. employs an administrative staff, which includes the administrative director, three assistant directors and a number of subordinate officials in various capacities.

Each of the constituent associations, including the General Branch, also has its own executive board and administrative staff. To support them, the individual firms pay additional dues, each to its own association, amounting to from 3 to 5 kronor per worker per year. There is considerable overlapping of powers between the boards of the associations and that of the S. E. F. This situation is attributable chiefly to the clause in the S. E. F. statutes which stipulates that "if an associate or member of the Federation wishes to enter into a collective agreement with a labor organization, the draft agreement (proposal for agreement) shall be submitted to the board of the Federation, and no such agreement shall be concluded without the approval of the board." [16]

Offhand, one would think there would be frequent clashes as a result of this arrangement, since it is the duty of the constituent board to uphold the interests of the particular industry group, while the central board looks out for the interests of all groups. Then the question must inevitably arise: which entity — the industry group or the S. E. F. — has final word in the matter?

Such clashes of interest undoubtedly do occur, although the reticence of the leaders in both quarters makes it difficult to determine just how frequent and how serious they are. But the important thing is that they are practically always ironed out without resort to the question of final authority. In the usual case, the stand of the employer side in agree-

[16] Section 23, No. 1.

ment renewal movements is arrived at through negotiation and compromise between the heads of the subordinate group and the S. E. F. executives, much in the same manner as, at a later stage, the agreements themselves are concluded between the union and employer delegations. Most of this adjustment work is done at the so-called "*ombudsmannamöten*" — meetings of the S. E. F. chiefs with representatives from all the constituent associations, held once a month in the Federation's headquarters in Stockholm.

A relatively new institution within the S. E. F. is the "industry grouping" (*yrkesgruppering*) arrangement, under which the constituent bodies which operate in closely related industries — e.g., the sawmill, pulp and paper associations — are combined into what might be called inter-industrial employer cartels. This scheme is designed to bring about greater consistency of policy (and hence effectiveness of action) among employers within each major industrial subdivision. The functions of the *yrkesgrupper* are mainly coadvisory. For example, if one of the associations in such a group wishes to conclude a new agreement, the matter must first be discussed with the other associations in the group, the intention being to give the latter a voice in determining those terms of the bargain in which their interests, as well as those of the contracting association, are affected.

EMPLOYERS' ASSOCIATIONS AND SELLING COMBINATIONS

It is apparent from the foregoing description that one of the outstanding features of employer organization in Sweden is its highly centralized structural setup. No less significant, however, is the spirit of close coöperation with which the employers work together within this organizational structure. The most obvious manifestation of this spirit is found within the constituent industry groups, where, despite wide variations in efficiency and unit costs among the member firms, the principle of centrally determined wages and working conditions is adhered to practically throughout.[17] But it is

[17] This aspect of employer bargaining policy is discussed in Chapter IV (pp. 69–70) and in Chapter XVI (pp. 284–285).

even more strikingly demonstrated in the operation of the insurance scheme, through which all the adherent firms in the Federation, regardless of industrial affiliation, are banded together for mutual support. When manufacturers of, say, sugar are willing to contribute year after year to a fund which may be used to finance a lockout of iron miners or sawmill workers, it is difficult to avoid the conclusion that solidarity among the Swedish employers must be unusually high.

The centralizing influence of the Federation executive and administrative leaders, as exercised through direct personal contact with the heads of the subsidiary groups, plays an important part in promoting unified action on the employer side. For example, when the head organization has called on a particular industry group to join in a sympathetic lockout and the latter shows reluctance to comply, it falls to the lot of the S. E. F. officials to bring the recalcitrant employers into line. The method usually employed is that of applying "persuasive pressure" to the executive board of the subsidiary association. And it seldom fails to work.[18]

In view of the fact that the Swedish industrialists, through their Federation, work together so closely as *employers*, the reader will naturally ask whether they do not also use this medium for coöperation as sellers in the market. This question can be answered definitely in the negative, at any rate as regards the bulk of the country's manufacturing industry. Marketing and price-fixing combinations are by no means rare in Sweden, but for the most part these operate quite independently of the employers' associations. The principal reason is that the common interests in the two fields of activity do not, except in rare instances, coincide in scope. This can be illustrated by referring briefly to a few of the more important lines of manufacturing.

In the machinery trades, selling combinations of any great

[18] The heads of the S. E. F. also exert a centralizing and unifying influence through participating in agreement negotiations between individual industry groups and the corresponding national unions. Cf. Chapter X, p. 150.

size are obviously out of the question. As already observed, this is in reality not a single industry but a large number of small industries, with a range of products extending from wood screws to turbogenerators. There is, therefore, very little possibility of collusion as regards marketing in this sphere. In iron and steel the variety of goods produced, although not so great as in machinery, is still very considerable. For example, one steel mill produces flat cold-rolled stock, another high speed tool steel, and so on. Hence the room for large-scale price combinations is definitely limited here also.[19]

In the paper industry there are a number of central marketing organizations, but these are highly specialized, each one dealing exclusively in a particular kind of paper (e.g., newsprint, wrapping paper, stationery) — whereas the employer group, the Paper Mill Association, covers the whole industry. In wood pulp, on the other hand, the community of interests in selling covers a wider area than that in the field of employer-employee relations. The volume of annual pulp production in western Europe (and through it, to a considerable extent, the price of the product) is controlled by an international cartel covering Sweden, Norway, Finland, and Germany.

In textiles, finally, there are three "marketing combinations" — covering woolen manufacturing, cotton spinning, and cotton weaving firms. However, these can scarcely be called cartels, their chief purpose being to regulate the "conditions of sale" — i.e., period of credit extended, cash discounts, etc. Sweden also imports a considerable amount of cloth from various countries, and it is probable that the strong influence of prices in the world market precludes any possibility of effective internal price regulation.[20]

[19] However, there are selling organizations embracing particular segments of these industries — e.g., foundries, bicycles, and agricultural machinery.

[20] For a summary description of the character and scope of marketing combinations in Sweden, see E. Skoglund, "P.M. Rörande Kartellväsendet med Särskildt Avseende på Svenska Förhållanden," in *Statens Offentliga Utredningar, 1935:66*, pp. 225–234.

EXTENT OF EMPLOYER AND WORKER ORGANIZATION

In concluding, it will be useful to present a rough numerical picture of the extent of employer organization in Sweden at the present time, and to compare this with the extent of unionization, in terms of worker coverage. The table on pages 46 and 47 has been arranged to show, so far as possible, the degree of correspondence in industrial scope between the several employer groups and the national unions with which they carry on bargaining relations.

The two outstanding general observations which this table elicit are:

(a) That the industrial distributions of the employer and worker groups are highly symmetrical. In no less than seventeen industries there are single national organizations on both sides which correspond exactly (or nearly exactly) to each other. In at least eight others the correspondence is also close. In these latter industries, there are two or more organizations on one side or the other, but in most cases the several groups work as one body in many activities, especially in concluding agreements.[21]

(b) That the extent of organization is considerably greater among the workers than among the employers, even after account is taken of the relatively large proportion of S. F. T. U. members who are government employees (approximately 8 per cent). In only one industrial subdivision out of thirty — textiles — does the employer group cover more workers than the corresponding union. The smaller coverage of the employers' organizations in the other industries is due mainly to the S. E. F.'s refusal to accept small firms as members and the unwillingness of many firms (even some which are eligible in point of size) to pay the high S. E. F. dues and insurance fees.[22]

[21] In a majority of instances this close correspondence has come about as a result of union reorganization along industrial lines. (See Chapter III.)

[22] Nonadherence to the S. E. F. on one or other of these two grounds is particularly marked in lumber products, sawmills, clothing, logging, and the building and construction trades, where the number of small enterprises constitutes a very high percentage of the total number.

Extent of Employer and Worker Organization in Sweden, 1938

Employer Group	No. of Member Firms	No. of Workers Employed	National Union	Membership January 1, 1938
S. E. F. Associations [a]				
Middle Sweden Mining Assn.	18	3,300	Mine Workers' Union	8,180
Grängesberg Mining Assn.	3	4,200		
Master Pipe-fitters' Assn.	188	4,900	Metal Workers' Union	146,800
Auto Repair Shops Assn.	189	2,500	Molders' Union	8,750
Iron Masters' Assn.	73	40,000		
Machine Industry Assn.	525	88,900		
Sawmill Assn.	64	12,300	Sawmill Workers' Union	27,200
Paper Mill Assn.	42	14,900	Paper Workers' Union	36,900
Paper Pulp Assn.	45	14,600		
Wood Products Assn.	292	8,100	Wood Products Union	23,300
Textile Assn.	165	42,500	Textile Workers' Union	35,000
Ready-made Clothing Assn.	92	13,900	Clothing Workers' Union	23,400
Tanners' Assn.	30	2,200	Shoe & Leather Workers' Union	11,100
Shoe Manufacturers' Assn.	67	6,200		
Bookbinderies Assn.	110	4,800	Bookbinders' Union	6,500
Lithographers' Assn.	72	1,600	Lithographers' Union	2,500
Printers' Assn.	165	3,500	Typographical Workers' Union	10,700
Brewers' Assn.	110	4,800	Brewery Workers' Union	6,620
Flour Millers' Assn.	36	1,200	Food Industries Union	24,400
Chocolate Manufacturers' Assn.	28	4,200		
Stockholm Merchants' Assn.	90	1,600	Merchandising Workers' Union	32,100
Norrland Dockwork Assn.	22	1,500	Transport Workers' Union	32,000
South Swedish Dockwork Assn.	63	3,600		
Omnibus Owners' Assn.	143	2,200		
Granite Quarries Assn.	10	2,100	Stone Workers' Union	9,150
Road & Waterway Builders' Assn.	60	6,100	Road & Watercourse Workers' Union	21,200
Master Electricians' Assn.	248	3,500	Electricians' Union	8,600

Master Builders' Assn.	1,039	24,100	Wood Construction Workers' Union	31,600
			Masons' Union	10,600
			Building laborers in Laborers' & Factory Workers' Union	30,000
Building Materials Assn.	176	10,400[b]	L. & F. Workers' Union minus building laborers	50,000
"The General Group"	623	41,200[c]	"The United Unions"	11,050
"The General Employers' Assn." (Malmö)	404	8,600		
Miscellaneous Small Groups	62	6,400		
Total S. E. F.	5,254	390,000		
Associations not affiliated with S. E. F.				
Agricultural Employers' Assn.		22,000	Agricultural Workers' Union	34,100
Forestry Work Associations		15,000	Logging Workers' Union	39,800
Steamship Owners' Associations		14,000	Seamen's Union	15,800
Swedish Cities' Negotiating Organization		20,000	Municipal Workers' Union	37,500
Swedish Railways Assn. (private railways)		18,000[d]	Railway Workers' Union	37,800
			Locomotive-men's Union	5,000
Hotel and Restaurant Owners' Assn.		11,000	H. & R. Workers' Union	14,700
Master Painters' Assn.		5,000	Painters' Union	13,800
			Unions in state enterprises	25,600
Miscellaneous unaffiliated (estimated)		15,000	Miscellaneous minor unions	13,500
Total non-S. E. F. (approx.)		120,000	Syndicalist unions	35,500
Total S. E. F. & non-S. E. F. (approx.)		510,000	Total Union Members	880,700

Sources: S. E. F. Associations: ***Svenska Arbetsgivareföreningens Kalender***, 1938, pp. 444–446.
Non-S. E. F. Associations: Estimates based on number of workers covered *by agreements*, obtained from the State Mediation Office and from *Landsorganisations Verksamhetsberättelse* (*Tabellbilaga*), 1936, pp. 40–41.
Unions: *Landsorganisationens Verksamhetsberättelse*, 1937, p. 7.

[a] Data as of June 1, 1938.
[b] Practically all organized in Laborers' & Factory Workers' Union.
[c] Majority of workers divided among L. & F. Workers', Food Industries, and Transport Workers' Unions.
[d] The remaining 25,000 organized railway workers are employed by the state-owned railways.

However, it should be remembered that, so far as collective bargaining is concerned, the influence of the employers' organizations extends over a considerably wider sphere than that covered by the member firms themselves, owing mainly to the policy of most of the unions, in their dealings with unorganized employers, of demanding the same terms of employment as are specified in the national agreements. It must also be remembered that the S. E. F. wields more "bargaining power per worker covered" (to use a very crude parameter) than does the portion of organized workerdom with which it deals. The chief reason is that on the employer side the head organization can constitute itself the deciding entity in any important contingency, whereas on the worker side it is the individual national unions which have the final word.

CHAPTER III

THE EVOLUTION OF UNION STRUCTURE

CRAFTISM BETRAYS ITS WEAKNESSES

THE FIRST local unions of Swedish factory workers made their appearance in such industries as lumber, paper, pulp, and textiles — industries which had come into existence after the introduction of power-driven machinery. As already noted they were organized along industrial lines from the start. At about the same time, however, a number of the earlier organized craft occupations also began to feel the effects of mechanical progress and specialization. For example, with the introduction of woodworking machinery and division of labor in furniture making, expert cabinet makers were obliged to become woodturners or assemblers, while other and scarcely more difficult operations in the process were performed by erstwhile laborers and farm hands. Skilled bootmakers became machine tenders, working alongside women and boys with little or no training. And so on. Moreover, the factories employed many workers in other occupations — such as millwrights and mechanics to install and repair the machinery, enginemen and firemen to operate the power plant, and strong-arm workers to move materials and waste.

Difficulties were bound to arise when groups of wage earners belonging to different unions were thus brought together in the same workplace. In many cases, each group had its own separate agreement with the employer. When such an agreement expired, if the employer and the particular union affected were unable to agree on a new one, the union might call a strike of its members, forcing the employer to shut down and throwing the rest of the employees out of work — often against their will. Even though no actual stoppage took place, the mere fact of contracts with individual unions expiring at different times during the year made the carrying on of productive enterprise more uncertain, since the risk that a stoppage might occur was almost always present.

Equally troublesome were the quarrels which arose among the unions as to which should have jurisdiction over "borderline" fields of activity. For example, the carpenters would dispute the claim of the millwrights — members of the Iron and Metal Workers' Union — to the woodwork entailed in installing machinery. Similarly, when additional men were hired for such work, each would insist that it had the prior right to organize the newcomers.

The more farseeing union leaders soon perceived that this internal strife was weakening and disrupting the labor movement, and was thus preventing it from serving the workers' own interests to the best advantage. As early as 1901 the S. F. T. U. representative council (*representantskap*) passed a resolution adjuring the national unions to avoid such disputes and to work for a consolidation of closely related organizations.[1]

However, there was strong opposition at this time to any reorganization along industrial lines, especially among the rank and file in the "pure" craft unions. The molders would not hear of an *anslutning* with the other metal workers; the painters employed in factories insisted that they should remain in the painters' union; the woodworkers' *förbund* refused to give up its pattern maker members to any organization covering the machinery industry. Even the Metal Workers' Union, despite the fact that it already comprised several different trades and occupations, took an unfavorable stand toward industrialism. At the S. F. T. U. congress in 1906, a representative of this large and powerful organization declared strongly against a proposal to recognize the industrial type of union as being on a par with the craft union. Despite this objection, the congress voted to incorporate the concept of the *industriförbund* in the Federation's

[1] *Protokoll vid Landsorganisationens Representantskapsmöte*, March 22, 1901.

statutes, but the opposition was strong enough to prevent the passage of any definitive measures for creating such organizations out of existing craft bodies.

When the next congress convened in the fall of 1909 — soon after the petering out of the general strike — the proponents of a change-over to industrial unionism were stronger than ever. The disruptive influence of conflicting agreements and jurisdictional disputes still figured prominently in their list of arguments, but they now had an even graver indictment against the existing setup. The events of the three preceding years, especially the bitter experience of the summer just past, had shown conclusively that the unions were no match, either in bargaining or in open conflict, for the industrially organized employers' associations. The tendency of the several craft bodies to further their own individual group interests, and their inability to hold together in an emergency, had played directly into the hands of the common adversary.

The Metal Workers' Union, which had fought against industrialism three years previously, now became its strongest advocate. Even prior to the earlier congress the metal workers had experienced the disadvantages of craftism. In 1903–1905 they, together with three other nationally organized groups — the woodworkers, molders, and "laborers and factory workers" — had struggled through a long series of negotiations with the Machine Industry Association, interspersed with numerous local strikes and two major lockouts. All during this time lack of unity on the worker side had been painfully evident, and had been largely responsible for the meagerness of the concessions gained from the employers when the machinery trades national agreement was finally concluded in the fall of 1905. But apparently this lesson had not struck very deep.

In 1908, when the agreement expired, the employers demanded as a condition of its renewal that the masons', painters', tinsmiths' and transport workers' unions also become signatories to it, and when the three first-named bodies refused, they served notice that an industry-wide lockout would follow unless their demand was met. Peace was preserved on this occasion, for the leaders of the S. F. T. U. stepped into the breach and, by threatening the recalcitrant unions with loss of Federation support, finally induced them to sign. But the episode brought home to the metal workers, as the earlier one had not, the ineptitude of having eight separate and independent worker organizations within the same industry, and did much to swing the bulk of opinion within the union over to the proindustrial side.

"PLANNED INDUSTRIALIZATION" — THE FIRST STAGE

The upshot of the metal workers' conversion was that the 1909 congress resolved in favor of "a successive change-over to pure industrial unions, with instructions to the S. F. T. U. *sekretariat* and the union executive boards to work for the merging of the smaller groups in each industry with the union representing the majority strength." [2] It then elected a committee to make an investigation and work out a concrete proposal for the change-over.

The committee's program, which was laid before the sixth trade union congress, held in 1912, was thoroughgoing enough to suit all but the most rabid advocates of industrialism. The reorganization, it averred, should take place not immediately, but "successively," in accordance with the resolution of the 1909 congress. As guiding principles, it proposed (a) that the (revamped) unions should comprise all workers employed within the same industry; (b) that their jurisdiction should be made to coincide with the sphere of coverage of the collective agreements; (c) that, where circumstances permitted, smaller industries, closely related to each other, should be organized in the same national union.[3]

The "specific" part of the program called for a reconstruction of the forty-one then existing national unions into twenty-two *industriförbund*. The largest of these was to be the Metal Workers' Union, which was to take over the Molders'

[2] *Protokoll*, 1909 S. F. T. U. congress. Quoted in Hansson, *Den Svenska Fackföreningsrörelsen*, fifth edition, p. 52.

[3] Hansson, *Den Svenska Fackföreningsrörelsen*, fifth edition, p. 54.

Union *in toto* and (from their respective craft and multi-industrial organizations) all the masons, woodworkers, tinsmiths, painters, and unskilled laborers employed within the machinery and iron and steel industries. Workers in furniture and joinery factories, regardless of occupation, were to make up a "Wood Products Union."

The members of the Woodworkers', Masons', Plumbers', Painters', and Laborers' and Factory Workers' Unions employed in the building industry were to form a "Building Industry Union." Three new national organizations — to be called the Building Materials, Paper Industry, and Road and Watercourse Workers' Unions were to be "drawn out" of the Laborers' and Factory Workers' Union. The remainder of this body — comprising such minor industries as porcelain, chemicals, sugar and flour — would continue to function as a single unit, the "Factory Workers' Union." The typographers and bookworkers were to combine and form a "Printers' and Bookbinders' Union." The groups already "purely industrial" in makeup — including the Mine, Sawmill, Textile, Tobacco, Railroad, and Transport Workers' Unions — were to remain practically unchanged.

The congress, by a fair margin of votes, gave its approval to the committee's program. But the craft unionists — particularly the molders and those in the woodworking, building, and printing trades — made every effort to prevent its passage, and finally succeeded in putting through a "modifying resolution," to the effect that no existing *förbund* could be made to change its setup against the will of the majority of its members. Their objections were in essence the same as those which craftists in other countries, both before and since, have usually raised against industrial unionism. Results were what counted, they said; wasn't the average wage much higher in the craft unions? If they merged with the unskilled, the latter — by virtue of superior numbers — would be able to raise their wages at the skilled workers' expense. The unskilled workers' lack of solidarity, and the ease with which they could be replaced, lowered the union's "strike efficiency." And so on.

Whatever the justice of these arguments, most of the craft unions held fast to them, and in the ensuing years they followed the "modifying resolution" rather than the reorganization program itself. When the eighth congress convened in 1922, the molding, printing, and building trades unions were still separate and independent entities. Indeed, they remain separate to this day, although they have now formed alliances with each other or with related industrial unions which make them, so far as collective bargaining is concerned, constituents of larger bodies essentially industrial in character.

Despite this recalcitrance on the part of the strictly craft organizations, a substantial amount of "changing over" in accordance with the S. F. T. U.'s program took place during the first decade after its launching. According to Hansson's comparison of Federation statistics for 1908 and 1923, the proportionate strength of the pure industrial unions, in terms of membership, increased during the period from 46 to 64 per cent of the S. F. T. U. total, while that of the craft bodies shrank from 26 to 20 per cent. The multi-industrial group (composed of the Transport Workers' and Laborers' and Factory Workers' Unions, hence primarily industrial in structure) had also shrunk — from 28 to 16 per cent.[4]

The gain of industrialism had come about partly through a transfer of members from union to union. For example, a large number of woodworkers and laborers had gone over to the metal workers' organization. Another increase resulted from the formation of several new unions out of portions of existing bodies. In 1920, two groups of paper and pulp workers — one from the Sawmill Workers' Union and a much larger one from the Laborers' and Factory Workers' Union — united to form the Paper Workers' Union. Here

[4] *Den Svenska Fackföreningsrörelsen*, sixth edition, p. 66. The proportions were practically the same in 1912 as in 1908. It should be noted, however, that the figure of 46 per cent for industrial unions in 1908 includes the Metal Workers' Union, which was by no means completely industrialized at this time — and was, moreover, only just beginning to favor industrial unionism. If this union is left out of the reckoning, the "degree of industrialization" as of 1908 reduces to 30 per cent.

again, as in the case of the transport workers in 1897,[5] the L. F. W. U. served as an "organizational nursery." A third instance was that of the road and watercourse workers, who broke away and formed their own union (in accordance with the S. F. T. U. reorganization scheme) in 1922.[6]

The principal new unions among previously unorganized workers were those in the logging, farming, food products, and merchandising industries. Only one of the prescribed regroupings of *craft* bodies was effected during the period. This occurred in 1923, when the workers in the wood products factories seceded from the Woodworkers' Union to form the Wood Products Union (industrial), leaving the original craft organization in possession of the wood *construction* workers.

THE REVISED PROGRAM OF 1926

One might say that the industrialization program had succeeded, in part at least, among the unskilled and semiskilled, and among those groups of erstwhile craft workers whose occupations had been translated into factory jobs by the advance of mechanization — e.g., pattern makers and furniture workers. But the building tradesmen and other predominantly handicraft workers, whose services still had a high scarcity value, had refused to accept it. Nor did it help matters when the Federation, at its 1922 congress, decreed that the program must be carried to completion by the end

[5] See *supra*, p. 10.

[6] *Förbundskamraten* (Journal of the Laborers' and Factory Workers' Union), 1931, No. 4, pp. 19–20. Of all the national unions, the L. F. W. U. has shown the greatest willingness to carry out its part of the industrialization program. During the past quarter-century it has sacrificed at least 20,000 members to existing and newly-formed unions. Despite this, it has continued to grow steadily, and is today the second largest body within the Federation. Nevertheless, it is something of an anomaly as an industrial (or rather multi-industrial) union, since it still harbors some 30,000 building laborers. (The balance, approximately 50,000 in number, are practically all factory workers, and represent more than one hundred different lines of production.) The union has several times expressed its willingness to give up these building workers to the proposed building-industry union. The latter, however, has not yet materialized, and the building laborers have preferred to stay where they are rather than strike out for themselves.

of 1925. The perverse-minded builders, printers and molders persisted in their do-nothing policy — and with entire impunity, since the authors of the decree had failed to provide any punishment for nonfulfillment.

Realizing that all was not going according to plan, and was not likely to for some time to come, the S. F. T. U. executive board finally set about revising the program. In doing this it still held to the original main motivating principle — the need of a unified negotiating and contracting entity to represent the worker *kollektivitet*. But they wisely decided to modify certain of the earlier established objectives in the light of subsequent developments. For example, according to the 1912 plan the Merchandising Workers' Union (*Handelsarbetareförbundet*) was to be divided up among the Transport Workers' Union and several others. However, the clerks' organization not only failed to dissolve, but made a substantial gain in membership. The revisers now gave their approval to this obviously more "natural" setup, and in addition gave it jurisdiction over several other classes of workers, such as milk deliverymen, theater personnel, and insurance company employees.

An important modification was made also in the case of the building industry. The earlier scheme had called for the inclusion in a single union of "all workers employed on building construction projects." According to the new proposal, the building workers' *förbund* should comprise only those workers employed by the master builders — the members of the house carpenters' and masons' unions and the building laborer segment of the Laborers' and Factory Workers' Union. The painters, sheet metal workers, and electricians, employed mainly by subcontractors, should retain their individual organizations, while the pipe fitters should remain within the Metal Workers' Union.

In justifying this retreat from the original program, the board expressed itself as follows:

During the time when the 1912 industrialization plan was being worked out, both the master builders and the subcontractors engaged in house construction work were organized in the same employers' association. . . . A change has now taken place in this industry, and the employers are no longer all united in the same organization; a separate agreement has been concluded for the building trades proper, and one for each of the other worker groups. It has therefore seemed to the board that there is no longer so great a need to unite all the individual unions in a single building workers' union.[7]

It is apparent from this statement that the desirability of modeling the workers' bargaining units after those of the employers was still prominent in the union leaders' minds — as indeed it had been all along.[8] One suspects, nevertheless, that their chief reason for abandoning the earlier plan was the obvious unwillingness of the building unions to carry it out.

The executive board's revised program, which the 1926 congress approved by a large majority, also proposed two new "industrializations": the amalgamation of the custom tailoring, ready-made clothing, and hatmakers' organizations

[7] Landsorganisationen, *Utredning Angående Industriarbetareförbund*, 1926, p. 7.

[8] It is worth reëmphasizing here that the chief argument of the upholders of the change-over program has been that organization along industrial lines enhances union strength and effectiveness vis-à-vis the employers' associations. No less important, however, is the fact that the organized employers themselves have all along preferred to have the workers organized in industrial unions, and still do. It is interesting to note, in this connection, that the employers have an industrialization problem of their own. The Employers' Federation favors greater industrialization not only for the workers, but also for its own member associations. And as one might expect, the industry in which it has been least successful in this respect is building construction. In this industry each of the *sub-contractor* employer groups — i.e., the pipe fitting, painting, sheet metal work, and electrical installation firms — has its own separate association. The Federation, so one of its leading officials told the writer, would like to see these occupational groups unite with the Master Builders' Association (composed of *general* contracting firms) and form a Building Industry Association. But it is very difficult to get the sub-contractor groups to merge, the chief reasons being — according to the same informant — that they are old organizations, with well-established rules and policies, and that their members consider the present scheme quite satisfactory.

into a clothing workers' union; and of six occupational groups in water transportation — the firemen, seamen, radio telegraphers, stewards, "seafaring women," and Swedish-America Line employees — into a "Seaworkers' Union" (*Sjöfolksförbund*). On the other hand, the previously adopted proposal for a union covering building materials (brick, tile, and cement manufacture) was abandoned, experience having shown that the laborers' and factory workers' group was well adapted to serving the needs of the workers in this industry.

SWEDISH UNIONISM "GOES INDUSTRIAL"

The two mergers have gone according to schedule. So also have a number of proposed additional transfers. For example, approximately 1500 mechanics' helpers have been shifted from the Laborers' and Factory Workers' Union to the Metal Workers' Union, and nearly a thousand woodworkers — mostly pattern makers — from the Wood Products Union to the same body. The biggest single instance of such a shift-over occurred in 1934, when the Sawmill Workers' Union gave up 11,000 of its members to the Loggers' Union.

On the other hand, the prescribed consolidations in the printing and building trades, and in the metal industry (the molders with the Metal Workers' Union) still remain unfulfilled. But even here the trend toward making the industry the organizational unit is unmistakable. In 1927 the printers', bookbinders' and lithographers' unions formed a "graphic cartel" — a loosely knit arrangement for coördination of membership campaigns, mutual strike and lockout aid, and other similar functions. And in later years the constituent unions of the cartel have been concluding joint agreements with the employers' organizations. Six of the unions in the building trades have also formed a cartel, but the functions of this combination do not extend to coöperative agreement making. However, three of these groups — the carpenters, masons, and laborers — have accepted this principle, and are now common signatories to a national agreement with the master builders. Hence, so far as bargaining is concerned, this most important branch of the labor movement in the building industry may be said to be industrialized *de facto*, though not *de jure*.[9]

Even the Molders' Union, which has the reputation of being the most intransigent of all the anti-industrial worker organizations, has a cartel arrangement with the Metal Workers' Union and is a joint party with that body to the machinery trades national agreement. Except for this one group, the Metal Workers' Union now covers all the workers in both the machinery and iron and steel industries. However, it was not until 1928 that the transference of woodworkers, masons, laborers, etc., from other unions had proceeded far enough so that these unions were willing to relinquish their share in the agreement negotiations to the metal workers' organization.

We may conclude our account of the efforts to industrialize the S. F. T. U. by presenting a few figures showing the relative strength of craft and industrial unions within the federation at the present time.[10] Of the approximately 840,000 workers comprising the forty-one constituent national organizations as of December, 1937, some 110,000 or 13 per cent, belonged to craft unions; 607,000, or 72 per cent, to "pure" industrial unions; 123,000 (15 per cent) to multi-industrial unions.[11] Since the last named bodies are closely

[9] In the matter of a single industrial union for the building workers, the S. F. T. U. congress has again made a revision in its program. Instead of merely the three "building unions proper," the plan now takes in all the allied organizations connected with the building industry — just as the original 1912 plan did. This new revision was initiated by the leaders of the Carpenters' and Bricklayers' Unions, who insisted that a national industrial union for building could not succeed unless *all* building workers were in it. The painters, electricians, sheet metal workers still persist in their refusal to "submerge" themselves in such an organization. The other five unions, however, are going ahead with plans to complete the merger without them.

[10] The Federation comprises about 95 per cent of the organized workers in Sweden.

[11] Source of data: *Landsorganisationens Verksamhetsberättelse* (S. F. T. U.'s Yearbook), 1937, p. 7.

similar to the second group, both as to structure and functioning, we may say that 87 per cent of the Federation's membership is industrialized.[12]

In the above split-up, organizational structure has been taken as the criterion of classification — that is, all unions still retaining the unioccupational form of organization have been included in the craft group. If the scope of bargaining and the type of agreement concluded are taken as the criteria, we may legitimately shift the three printing trades unions and the Wood Construction Workers', Masons', and Molders' Unions over to the industrial column.[13] The figures for the relative prevalence of craft and industrial bargaining — in terms of union membership — then become 39,000 (4.5 per cent of the S. F. T. U. total) and 801,000 (95.5 per cent) respectively. It is no exaggeration, therefore, to say that the industrialization of employer-employee relations in Sweden is practically completed.

OCCUPATIONAL GROUPS WITHIN THE INDUSTRIAL UNIONS

Despite the blurring of the old occupational boundaries which accompanied the advent of mechanization, distinctive craft groups are still to be found in most industries. Moreover, specialization and the division of labor have created many new lines of demarcation, particularly in the sphere of manufacturing. It is necessary, therefore, to give some account of the extent to which suborganizations, based on occupational differences, occur within the industrialized unions.

So far as organizational makeup is concerned, there are no longer any national divisions along craft or occupational lines. Each industrial union is a single, cohesive unit, with a single set of executive officers, a single central headquar-

[12] Exception should perhaps be made for the 30,000 building laborers in the L. F. W. U., who may be designated as a non-industrialized group organized in a multi-industrial union. The above figure then reduces to 84 per cent.

[13] This leaves only the electricians', painters', mail-carriers' and four other much smaller unions in the craft category.

ters, a single schedule of dues payments for all members, etc. Only in respect of the contract-making function is there any occasion for segregating the membership into groups nationally, and even this is confined to a relatively small number of unions.[14] However, the local organizations not infrequently take the form of occupational groups, particularly in those national unions which cover the more "diversified" industries. For instance, the Wood Products Union has six locals (*avdelningar*) in Stockholm: No. 1, comprising furniture, joinery, and box factory workers; No. 3, boat builders; No. 4, wagon makers; No. 5, (glass) facet polishers; No. 7, basket makers; and No. 82, brush factory workers. The Transport Workers' Union suborganizations in the same city include locals representing dockworkers, coal carriers, teamsters and truck drivers, inland freight boat workers, and newsboys.

The Metal Workers' Union has come the nearest of any to eliminating occupational distinctions entirely from its organizational setup. Each of the locals making up this largest of all the Swedish unions covers an entire city or town, and comprises all members — in all workplaces and occupations — within the designated area. The segregation necessary for efficiency in local bargaining is attained by splitting up the locals into *verkstadsklubbar*, or shop unions. For example, in Gothenburg all the pipe fitters (employed by pipe fitting concerns) make up one such *klubb*, all garage mechanics another. In metal manufacturing, the workers in each factory have their own separate shop union.

In practically all cases, the chief reason for basing the local subdivisions on occupational or individual workplace con-

[14] In the Metal Workers' Union for example, each of the four constituent groups — the pipe fitters, automobile repairmen, iron and steel workers and machinery manufacturing workers — concludes a separate agreement with the corresponding employers' association. Each selects its own negotiating delegation, and in the final balloting on acceptance or rejection of the negotiated terms, only the group members vote. It should be noted, however, that the pipe fitters' agreement covers only plumbers and other workers in the employ of *pipe-fitting entrepreneurs* — not those in metal manufacturing or other industrially organized industries.

siderations is that it makes for greater convenience and effectiveness in bargaining over the terms of employment, or in straightening out interpretational disputes and other local difficulties. In some cases community of interest founded on knowledge of the trade or operational process undoubtedly enters in; but on the whole this is a relatively weak and insignificant factor in the Swedish industrial unions.

THE EFFECTS OF INDUSTRIALIZATION

How has the progressive change-over to industrial unionism affected worker-employer relations in Sweden? Has it benefited the workers? The employers? The country as a whole?

No complete and definitive answers can be given to these questions. Many other dynamic influences have been at work during the period under survey, and it is extremely difficult to ascertain the part which any one of them has played in bringing about a given event or trend. In one or two instances, however, the effect of industrialism's advance is unmistakable.

The replacement of several craft agreements with a single industrial agreement, in such industries as machinery, iron and steel, and building construction, has undoubtedly been beneficial, on balance, for all concerned. To be sure, the difference between the hourly rates of highly skilled workers and those of day laborers, as established in these industrial agreements, is smaller than it was when the former were still organized by crafts. But so far as actual earnings are concerned, the skilled members of the industrial unions have probably fared quite as well as they would have under a continuance of craftism.

No less unmistakable is the reduction in jurisdictional disputes which has resulted from the consolidation of craft groups into single unions. True, squabbles over the right to particular kinds of work, or to particular groups of workers, still occur — even among industrial unions. For example, there is still disagreement as to whether certain types of deliverymen rightfully belong to the transport workers or the merchandising workers. And the Laborers' and Factory Workers' Union is having considerable difficulty in persuading the so-called United Unions (*De Förenade Förbunden*) to give up certain groups of chemical and rubber workers. It is significant, however, that in recent years the number of such quarrels occurring between the craft-organized building trades unions, and between one or another of the latter and certain other unions in closely related fields, has been far greater than all the inter-industrial union disputes combined.[15]

As to the effect of the "progressive change-over" on the prevalence of strikes and lockouts, the presence of other contributing factors makes it impossible to draw any definite conclusions. One can merely observe that since the beginning of the thirties, with industrial unionism considerably farther advanced than ever, stoppages of work have decreased markedly both in number and duration. One might note, also, that the most severe stoppage in recent years — the building trades strike of 1933–1934 — was prolonged for many weeks because one of the participating craft organizations (the Masons' Union) refused to concur in a proposed settlement which the other participants had already accepted.

All in all, it is difficult to escape the conclusion that in choosing the industrial form of organization, the Swedish workers chose wisely. And this conclusion is strengthened when one discovers, as the writer did on a recent visit to Sweden, that the great majority of employers and disinterested outsiders are also convinced of its superiority over the craft union as a bargaining agency.

[15] See Landsorganisationen, *Beslut i Frågor Rörande Organisationsgränserna* (1936), *passim.*

CHAPTER IV

THE DEVELOPMENT OF BARGAINING AND AGREEMENTS

UNION ASCENDANCY AND WRITTEN AGREEMENTS

During the first years of the Swedish labor movement, negotiations between employers and organized wage earners were practically unknown. Nor is this to be wondered at, in view of the newness of unionism and the workers' inexperience in collective conduct. When dissatisfaction with prevailing conditions reached the point of active protest, they practically always struck, either in the first instance or after their demands had been refused. The employer usually preferred to let them strike, on the theory that exhausted resources would soon drive them back to work. And indeed this proved to be the case — most of the strikes of the early eighties lasted only a few days, or a few weeks at the outside.

As the union movement gathered strength during the late eighties and early nineties the situation altered materially, for by this time the older unions had acquired a well-defined organizational setup, with responsible leaders and some measure of discipline among the rank and file. And with this eventuation it became more and more the accepted practice to present formal demands to the employer before calling strikes. Moreover, many unions had by now built up strike funds, and when strikes did occur, it became increasingly difficult to starve the men out.

The employers soon woke up to the fact that protracted strikes raised their costs and drove customers away. And the more farseeing among them, realizing that this might prove ruinous in the long run, began to change their tactics. Instead of letting strikes take their course or flatly refusing the demands of the workers and thus encouraging them to strike, they offered to get together with their representatives and "talk things over."

One of the earliest recorded instances of this occurred in Stockholm in 1890.[1] The molders in Moberg's foundry, being dissatisfied with the employer's response to their demands for better wage terms, had walked out. The association of machine shop and foundry owners in Stockholm, of which the Moberg firm was a member, had previously made a rule that in the event of a strike at any workplace, all constituent plants were to be shut down. In the present instance, however, this was not done. Instead, the association delegated to three of its members the task of ending the conflict by peaceful means. This committee, after studying the situation for several days, discovered that the discontent was by no means confined to Herr Moberg's establishment, and it therefore invited the managers and foremen of all the foundries in the city, together with three union representatives from each plant, to meet in a conference for the purpose of "freely and openly discussing" working conditions. The result of this "first Swedish Mond conference" was the following written agreement:

(1) The time rate shall be the basis of all wage payments. It shall be determined by agreement between the individual molder and his superior, and may thereafter be raised or lowered by the said superior in accordance with the worker's ability and current business conditions.

(2) Overtime work shall as far as possible be avoided.

(3) Payment shall be by the hour or by the piece, as agreed upon between the molder and his superior.

(4) For overtime work, molders shall be paid at a higher rate than for regular work, on the same basis as other workers in the plant.

(5) For piecework, the rate shall be established beforehand by agreement between the individual molder and his (immediate) superior, and shall apply for a determined number of pourings. The piece wage for any molder may be as high as 50 per cent above his time rate, and the rate shall be such that he will be able to earn his time rate.

(6) The full time rate shall be paid for all work done on the time basis, whether or not the product is free from flaws.

[1] See Styrman, *op. cit.*, pp. 56–57.

(7) Piecework product which is spoiled through the molder's negligence shall not be paid for, but in cases where the molder is not at fault, payment shall be made according to agreement with his immediate superior.

(8) The total wage, time rate, hours worked, and a reckoning of all piece wages shall appear on every pay envelope.

This contract was obviously not very favorable to the workers. But it must be remembered that it was the first document of its kind ever concluded in Swedish manufacturing industry and therefore any provisions which the workers had had a voice in determining were almost certain to be an improvement. It will also be noted that the agreement is entirely taken up with methods and rates of payment. Indeed, most of the early agreements consisted almost exclusively of small concessions to the workers regarding wages, overtime, and hours of work.

As consolidation of the local unions into national bodies proceeded, the bargaining position of the organized wage earners in their dealings with the employers (the great majority of whom were still unorganized) improved correspondingly. Nor were they slow to take advantage of this growing strength. Their policies became increasingly more militant, and their demands more insistent. As a result, there was a rapid increase in the number of agreements; the concessions in wages and hours became more and more substantial; and, not least, provisions concerning safety, sanitation, medical attendance, and other conditions over which the workers had previously had no control, were introduced. As one early commentator put it, "The tables became so completely turned that the isolated employer soon found himself in the same disadvantageous position relative to the unions that the unorganized worker had previously occupied relative to him." [2] The figures summarizing the outcome of stoppages of work before and during the "consolidation period," shown on the following page, indicate the extent of this shift in bargaining advantage.[3]

[2] G. Olin, *Kollektivavtal i den Utländska Lagstiftningen* (1911), p. 5.

[3] Taken from the official government statistics (Kungliga Kommerskol-

It will be observed that the ratio of worker to employer victories was considerably greater after 1895 — when the consolidation process was well advanced — than in the preceding five years. From 1885 to 1889 the honors were about even.

However, less than a decade was to elapse before the employers had built up organizations of their own, which in

OUTCOME OF STOPPAGES, 1863–1902

	Number of Stoppages				
Outcome	1863–1884	1885–1889	1890–1894	1895–1899	1900–1902
In favor of employer	22	26	41	39	24
In favor of workers	7	29	74	150	93
Compromise	14	16	29	102	82
Total	43	71	144	291	199

scope and bargaining strength were nearly on a par with the unions and in centralization of responsibility were, on the whole, superior to them. The employers' main and immediate objective in organizing was, of course, to halt the workers' forward push. But it is significant that in launching their counteroffensive they did not try to destroy either the unions themselves or the bargaining institution which union initiative had brought into being. They had discovered that the existence of a mutually agreed upon written document, specifying the important wage and working conditions, held certain advantages for them as well as for the workers. For one thing, it provided a reasonably good insurance against strikes during the life of the agreement. It also lessened materially the number of complaints and demands from individuals and small groups of workers — necessarily a considerable item in a country with an enlightened and independent worker population. In fact, the most important developments in the evolution of the written agreement occurred immediately *after* the formation of the employers' associations, and largely as a consequence thereof. Just as the unions were chiefly instrumental in introducing

legium, *Arbetsstatistik, E:1, Arbetsinställelser i Sverige, 1863–1902*) as reproduced in Hallendorff, *Svenska Arbetsgivareföreningen*, p. 18.

the collective contract into Swedish industrial relations, so the employers' organizations played the leading part in giving it the form and content which it has today.

FROM LOCAL TO NATIONAL AGREEMENTS

The first of these developments, the transition from local to national agreements, was in a sense a necessary result of the employers' banding together. A strong sentiment for uniformity of wage and working conditions over all plants producing the same product was already in evidence on both sides. The more highly paid workers saw that their jobs were endangered by the existence of lower wage rates in other workplaces; similarly, their employers realized the difficulties of competing with these establishments.[4] With the workers already nationally organized and the employers forming associations equally broad in scope, it was almost inevitable that negotiations between the corresponding national bodies should take place sooner or later, and that the question of uniform agreement provisions for all plants should be one of the first to be taken up.

The national negotiations came about in various ways. Sometimes it was the employers who issued the invitation, but quite as often the unions took the initiative. Sometimes they were of peaceful origin, but more frequently they were called only after serious strikes or lockouts had occurred.

One of the first, and in many respects the most significant, of these conferences took place between union representatives and the executive committee of the Machine Industry Association in 1903, less than a year after the formation of the latter body. The Association, convinced that the time had come to put a stop to what it termed the "tyranny of the unions' demands," had taken the occasion of a number of minor strikes to declare an industry-wide lockout — the first of its kind in the country's history. Two weeks later the four principally affected national unions — those of the metal workers, molders, woodworkers, and laborers and fac-

[4] Cf. Kungliga Kommerskollegium, *Arbetsstatistik, A:5, Kollektivavtal* (Stockholm, 1910), vol. I, p. 95.

tory workers — proposed a conference with the Association, which the latter, after some delay, accepted. As a result of this conference the lockout was called off and the minor strikes settled, but it required more than two years of further negotiations — during which period another big lockout, this time of five months' duration, took place — to iron out the difficulties regarding the industry as a whole. In November, 1905, a committee composed of two employers and two union representatives, with a government conciliator as chairman, finally worked out a national agreement which both sides were willing to accept. By it minimum wage rates, uniform hours of work, overtime payment schedules, and rules for settling disputes were established in all plants owned by members of the Machine Industry Association.[5]

Although this was the first national agreement of outstanding importance to be concluded, other industries were not far behind.[6] By 1909 similar covenants were in force for iron and steel, sawmills, bottle manufacturing, construction materials, wood products, shoe factories, the building trades, and the privately owned railways. Four more industries — paper, pulp, textiles, and ready-made clothing — followed suit within the next few years.[7]

In view of the reluctance of many American employers to form combinations and become joint parties to wage con-

[5] While the settlement included a number of concessions by both sides, on balance the employers appear to have had the better of the bargain. Wage rates were, to be sure, increased somewhat, and hours slightly reduced. But over against these gains one must set two provisions which the employers succeeded in getting incorporated in the agreement: a prohibition of stoppages based on grievances and interpretational disputes; and a stipulation that "for all piecework not established in fixed price lists, the terms of payment shall be decided on, in each instance, through free negotiation between the employer or his representative and the particular worker or workers to whom the job is offered" — i.e., without the intervention of the union. For a fuller account of this episode see John Lindgren, *Svenska Metallindustriarbetareförbundets Historia* (Stockholm, 1938), vol. I, pp. 550–638; see also Styrman, *op. cit.*, chapter iv.

[6] The only earlier ones of any significance were those concluded in the printing and tobacco-products industries, in 1903 and 1904, respectively.

[7] Cf. *Arbetsstatistik, A:5*, vol. I, p. 97.

tracts covering wide geographic and economic areas, it may seem strange that national agreements should have made such rapid headway in Swedish industry. It must be remembered, however, that in the past most American unions have had no great bargaining advantage over local employer groups, or even over individual concerns. Hence when the question of joining a national combine and subscribing to a joint agreement has arisen, the employers have been more or less free to choose between nationally determined and local wage scales.

But in the period when the Swedish employers' associations were being formed, the situation was quite different. The national unions were already very strong — so strong, in fact, that they were able to force individual enterprises to pay much higher wages than they had been paying prior to the advent of organization. True, the leveling process of negotiation would also result in higher wage scales *for the relatively low-paying employers*, if they joined an association and became signatories to an industry-wide contract. But these prospective increases seemed less formidable than those which they foresaw the unions forcing on them if they remained unorganized. In other words, it was the desire to sacrifice as little as possible which led the low-wage employers to band together with those who were paying better and to seek national agreements with uniform wage rates.

FROM CRAFT TO INDUSTRIAL AGREEMENTS

A second and no less important consequence of the formation of employer combines was the development of what may be called industrial agreements (*industriavtal*), and here we find the employers pursuing a deliberate and preconceived policy. From the start the unions — and especially the craft unions — had insisted on negotiating agreements with the employers independently of other bodies represented in the same plants. The employers, however, had always been opposed to this arrangement, mainly because of the time and trouble involved, and the element of uncertainty introduced when the several contracts expired at different times during the year. Soon after they became organized, therefore, they began to force the issue on this point, and with considerable success. In the above-mentioned case, for example, the Machine Industry Association was able to bring together the four national craft unions which had taken part in the conferences under the same contract. And, as noted earlier, when this contract expired in 1908 the employers succeeded in forcing the inclusion of four additional organizations as signatories to the new agreement. The machinery trades national agreement thus became also a full-fledged *industrial* agreement, in that it covered practically all types of wage earners within the industry.

In the same manner, the Iron Masters' Association, in 1907, induced the metal workers and the laborers and factory workers to act together in negotiating the first national covenant for the iron and steel industry.[8] Since then, practically all the employers' organizations have taken up this policy, and, as a result, the industrial agreement is today the dominant, not to say the almost universal type of labor contract in Swedish industry. Moreover, employer pressure in this direction has been one of the important influencing factors in the "successive change-over" of the Swedish unions from craft to industrial unionism.[9]

As regards the wage contract, the major consequence of combination among the employers was the reëstablishment of piecework as the principal method of determining wages in the agreements. During the nineties the consensus of worker sentiment was overwhelmingly in favor of eliminating this form of payment. The then prevailing practice in industrial concerns was to revise the piece rates whenever a given job or batch of work was completed and, owing to the constant introduction of improved machinery, the revisions were usually downward. It was this feature that constituted the chief grounds for the workers' hostility. Most of the unions had adopted by-laws or resolutions calling for

[8] Sundholm, *op. cit.*, p. 40.

[9] See Chapter III, esp. pp. 51–52.

the abolition of piecework,[10] and by the turn of the century they had succeeded in introducing into many of the agreements clauses expressly forbidding its use.

One of the chief reasons for the employers' banding together was their desire to combat this movement. But in doing so they were sensible enough not to insist on retaining the rate revision practice. Instead they agreed to the adoption of fixed rate lists, arrived at through central negotiations and remaining in force for a definite period. With the main source of dissatisfaction thus eliminated, the employers found it much easier to persuade the workers to accept the piecework system. By 1907 its use was specified in all the important agreements in manufacturing, mining and construction, and in a number of service industries as well.[11]

THE GROWTH OF AGREEMENT COVERAGE

While the employers were establishing their organizations and consolidating their position against the unions, the bargaining institution itself had been making steady progress. Between 1902 and the beginning of 1909 the collective agreement had come into widespread use in all branches of economic activity except agriculture, logging, and merchandising, and the number of workers covered by agreements had more than trebled. During 1908 the upswing was especially marked, the total coverage being nearly 320,000 workers at the end of the year, as against 250,000 at the beginning — this despite the fact that the country was in the grip of a severe depression.

But with the general strike of the following year the cause of collective bargaining received a severe setback. The strike ended in defeat for the workers — a defeat of attrition which left the unions practically bankrupt. The morale of the rank and file was undermined, and membership fell off sharply. It was this latter circumstance which, more than

[10] Cf. Landsorganisationen, *Fackföreningsrörelsen* (Stockholm, 1912), vol. I, pp. 63, 111–112; Styrman, *op. cit.*, p. 90.

[11] *Arbetsstatistik, A:5*, vol. I, p. 330. A fuller description of the piecework system's development is given in Chapter VIII.

any other factor, brought about the slump in collective employer-employee dealings. Many local agreements expired and were not renewed because the party on the worker side no longer existed. In other instances the employers, realizing that the unions no longer commanded sufficient strength to enforce observance, repudiated the contracts they had made. By the end of 1909 the number of agreement-governed workers had fallen to 250,000, where it had been at

COLLECTIVE AGREEMENTS IN SWEDEN, 1902–1937

Year	Workers Covered by Agreements (*thousands*)	Year	Workers Covered by Agreements (*thousands*)
1902	73	1920	438
1903	87	1921	349
1904	106	1922	313
1905	115	1923	392
1906	200	1924	413
1907	256	1925	452
1908	318	1926	465
1909	254	1927	495
1910	252	1928	513
1911	230	1929	541
1912	227	1930	581
1913	233	1931	618
1914	244	1932	636
1915	256	1933	636
1916	266	1934	675
1917	297	1935	719
1918	317	1936	769
1919	379	1937	911

Sources: Kungliga Socialstyrelsen, *Arbetsinställelser och Kollektivavtal samt Förlikningsmännens Verksamhet*, 1931, p. 32, and 1937, p. 28. Figures for 1902–1906, inclusive, estimated on basis of growth in total union membership. (Landsorganisationen, *Sifferuppgifter och Grafiska Framställningar, 1888–1912*, p. 8.)

the beginning of 1908; it did not rise above this figure again until 1916.

With the labor movement in a state of semicollapse, it might be expected that the employers who continued to negotiate and sign contracts with the unions would have seized the opportunity to force their adversaries to accept a worsening of the terms. The available evidence indicates, however, that the agreements renewed during 1910 and 1911 were little if any more unfavorable to the workers than they had been before the strike. In fact, so far as wages and hours are concerned, a slight gain was recorded by the end of 1911.[12] It is difficult to account entirely for this, but the business leaders' alarm at the magnitude of the general strike probably had a good deal to do with it. At any rate, it is certain that few of them had any desire to see the performance repeated.[13]

With the revival of union activity shortly after the outbreak of the war, collective bargaining also began to show signs of renewed life, and by 1919 a full-fledged upswing in agreement making was again under way. A brief recession accompanied the postwar depression, but shortly afterwards the upward trend was resumed. As the table on page 73 shows, it has continued practically unabated ever since.

EXPANSION IN PARTICULAR INDUSTRIES

In examining some of the features of this expansion, it will be convenient to draw a line first at the year-end of 1920, at which time the Social Board conducted a comprehensive survey of the currently operative collective agreements — the only one that has been made since the original study by the *Kommerskollegium* at the close of 1907. The survey shows that the increase in bargaining during and immediately after the war was by no means a general one, but was confined in the main to half a dozen important industries. The following table shows the extent of use of agreements in these industries in 1920 as compared with 1907.

In each of these industries except textiles, it will be noted, the coverage was considerably more than doubled, and in the case of agriculture it was increased nearly sixteenfold. The causes of this selective growth were no doubt various, but two factors appear to have been predominant: the rapid development of Sweden as an exporter of industrial products during the period and the increase of organization among

[12] See Kungliga Socialstyrelsen, *Kollektivavtal i Sverige År 1911* (Stockholm, 1913), pp. 15–31.

[13] The fact that 1910 and 1911 were relatively prosperous years, as compared with 1908, was undoubtedly another contributing factor.

the workers. In iron and steel and machinery the rapid rise in the volume of production during the war and postwar years was unquestionably the major item. Union membership and collective bargaining had been quite general in these industries for more than a decade, and once the dis-

COLLECTIVE AGREEMENTS IN SELECTED INDUSTRIES, 1907 AND 1920

Industry	NUMBER OF WORKERS COVERED BY AGREEMENTS (*in thousands*) 1907	1920
Iron mining, and iron and steel manufacture	16.0	43.8
Machinery	26.2	62.5
Sawmills	10.5	24.5
Pulp and paper	8.4	28.8
Textiles	12.5	23.5
Agriculture	1.7	26.4

Sources: *Arbetsstatistik A:5*, vol. I, and Kungliga Socialstyrelsen, *Kollektivavtal i Sverige vid Årsskiftet 1920/21* (Stockholm, 1922).

couragement engendered by the failure of the general strike had been dispelled, it was a relatively easy matter for the unions to bring the new workers into the fold.

Pulp and paper manufacturing also expanded rapidly during this period, but here there had been little effective organization, and it required vigorous efforts on the part of several national unions as well as the S. F. T. U. to build union strength up to the point where the bargaining privilege could be demanded and obtained. This was even more true of the sawmill industry, where the small size of the plants and their wide dispersion through the northern half of the country made the work of organizing especially difficult.

In agriculture the introduction of agreements must be attributed almost entirely to organizational activity. The large-scale farmers had had an employers' association for many years, but except for a brief outbreak in 1907 and 1908, combinations among the agricultural laborers had been practically nonexistent. However, in 1918 the S. F. T. U. conducted an intensive campaign in the rural districts, and within a year the Agricultural Workers' Union — its membership now increased to a figure comparable with that of the other national bodies — had signed a country-wide agreement with the organized employers, embracing a majority of the larger farming estates.[14]

From the postwar depression to 1935 the agreement system underwent a further expansion of approximately 65 per cent, measured in number of workers covered. During this period the most rapid progress occurred in logging.[15] In 1921 the number of people working under agreements in this industry was practically negligible, but by 1935 it had increased to 56,000 — nearly 70 per cent of the total gainfully occupied wage earners.[16] The small size and inaccessibility of the enterprises and the seasonal character of the work constitute serious obstacles to organization among the loggers, which accounts in large measure for the industry's tardiness in adopting the bargaining institution. Even now most of the contracts are purely local. Nevertheless, the work of organizing, and of consolidating organizations, is being steadily pushed on both sides, and it may well be that before the decade is out wages and working conditions in logging, as in manufacturing, building, and other productive fields, will be governed by a central document.

Meanwhile a number of other industries, already well organized in 1920, have greatly increased their use of collective bargaining. The most noteworthy of these increases are shown in the accompanying table.

In the main these increases reflect gains in worker organization and concomitant union agitation for contracts with the employers. In building, pulp and paper, however, industrial expansion has played a not unimportant role, while the taking over by the state of a large part of both the rail-

[14] Cf. *Kollektivavtal vid Årsskiftet 1920/21*, Part 1, pp. 143–144.

[15] The term logging, as used here, includes the felling of trees, cutting them into logs, and transporting the logs to market (sawmills and pulp factories) usually by floating them down the streams.

[16] Data from *Statistisk Årsbok* (official statistical yearbook of the Swedish Government) for 1937, and from the files of the State Mediation Service (*Förlikningsmannaexpeditionen*).

way and the power systems accounts for some of the increase in government service.

One of the outstanding features of the extension of the scope of bargaining during this period has been the large increase in the number of agreements signed with unorganized manufacturers. This has occurred mainly in the machinery trades, but it has been considerable also in sawmills, wood products, construction, textiles, and a number of other lines. Most of these employers are small scale producers who cannot afford to belong to employers' associations, but who nevertheless find themselves obliged to conclude contracts because their employees are practically all organized. An account of the unions' policies in dealing with these isolated entrepreneurs is given in Chapter VI.

COLLECTIVE AGREEMENTS IN SELECTED INDUSTRIES, 1920 AND 1935

Industry	Number of Workers Covered by Agreements (*in thousands*)	
	1920	1935
Agriculture	26.4	59.7
Building	24.0	83.1
Government Service (National and local)	14.6	48.0
Pulp and paper	28.8	44.7
Textiles	23.6	40.8

Sources: *Kollektivavtal vid Årsskiftet 1920/21*, and *Arbetsinställelser och Kollektivavtal samt Förlikningsmännens Verksamhet, 1935*.

Wholesale and retail trade are the only important branches of business activity in which collective bargaining has not yet come into general use. In neither line are more than 20 per cent of the workers organized or covered by agreements. As in logging, the establishments here are almost always small. Moreover, some two thirds of the employees are young women and boys, working at relatively low rates of pay. It is no easy matter to weld such workers into strong unions. Finally, the employers have also been reluctant to join organizations, and this has rendered the development of bargaining in the trading occupations still more difficult.

In summary, it may be said that the chief factor influencing the spread of collective agreements in Sweden has been the growth and spread of unionism itself. The correlation between the trend of S. F. T. U. membership and that of worker coverage of agreements, especially during the past fifteen years, is too close to be accidental. As for the employers' associations, we have seen that one of the principal consequences of their entry into the bargaining arena has been the establishment of national industrial agreements as the predominant type of labor contract. The employers' influence on the contents of these compacts will be discussed in Part Two.

PART TWO

THE COLLECTIVE AGREEMENTS

CHAPTER V

AGREEMENT CONTENTS: "GENERAL" PROVISIONS

IN THE FOUR preceding chapters we have seen how the Swedish trade unions and employers' associations have been built up over the past forty or fifty years, and how, through the process of collective bargaining, these organizations have worked out a system of written agreements, defining the terms of employment for each major industry. With this historical bird's-eye view as a background, we may now proceed to the main object of our study, which is to describe the makeup and functioning of the Swedish bargaining institution as it exists at the present time. First, we shall examine the principal contents of the agreements. Following this, we shall look into the process of negotiating and concluding agreements. Finally, we shall make a brief survey of the methods by which bargaining is carried on while the agreements are in force.

As has been noted, the terms of work in most branches of economic activity are contained in *national industrial* agreements, governing all organized plants and all wage earner occupations within a given industry. Each of the twenty-eight employers' associations of nation-wide scope concludes such a contract with the corresponding national union.[1] Some fifteen more, covering smaller industries and state-owned enterprises, also fall in this class, bringing the total of national agreements to forty-three. These sets of standards, which make the conditions of work uniform throughout each industry, may therefore be said to constitute the essential framework of the Swedish bargaining system.

In the present chapter we shall examine some of the more important "general" provisions (*allmänna bestämmelser*) in the agreements — e.g., those relating to the adjustment

[1] See *supra*, pp. 46–47.

of disputes, hiring and termination, hours of work, overtime, vacations, and sick leave compensation. We shall then turn our attention to the other main subdivision of agreement subject matter — namely the terms of payment for work.

THE ADJUSTMENT APPARATUS

Taking the complex of collective contracts as a whole, "fixed rules" are unquestionably predominant over "adjustment machinery." The Swedes are a methodical and formality-loving people, who prefer to behave according to well-defined precepts — albeit they like to have a hand in determining what these precepts shall be. This explains, in part at least, the fact that the agreements are largely taken up with detailed stipulations regarding wages, hours of work, overtime, and other conditions of employment.

However, rules are seldom entirely unambiguous; nor is it possible to include them in sufficient number and detail to cover all situations which may arise in connection with the employer-employee relationship. It has, therefore, been found necessary in most agreements to set up some sort of mechanism for handling difficulties which cannot be settled by literal application of the written provision.

With respect to this feature, we find that in the majority of the contracts where one of the parties is a constituent firm or association of the Swedish Employers' Federation, the stipulations are practically identical — a circumstance which further attests the powerful unifying influence exerted by the central employers' organization. Indeed, the Federation's influence has extended considerably beyond the sphere of its own membership in this regard, for essentially the same provision is found in most of the agreements concluded by "unaffiliated" firms and associations as well.

In its most common formulation, the "disputes clause" reads as follows:

> When differences arise as to the meaning or application of this agreement, negotiations shall be instituted first between the immediately affected parties, thereafter (if no settlement can be

reached) between the respective central organizations. Such differences may not be made the occasion for stoppages of work, whether by strike, blockade, lockout, or any other method, until an attempt at peaceful settlement has been made in the manner prescribed above.

It will be noted that this provision gives only general information as to how, and by whom, the negotiating is to be done.[2] In a few contracts, however, the procedure to be followed is specified in greater detail. For example, the machinery trades national agreement states that if a dispute has not been cleared up through local negotiations within fourteen days, either party may "appeal" to higher authority by communicating its desire to the other party, in writing, within an additional period of eight days. When this has been done, each of the central organizations — national union and employers' association — must designate from two to six delegates, "who through negotiation shall attempt to adjust the dispute." It is then up to the joint committee to agree on one of their number as chairman, to lead the proceedings. If this proves impossible, an "outside impartial person" is chosen. This committee must have completed its work (reached a settlement or declared the negotiations broken down) within fifteen days after the date of the written communication.[3]

It will be observed that neither of these clauses states what is to be done if the *central* negotiations fail. Until a

[2] In practice, the parleys are usually conducted according to "unwritten rules" — established and mutually accepted methods which vary only to a minor degree from industry to industry. Cf. Chapter XII, pp. 194–195.

[3] *Kollektivt Avtal mellan Sveriges Verkstadsförening och Vedërbörande Fackförbund, 1938* (Stockholm, 1938), pp. 3–4. It should be noted that in the machinery trades, where the diversity of products and occupations makes the frequent setting of new rates of payment unavoidable and where, consequently, local differences are continually arising, the "adjustment machinery" method of bargaining occupies a central position. In most other manufacturing lines, however, the productive processes are much more nearly uniform, both over time and from place to place. It is therefore easier, in these industries, to make semi-permanent stipulations which will be satisfactory to both sides.

decade ago approximately two thirds of the national agreements contained no provision for final settlement; hence the parties to these covenants were free to take coercive action at this stage. The remaining third specified arbitration as the last instance, but even here the degree of compulsion was limited, since the method was to be resorted to only if either party so desired.[4]

However, with the passage in 1928 of the Collective Agreement and Labor Court Laws, adjudicative disposal of disputes concerning the meaning and application of agreement subject matter was made compulsory for all industries. Since then most of the "arbitration provisions" have been struck out, and new clauses, either expressly or impliedly specifying the Labor Court as the final resort, have been added to practically all the national agreements.[5]

SAFEGUARDS IN AGREEMENT-MAKING

Although the "adjustment clauses" described above refer only to interpretational disputes, in practice they apply to *all* intra-agreement period differences, whether specifically alluded to in the agreements or not. But there is another and even more important class of disputes which they do not cover — those which arise after an agreement has expired and before a new one has been concluded. In the great majority of instances there is no express prohibition of strikes or lockouts on such occasions. What is more, both sides strongly insist that the right to take drastic measures shall be left unimpaired.

But this does not mean that either of the parties to an agreement is free to allow its contract to expire and then to declare a stoppage immediately and without warning. On the contrary, the dissatisfied party is obligated to initiate the proceedings for negotiating a *new* contract. This is accomplished through the "termination clause," which, like

[4] Cf. *Statens Offentliga Utredningar, 1927:4* (*Utredningar till Belysande av Arbetsfredsfrågan*) (Stockholm, 1927), p. 120.

[5] Regarding this subject see further Chapter XII, pp. 195–196, and Chapter XV.

the disputes arrangement, is practically universal. It provides that if either side wishes to terminate the agreement at the stated (optional) expiration date, it must notify the other side of its intention a certain period in advance — usually three months. In addition, the aggressor party must accompany its termination notice with a "complete and comprehensive proposal for a new agreement."[6] In many cases it is also stipulated that the opposing party must submit a counterproposal within a stated period and that negotiations shall begin within a certain interval after that.

It is thus evident that even in these "interest disputes," as they are called, some attempt at peaceful adjustment is guaranteed. To be sure, the renewal conferences which follow the termination of agreements are not always successful. The issues at stake here are usually more vital and the opposing parties' views more divergent than in interpretational quarrels, and despite the existence of a well-worked-out negotiation procedure — including eventual mediation by the state — breakdowns and stoppages not infrequently ensue.[7]

A few agreements, notably those for newspaper printing, the private railways, and municipal works, contain provisions which practically preclude *all* strikes and lockouts, whatever the cause or occasion. Peaceful settlement of interest disputes in these industries is attained, in the last instance, through arbitration. The first step in concluding a new agreement, after the old one has been terminated, consists in ordinary negotiations across the conference table. If this attempt fails, the entire matter is placed in the hands of a board of judges, composed of an equal number of union and employer representatives, together with one or more impartial members. The decision of this board is final and binding.

In the newspaper industry, prohibition of stoppages is unequivocal and the settlement by arbitration of differences

[6] See, e.g., the wood products national agreement.

[7] A more detailed discussion of the negotiation procedure is given in Chapter IX.

regarding new agreements compulsory. Similar rules were laid down in the original private railways agreement, but in 1918 these were modified, the arbitration process being made voluntary rather than obligatory. This was followed by several minor strikes, which caused some disruption over a period of three or four years. For more than a decade past, however, there have been no stoppages on the railroads. The practice of the earlier years is still followed, but by choice rather than compulsion.

Voluntary arbitration is also stipulated in the municipal works agreement,[8] and here too stoppages are practically unknown. As a means of insuring smooth continuance of operations, it is further specified that if accord has not been reached on a new contract when the expiration date arrives, the old document shall continue in effect until all disputed points are settled.

SYMPATHETIC STOPPAGES NOT A BREACH OF CONTRACT

From what has been said above, it must not be concluded that all provisions connected with disputes in Swedish agreements are of a peace-conducing nature. On the contrary, some of them are designed primarily to avoid the necessity of keeping the peace.

As noted, both sides insist on having a free hand to take strong measures, if and when the initial attempt at negotiating a new contract has failed. This idea of freedom of action is carried even further in the so-called "sympathy clause," contained in all the S. E. F. agreements and many others. According to this provision, "lockouts ordered by the central employers' association, and strikes or blockades ordered by the central workers' organization, shall not be considered a breach of this contract." It is usually invoked for the declaration of sympathetic strikes and lockouts, which have been used with great effectiveness in Sweden in the past, and still are to a considerable extent. For example, if a local union has terminated its agreement with an employer and the national union decides to apply pressure to make him

[8] See *supra*, p. 38.

come to terms by calling out all the other workers in the same industry, the agreements covering these other workers are not thereby violated. Similarly, if two employers' associations go to the aid of a third, which is trying to impose its will on the corresponding national union in negotiations over a new national agreement, the former do not thereby break their contracts.

It is important to note that the effective use of this method of applying pressure became possible only after strong centralization over a wide sector of the industrial field had been accomplished. It seems fairly clear that no sympathetic stoppage, on a scale involving one or more entire industries at any rate, can really be made to work unless the organizations declaring it are under some obligation, either statutory or moral, to render aid to others with which they are allied. And indeed, the available evidence bears this out. The S. E. F., with its highly integrated central control, has made frequent and successful use of sympathetic lockouts — involving as many as six major industries at once — whereas sympathetic *strikes* (if one excepts the great conflict of 1909) have seldom been extended beyond the individual national union concerned.

The employers were, in fact, the initiators of both the practice and the provision. The associated machinery manufacturers adopted the idea at the very outset. In 1903, as we have seen, they declared an industry-wide lockout as a means of forcing the national unions to call off a number of minor strikes; and in 1905 they repeated the performance, this time in deadly earnest. The other employers' organizations, which had put the major emphasis on strike insurance at the start, soon saw the advantages of the machine makers' methods. In 1907, when the workers balked at accepting the unsavory "December compromise," the S. E. F. made its first threat of a general shutdown. The threat proved to be all that was necessary.[9]

At about this time too, the S. E. F., through its member associations, began to demand the inclusion of the sympathy

[9] Cf. *supra*, p. 31.

clause in the agreements.[10] Ostensibly this was a defensive move to protect the employers' rights. The workers, it was claimed, "never consider themselves prohibited, by their contracts, from taking part in any sympathetic strike . . ." so why shouldn't the employers be equally free?[11] One may suspect, however, that the superior possibilities of the sympathetic stoppage, from their own standpoint, had a good deal to do with their insistence.

In 1908 the employers wielded the lockout threat weapon on three different occasions, each time substantially attaining their end.[12] And during the ensuing twenty years or more they lost no opportunity to avail themselves of it. Sometimes they had to carry out the threat, but even in these instances they were, on the whole, successful.[13] All in all, the employers have little reason to regret the sympathy clause.

THE "SECTION 23 CLAUSE"

Along with the disputes clauses there are a number of other provisions, dealing with general features of the employment relationship, which are identical in the great majority of Swedish agreements. Most prominent among these provisions, perhaps, are the two which guarantee the employer's right to "run his business in his own way" and the workers' right to organize. The source of the former is Section 23 of the S. E. F.'s statutes, according to which every collective agreement entered into by a member association or firm of the Federation must include a stipulation to the effect that the employer shall have "full freedom to take on and to employ workers regardless of whether they belong to organizations or not." Heavy fines are levied on the S. E. F. members for nonobservance of this rule.

The second of these two clauses, it will be remembered, was the employers' counterconcession to the unions' acceptance of Section 23 in the famous compromise of Decem-

[10] Cf. Landsorganisationen, *Minnesskrift, 1898–1923*, p. 123.

[11] Hallendorff, *op. cit.*, p. 78.

[12] *Ibid.*, pp. 97–103.

[13] For a fuller description of this episode, see Chapter X, pp. 162–165.

ber, 1906. As customarily formulated, the clause guarantees the right to organize to both workers *and* employers. Obviously, however, the important right in this connection is that accorded to the workers. The "right to organize" provision is invariably followed by an auxiliary stipulation to the effect that if a worker believes he has been discharged because of his union affiliations he may demand an investigation, through his union, as a means of obtaining redress.

So far as *hiring* is concerned, the "Section 23 clause" is of relatively minor significance today. With more than 90 per cent of all the workers in manufacturing, mining, and construction organized, employers in these branches of activity have little choice but to hire union men. Its import with respect to *dismissals* and *layoffs* is considerably greater, for this feature of Section 23 is intimately bound up with the "right to organize" clause. However it is in connection with union *activity*, rather than the mere fact of belonging to a union, that the latter clause is usually invoked in disputes over dismissals and layoffs. The adjustment of such disputes, and of those relating to the employer's "right to lead and allot" in general, is discussed at some length in Chapter XII.[14]

It may be mentioned in this connection that limitations on the introduction of labor-saving machinery are almost totally absent in Swedish collective contracts;[15] and in practice there has been little active opposition to innovations by the workers. The most common, and indeed practically the only stipulation concerning this aspect of the conduct of enterprise provides that "if the employer introduces a new method of production, or improved machinery, the rates of payment (piece rates) may be changed, through negotiation, even during the life of the (agreed-upon) piece rate schedule."[16] The implication here is, of course, that the rates will

[14] Pages 197–201.

[15] Such limitations would — according to the conception prevalent in Sweden, at any rate — be incompatible with the "Section 23 clause."

[16] National agreement for the iron and steel industry (*Järnbruksavtalet*), 1936, p. 3.

be *lowered*, although the bargaining feature may enable the workers to prevent a reduction in full proportion to the increased output. However, no provision is made for taking care of workers displaced by labor-saving devices.

HOURS OF WORK

A working week of 48 hours, usually divided into five days of 8½ hours each and one of 5½ hours, is specified in all major industries except agriculture and forestry, retail trade, and railroad and water transportation. Since 1920 this has been stipulated as the *maximum* week by law,[17] and from this standpoint the clause has no great significance at the present time, being merely a confirmation of the statutory requirement. That 48 hours still remains the *standard* week is, nevertheless, of considerable interest, indicating as it does the relative rarity of agitation for shorter hours in Sweden as compared with other countries in recent years.

Within a year after the passage of the Forty-eight Hour Law, the hours clauses of most of the agreements had been changed to conform to it. However, this was accomplished only after a great deal of bickering and many open conflicts. When one considers that the average week in the affected industries had been more than 54 hours, with as high as 60 hours obtaining in particular trades, it is evident that a sudden and drastic readjustment in the productive setup was called for. It involved, on the one side, the question of "compensation" to the workers for the decrease in weekly working time and, on the other, such problems as the revision of shifts and the procurement of additional personnel to supply the man-hours lost through the curtailment.[18]

[17] The unions had long been agitating for a legal forty-eight hour week, but the succession of conservative governments had refused to entertain the idea. In 1917, however, a coalition of Liberals and Social-Democrats gained control of the government; and when, two years later, they also succeeded in getting a majority in both houses of the Riksdag, it was a foregone conclusion that the Forty-eight Hour Law would be one of the first acts passed. V. Spångberg, *Från Arvid Posse till per Albin Hansson* (Stockholm, 1936), pp. 154, 159; see also Hansson, *Den Svenska Fackföreningerörelsen*, sixth edition, p. 282.

[18] Cf. Styrman, *op. cit.*, pp. 184–187.

The final outcome, after the controversies and stoppages were over, was what might have been expected in a situation where the opposing parties were of approximately equal strength.[19] In the main, pay rates were raised, but in a smaller proportion than the reduction in hours. "Time out" periods were eliminated, in the interests of a more effective utilization of the shortened day, and "plus percentages" for overtime were increased, both as compensation to the workers and as a means of making the employers reduce the actual work week to 48 hours as soon as possible.

The compromise features of the new machinery trades agreement concluded in March, 1920, after a stoppage of two months, may be regarded as fairly typical of these adjustments. The time rates, in places where the regular week had been 52 hours, were increased by 8½ per cent — i.e., in full proportion. But the piece rates (which were what really counted) were raised by only 4 per cent, with the qualification that "in cases where increased working efficiency cannot be attained nor reduction of earnings prevented through introduction of better methods or machines (as determined by joint investigation by the parties), piece rates shall be adjusted in the same proportion as the time rates." [20] The reduction in hours, fairly sharp even here, was moderated by the elimination of rest periods, washing-up allowances, and other non-work intervals, previously included in the paid working day.[21]

There are a number of occupations to which the Forty-eight Hour Law does not apply. In general, a somewhat longer and more flexible work week has been retained in these lines. In agriculture the hours vary according to the season of the year, being 46 in winter and 56 in summer.

[19] Largely because of the rapid cyclical downswing which set in late in 1920, it is difficult to isolate the compensation adjustments from the gamut of other changes made during this period. Only in those cases where the adjustments were completed before the depression began is it possible to say with any certainty how large they were.

[20] Kungliga Socialstyrelsen, *Kollektivavtal vid Årsskiftet 1920/21*, vol. I, p. 69.

[21] *Ibid.*, p. 70.

At the employer's discretion the summer schedule may be increased by eight hours per week, but not for more than a total of twelve weeks. For railroad traffic personnel (station attendants, conductors, engineers, etc.) a 208-hour month is specified, which is equivalent to 48 hours a week, but here also the employer is given considerable leeway in extending the working time.[22] In the category comprising retail trade, restaurants, barber shops, and other similar enterprises, the average work week for establishments operating under agreements was approximately 54 hours in the early twenties. This figure has undoubtedly been reduced considerably since then,[23] but many tradespeople *not* covered by agreements still work 54 hours or more.

Since the political campaign of 1918–1919, which resulted in the passage of the Forty-eight Hour Law, the unions have made no serious efforts to obtain further reductions in the hours of work and, consequently, the standard week still coincides with the legal maximum. It seems strange, at first, that this powerful worker machine should leave almost unnoticed an issue which weaker organizations in other lands make one of their foremost objectives. Yet there is no doubt that the policy reflects the average sentiment of the rank and file as well as the leaders. To most Swedish workers a high material standard of living means more than quitting work at an early hour. The relative scarcity of labor — due, in large part, to the low birth rate — also tends to work counter to the desire for shorter hours. With wage earners' services in demand and low unemployment,[24] there is little occasion to push the idea of "spreading out" the available work.

[22] National agreement for the privately-owned railways — reproduced in *Landsorganisationens Verksamhetsberättelse*, 1930, p. 83.

[23] Examination of a large number of single-place agreements indicates that the average today is only slightly above 48 hours.

[24] In some occupations there is actually a shortage. During the spring and summer of 1937, for example, agricultural laborers and building workers had to be imported from nearby countries to meet the demand.

OVERTIME

Most of the collective agreements stipulate higher wage rates for overtime than for work done during regular hours. These provisions do not conflict with the Forty-eight Hour Law, since they refer to services performed after the completion of the regular working *day* (as specified in the agreement) or on Sundays or holidays. Moreover, in cases of "preparation and finishing which must of necessity be done to assure unhindered operations," the law allows overtime work beyond the statutory limit, up to a maximum of 48 hours during any four-week period and up to 200 hours a year.[25]

The overtime rate is usually expressed as a certain percentage above the regular rate and varies (if one excepts scattered minor instances) from time-and-a-quarter to double time. In the great majority of cases, a distinction is made between "ordinary overtime" (customarily limited to two hours after the close of the regular day), night work, and Sunday and holiday work. The most frequently occurring "overpercentages" for these three categories are 35, 70, and 100 per cent. Among the lowest of the overtime allowances in the larger industries are those paid in the machinery trades — 25, 50, and 50 per cent — while those for the printing industry — 50, 100, and 100 per cent — are among the highest.[26]

According to most of the larger agreements, overtime work ordered by the management is mandatory. Frequently, however, the qualification is made that the employer is obligated to limit it to work which cannot be done during regular hours without serious inconvenience.[27] In practice,

[25] Section 7, par. 2. The law is reproduced in A. Molin, *Svensk Arbetslagstiftning* (Stockholm, 1934), p. 139.

[26] Data obtained from latest national agreements. These documents, and most of the other large-scale agreements referred to in this study, are reproduced in the current and recent issues of *Landsorganisationens Verksamhetsberättelse*.

[27] See, e.g., latest national agreements for the sawmill, wood pulp, and textile industries.

overtime is largely confined to repair and maintenance work, except during periods of unusual business activity.

VACATION PROVISIONS

Another provision found in practically all the major agreements is the one providing for a week's vacation with pay. Paid vacations have long been an established feature of the Swedish agreement system. They were first introduced in the printing industry in 1903, and by the eve of the general strike had gained a foothold in at least three other major lines. But the real upswing in the "vacation movement" did not come until after the close of the war. Beginning in 1919 the unions, now fully recovered from the setback of the general strike and the attenuating effects of the war years, made a determined drive for a contractually established recreation period, and within two years had succeeded in obtaining it for more than 70 per cent of the agreement-governed workers.[28] Since then, the institution has been extended still further, and today it is accepted as a matter of course in all but the most highly seasonal branches of economic activity.[29]

The most common practice in the manufacturing industries is to close the plants — usually during the week in which midsummer day (June 21) falls. Advantage is taken of the shutdown to make necessary major repairs and changes, and those who do this work are given vacations at other times during the summer.

The emolument is usually based on the individual wage earner's time rate; hence the strictly time worker gets his regular full week's pay. The majority of workers, however,

[28] *Kollektivavtal vid Årsskiftet 1920/21*, vol. I, p. 47.

[29] Since this chapter was written a statutory *two*-week holiday has replaced the contractual "week off with pay." In June, 1938, a law was passed (chiefly on the strength of support from the unions) which establishes twelve working days as the minimum paid vacation for all manual and clerical workers. This law, which became effective in 1940, extends the vacation privilege to *seasonal* workers, provided they have been occupied for a period of four months or more during the current year. Cf. *Fackföreningsrörelsen* (official journal of the S. F. T. U.) for June 10, 1938.

are paid on a piece or tonnage basis, and since the piece rates are customarily set to yield a larger return than the time rates, the average vacation pay is lower than the regular weekly wage. In a few of the more highly paid occupations — such as printing — the workers provide their own vacation allowances, by having a fixed sum deducted from their pay each week throughout the year.

ACCIDENT INSURANCE AND SICKNESS ASSISTANCE

We come now to a group of provisions which, while not included in all or even a major proportion of the agreements, are nevertheless sufficiently common to have an appreciable influence on the average working conditions prevailing in the country. Among the more significant of these are the stipulations regarding accident insurance. Swedish employers have been obligated by law to provide compensation for industrial accidents since 1901. However, the payments provided for at this time were entirely inadequate, and it was not until 1916 that this defect was remedied. According to the revised statute, which is still in effect, employers are required to *insure* their workers — in the state-owned *försäkringsanstalt* or other approved insurance enterprise — "for all injuries resulting from mishaps occurring at the workplace."[30] The stipulated minimum compensation amounts, for full incapacitation, to something over one-half the worker's yearly earnings. This compensation becomes an annuity for life in cases where the inability to work is permanent. For less than full incapacitation the required payments are proportionately lower.

Approximately 50 per cent of the agreements merely corroborate the statutory requirement, or carry no provision at all in this regard. In the remainder, various responsibilities

[30] *Lag om försäkring för olycksfall i arbeten*, Section 1 (reproduced in Molin, *op. cit.*, p. 169). This phrase is interpreted to include *sickness* resulting from "mishaps," as well as accidents in the ordinary sense of the word (Section 6). It is not clear, however, whether it also covers occupational diseases contracted through contact with conditions or materials in the workplace.

beyond those stipulated in the law are placed on the employer. Chief among these, perhaps, is the obligation to afford compensation during the "waiting period" (i.e., the three-day interval for which no payments are required under the law), which is included in approximately a fourth of the agreements. This clause is by no means unimportant, since it applies to accidents in which the time lost from work amounts to *less* than three days; these are, as one might expect, among the most numerous. The employers in the machinery industry also contract to insure their workers for injuries sustained outside of working hours, but this type of insurance is permissive and the expense is borne by the worker himself.

Closely allied to the accident insurance provisions, yet involving no legal compulsion, are the "sick leave clauses," by which workers are afforded compensation during absences from the job because of illness. Such clauses occur in approximately 30 per cent of the agreements. Most frequently direct disbursements by the employer are called for. However, in a few cases it is done through benefit funds, to which the employer makes periodical contributions. The sick leave payments usually amount to about half the worker's regular pay and continue, on the average, about three months. Exceptions are often made for "self-inflicted" sicknesses, such as alcoholism and venereal diseases, and for chronic ailments. Provisions of this kind are confined mainly to the clothing trades, municipal workers, telephone and telegraph personnel, and certain food industries. They are rarely found in mass production manufacturing.[31]

In practically all the agreements with sick leave clauses as well as in several hundred others, provision is made for free medical care. All in all, approximately 350,000 workers are accorded this advantage. It includes, as a rule, both doctor's services and medicine, and not infrequently hos-

[31] Comprehensive statistical analyses of the status of accident insurance and sick-leave compensation in the Swedish agreements are given in *Arbetsstatistik, A:5*, vol. I, pp. 201–209; and *Kollektivavtel vid Årsskiftet 1920/21*, vol. I, pp. 54–57.

pitalization. The industries in which medical attendance stipulations occur most commonly are (in addition to those already mentioned) agriculture, iron and steel, coal mining, glass, sawmills, paper and pulp.[32] These industries, it will be observed, are all found predominantly in rural communities, where doctors are relatively scarce and where, consequently, some special provision for medical care is more or less a necessity.

OTHER NON-WAGE PROVISIONS

In the foregoing survey, attention has been confined to the more common provisions — those which are in some sense characteristic of the agreement system as a whole. If one were to examine those of less frequent occurrence, a much larger space would be required. It is doubtful, moreover, if such an examination would serve any very useful purpose in the present study. However, one or two of these provisions may be mentioned as being indicative of the way in which certain special phases of the employment problem are handled.

To take one example, regulations regarding apprenticeship still occur in Swedish agreements, but to a considerably smaller extent than formerly. They are confined almost exclusively to craft agreements, which comprise only a small proportion of the total number at the present time. The only occupations of appreciable importance in which the employment of apprentices is in any way regulated are printing, engraving, bookbinding, baking, custom tailoring, cabinetmaking, and the painting trades. Customarily the apprenticeship clause is limited to stipulations concerning wages and the length of the training period. In baking, tailoring, and painting, however, limitation of the number of

[32] *Kollektivavtal vid Årsskiftet 1920/21*, p. 57; the estimate of 350,000 is based on the statistics given here (for the year-end of 1920), and on the increase in agreement-governed workers in the above-mentioned industries since then, as shown in Kungliga Socialstyrelsen, *Arbetsinställelser och Kollektivavtal samt Förlikningsmännens Verksamhet År 1936* (Stockholm, 1938), pp. 30–37.

apprentices is also specified. As for manufacturing, the question of restricting entrance to trades or occupations is scarcely ever mentioned. The bulk of Swedish workers have long since ceased to consider this as a reasonable possibility — if indeed they ever did.[33]

In a number of industries — notably agriculture, railway transportation, municipal works, printing, and chemicals — a "notice period" for the termination of the individual employment contract is specified. The obligation to give due notice applies to workers and employers alike, and the period — varying from a week to two months — is practically always the same for both. In most cases some form of fine is included for breach of this provision by the worker. One such is the so-called *decomptesystem*, whereby the employer can withhold a portion of the worker's uncollected wages. Newspaper printing is the only industry in which the payment of fines by the *employer* is explicitly provided for.

CONCLUSION

If one looks at the non-wage provisions of the Swedish agreements as a whole, it is apparent that they reflect, with reasonable accuracy at any rate, the strictly businesslike nature of the relations between organized labor and organized ownership. There is not, nor has there ever been, much love lost between the parties to the collective contract. The only features that show any evidences of paternalism are

[33] Cf. *Kollektivavtal vid Årsskiftet 1920/21*, vol. I, pp. 58–60; also latest national agreements for the above-mentioned trades. An exception to the general rule of omitting apprenticeship clauses in the manufacturing agreements is the "arrangement concerning apprentices" recently concluded between the Machine Industry Association and the Metal Workers' Union. This compact stipulates a training period of three years for "apprentices proper" — i.e., young workers hired with the express intention of training them for a skilled trade; and establishes a schedule of minimum hourly rates, graduated according to period of service. It provides further that "the number of apprentices (in relation to the total of skilled workers) may not be so large that it militates against their receiving proper training." As a basis for limiting the number of apprentices, this clause is obviously amenable to wide differences of interpretation; and it is safe to predict that no serious "artificial" shortage of skilled help will result from it.

those regarding sick leave and medical care, and even these are the result of union initiative and bargaining power — not of employer charity. For the most part, the provisions are of the nature of guarantees by one party, wrung from it by the other — not infrequently by the threat or fact of coercive measures. We shall see that this is even more true of the provisions relating to wages.

Particularly noteworthy is the infrequent occurrence of "restrictive rules" — i.e., provisions defining layoff and rehiring procedure, the rate of introduction of new machines and methods, etc. This circumstance is closely associated with the well-nigh universal stipulation according the employer a free rein in "running the business." The organized managers' insistence on retaining this clause in the agreements has long been a source of tension between the two sides. Within recent years, however, the employers have modified their stand and, as a result, there is considerably less hard feeling on this score today than formerly.[34]

[34] See *infra*, pp. 445–452.

CHAPTER VI

AGREEMENT CONTENTS: WAGE PROVISIONS

WAGES are usually the chief point at issue in employer-employee dealings, and in Sweden this question comes in for even more than its customary share of attention. Moreover, certain features of the wage contract as found in Swedish agreements are so nearly unique that the subject deserves separate consideration. The two most distinctive of these features — the piece wage system and the use of cost-of-living indices in determining wage rates, will be dealt with in detail in subsequent chapters. For the present we shall confine ourselves to the simpler and more familiar criteria for setting the terms of payment, chief among which are age, experience, and occupation. We shall consider first only the fabrication industries (manufacturing and construction), since it is mainly in these spheres of activity that wages, in the narrow sense of payment by the hour or piece, constitute a predominant part of costs. For most purposes mining may also be included in this category.

MINIMUM TIME RATES

Hourly rates (*tidlöner*) usually constitute the basic wage determinants. Practically all of the national agreements in manufacturing, construction and mining contain schedules specifying one or more such rates for each category of workers. True, the basis on which most wage payments are computed is the amount of work done, rather than the time spent, but the time rates establish definite minima for piece-work earnings. In only a relatively few industries are they actually termed minimum rates and specifically defined as such. More frequently they are given some such designation as "hourly earnings" or "time wages," and no express reference is made to any low limit. In practice, however, these also are true minimum rates, since no "average competent workers" are ever paid on any lower basis. A clause is usually included permitting exceptions to be made for very young workers (apprentices or others) and for "those who, because of age, sickness, or disability have had their capacity to work reduced." But in most plants these constitute only a very small proportion of the total worker force.

In a number of major industries, notably iron and steel, machinery, and building construction, the time rates are used as guarantee base rates which pieceworkers are assured of being paid, regardless of the amount of their output. Again, when production workers are temporarily shifted from piecework to "day work," their time rates become applicable. Still again, the wages of non-pieceworkers — such as repair and maintenance men and workers on special or "high quality" products — are frequently specified as a certain percentage or amount above the standard time rate. Most important of all, perhaps, is their use as a basis for the "average earnings" on piecework production itself. In practically all the larger industries the agreements provide, either explicitly or by implication, that under "normal working conditions" an average competent pieceworker shall be able to earn a given amount or per cent more than his time rate. This *överskott*, as it is called, varies from about 12 per cent in the paper mills to 30 per cent for outdoor workers in the pulp industry. The average for all industries is somewhere between 20 and 25 per cent.

Most of the agreements specify not one time rate but several — or, more accurately, several *scales*. Aside from the cost-of-living differentials,[1] the chief criteria for determining these different scales are sex, age, experience, craft or occupation, and ability (i.e., degree of skill and diligence). We shall consider each of these, so far as possible, separately and in order.

The question of sex may be disposed of at once. The only major fabrication industries in which women are employed in appreciable numbers are textiles, clothing, shoes, paper,

[1] See Chapter VII.

and wood products. In the two first named, they are predominant; in the latter three, decidedly in the minority. The national agreements for all these industries contain separate time rate schedules for women; and, as in most other countries, their wages run much lower than those of the men, for comparable kinds of work. Moreover, the differences are strikingly similar from industry to industry. Aside from one category in the clothing agreement, called "regular workers," the proportion which the time rate of "mature and experienced" female workers bears to that of males is almost exactly 67 per cent for all five of the abovementioned industries. In the exceptional case it is 76 per cent. For less mature workers the difference between the rate for males and that for females is smaller, and when specific rates are given for very young workers (e.g., 14–15 years — as in the textile industry), there is almost no difference at all.

One factor often considered in fixing time rates is a combination of age and experience.[2] Most commonly, *two* age-and-experience classes are established; all workers under 20 (or 21) and with less than 3 (or 4) years of practice in their trade are placed in the lower class, all those meeting or exceeding these requirements in the upper class. In iron and steel, machinery, and a number of other industries where long training is required for certain jobs or operations, workers over 24 and with more than 6 (or 7) years' experience constitute a third group, with a higher time rate level.

In certain lines where the average training period is relatively short, the gaps between the successive time rate classes are correspondingly narrow. In the textile industry, for example, the age steps are only one year apart, beginning with 14-year-old boys and ending with adult male workers (21

[2] The term experience, as used here, refers to the length of time spent at a particular trade or occupation. The period of employment with the *particular employer* is of very minor significance as a determinant of time rate differentials in the Swedish agreements. Of the major industries, only the railroads have any formal arrangement for increasing the pay of workers on the basis of length of service. *Landsorganisationens Verksamhetsberättelse* for 1930, pp. 90, 112.

and over). In the garment trades the dividing lines are still closer together, different rates being specified for people with ¼, ½, 1, 1½, 2, and 2½ years' experience.[3]

Even more common than age-and-experience differentiation is the practice of grading workers according to the degree of skill required in their respective trades or occupations. This criterion is especially important in the mass production industries — such as wood pulp, paper, and lumber — and we shall have occasion to discuss it at some length in a subsequent section of the present chapter.

TIME RATE CRITERIA: AGE AND EXPERIENCE

In trying to generalize about the wage provisions of a large number of agreements showing marked dissimilarities of detail, one runs the risk of overstressing the features they have in common. In order to avoid this danger, it may be well to summarize, industry by industry, the basic criteria for establishing time rates in a few of the more important national covenants.

Let us take first the industries employing mainly skilled help. In the *machinery trades agreement*, workers are divided into two general classes: skilled and unskilled. The former are split up into two subclasses: those over 24 years of age and with at least 7 years' experience in their trade, rated at 88 öre; those over 21 and with at least 4 years' experience, rated at 82 öre.[4] In the unskilled class, age alone is considered, the rates being 75, 70, and 55 öre for workers over 20, between 19 and 20, and between 18 and 19. Skilled workers under 21, or with less than 4 years' experience, are classed as unskilled. It is specified that the actual hourly pay of non-pieceworkers shall exceed these *minimum* rates by at least a certain amount, varying from 15 to 25 öre, according to the "dearness class" (*dyrortsklass*)

[3] In textiles, experience is left out of the reckoning, whereas in clothing comparatively little attention is paid to the age factor.

[4] These minimum rate figures apply to the Stockholm area — the highest group of communities in the cost-of-living classification (*dyrortsgrupperingen*). See *Landsorganisationens Verksamhetsberättelse* for 1937, p. 432.

in which the particular community falls. Unlike the majority of agreements, this one does not stipulate the average excess of piece rate earnings over the minimum hourly rate, but in point of fact it runs considerably higher than the margin specified for non-pieceworkers.[5]

In the national agreement for the *iron and steel industry*[6] the major classification is made by separating non-production workers (machinists, molders, woodworkers, and electricians, as well as general maintenance men) from those engaged in turning out the regular mill product. The rates for skilled non-production workers are set according to a combination of age and experience, while for production workers over 20, degrees of skill (high, low, or none) are the determining factors. For unskilled maintenance men, and for production workers below the 20-year mark, age alone is the criterion. As in the machinery industry, the amounts specified in the agreement are truly minimum rates, the actual earnings, whether for piece or time work, being on the average some 30 to 40 per cent higher.

Another national document in which both age and experience are taken into account is that for the *wood products industry* (furniture factories, builders' finish plants, etc.). Here the starting point is the "fully competent craft-trained worker" — one who is 20 years old or more and has worked at his trade at least 3 or (in some cases) 4 years. A single time rate of 126 öre applies to practically all such workers, the principal exception being assemblers of "standard house" parts, who are rated 3 öre lower. All workers below 20 are classified according to age, in a series of one-year steps, the rating of the 15–16 year group being approximately one third that of mature workers.

The time rates contained in the *building trades agreement*[7] are not true minimum rates in the same sense as those used in the machinery and iron and steel industries. The differ-

[5] Information obtained from Herr Hjalmar Engström, Chief Statistician of the Metal Workers' National Union.

[6] See *Landsorganisationens Verksamhetsberättelse* for 1937, p. 423.

[7] *Ibid.*, pp. 312–339.

ence lies in the fact that the building workers, when not engaged in piecework, are remunerated strictly in accordance with their specified ratings, whereas non-piecework jobs in machinery and steel are usually paid for at rates higher than the stipulated minimum figures. Largely because of this feature, the time rates for building construction are at a considerably higher level than those found in most other national agreements. However, the major proportion of construction work is done on a unit area or unit volume basis, and the actual hourly earnings average at least 25 per cent higher than the time rates. Hence the latter constitute, for most purposes, a definite lower limit of payment specifications.

As regards age and experience standards, the building trades agreement is much simpler than those previously described. To merit the regular "craft" time rate, a skilled building worker (carpenter, plasterer or bricklayer) [8] must present evidence of having worked at the trade at least three years. Building laborers (*byggnadsgrovarbetare*) [9] must be at least 18 years old to be accorded the time rate specified for them. These are the only specific limitations. For all workers not meeting these requirements the time rate can be set at a lower figure, but not by more than 15 per cent.

TIME RATE CRITERIA: OCCUPATIONAL GRADING

Coming now to the industries in which the number of highly skilled workers is small compared with those whose jobs require relatively little training,[10] we find that the age-experience criterion occupies only a minor position. Length of experience is, in fact, scarcely considered at all in the agreements governing these industries. Some account is usually taken of the age factor, but the worker ordinarily

[8] Other strictly craft workers in the building trades, such as plumbers, painters, and electricians, are governed by separate agreements, covering only their particular phase of the work.

[9] See *infra*, p. 214 (footnote).

[10] The principal ones are those producing pulp, paper, lumber, textiles, and construction materials (brick, tile, cement, etc.).

reaches the top of the time rate scale at a considerably earlier age than is the case in the "skilled trades." On the other hand, time rate differentials based on differences in *occupation* are very common in the mass manufacturing lines, even though the great majority of the workers in a given plant may be doing the same kind of work.

In the national agreement for wood pulp, for example, no mention is made of age or experience,[11] the steps in the time rate schedule being based entirely on occupational and cost-of-living considerations. Three main groups of wage earners are distinguished: production workers, repair and maintenance workers, and outdoor laborers. Each of the

TIME-RATE SCHEDULE FOR THE SWEDISH WOOD PULP INDUSTRY

Group	Grade		Classification of Factories [a]				
			I (100%)	II (97%)	III (94%)	IV (90%)	V (85%)
I and II	A	(110%)	100	97	94	90	85
	B	(105%)	96	93	90	86	81
	C	(100%)	91	88	86	82	77
	D	(95%)	86	84	81	78	73
	E	(90%)	82	79	77	74	70
	F	(85%)	77	75	73	70	66
III			85	82	80	77	72

Source: *Kollektivavtal mellan Pappersmasseförbundet och Svenska Pappersindustriarbetareförbundet, 1928, med Ändringar och Tillägg, 1936* (Stockholm, 1937), p. 33.

[a] This classification corresponds to the groupings by localities according to cost of living, found in most other national agreements.

first two groups is divided into six *grades*, according to the type of work or the operation performed. Grade A comprises the jobs requiring the highest degree of skill and responsibility, Grade F those requiring little or none. The time rate for Grade A is approximately 30 per cent above that for Grade F.

The degree to which wage scales in the mass production industries have been systematized is so well illustrated by the national time rate schedule for wood pulp that it has seemed worth while to reproduce it in full. (See table above; the figures are in öre except where otherwise specified.)

[11] Except in the case of outdoor laborers, who must be 18 or over.

It will be seen that the key to the time rates for the several grades of workers and the several groups of plants lies in the two sets of percentages, with Grade C and Class 1 as the respective bases. With the relative wage levels thus fixed, a wage revision for the entire industry can be made by simply changing one figure. A similar scheme is used in the paper industry, except that here there is no special classification for laborers. All male wage earners are included in one or another of seven time rate grades, arranged in order of skill and responsibility, without regard to age or experience.[12]

The grading device merits a further word of attention because of the important place it holds in Swedish wage-making practice. Even in those branches of activity where age and experience criteria are used, the degree of skill required in different trades and occupations is also taken into account in setting rates of pay. Thus the agreement for the state-owned railroad shops specifies three time rate grades; the first including apprentices and all unskilled laborers; the second, such "medium skilled" workmen as drill hands, automatic lathe operators, timbermen, and spray gun painters; the third, all the more highly skilled workers — e.g., forgemen, toolmakers, tinsmiths, molders, electricians, and carpenters. The time rate differential between adjacent grades is about 6 per cent in each case, making a total spread between the highest and lowest of approximately 12 per cent.[13]

The particular classifications differ from industry to industry. In wood pulp, where no less than six grades of "indoor" workers are distinguished, carpenters and machinists are paid at a lower rate than molders and electricians. However, the general method is much the same throughout.

Some such arrangement as this is obviously necessary

[12] Wage payments in the pulp and paper industries are based partly on time rates and partly on the individual worker's output. See Chapter VIII, p. 138.

[13] *Statens Järnvägars Författningssamling, Särtryck nr. 28* (Stockholm, 1937), pp. 16–17.

when workers in many different occupations, requiring varying degrees of skill, belong to the same union and have their wages regulated in the same contract. In a sense the wage grades are quasi-craft bodies within the industrial unions, but their resemblance to the traditional craft union is mainly superficial, not only because several trades are lumped together in the same grade, but also because they exist solely for wage-making purposes.

It will be recalled that in the days when the question of adopting industrial unionism was first being debated in Sweden, many craft unionists opposed it on the ground that it would permit the numerically superior unskilled workers to command higher wages at their expense.[14] That their fears were not entirely unfounded is evidenced by the fact that the difference between the hourly rates of highly skilled workers and those of day laborers is considerably smaller today than it was during the first decade of the century.[15] But, as the above example indicates, it has by no means disappeared. It must be remembered, too, that the higher time rate assigned to a worker in one of the upper grades is merely intended to compensate him as a "member" of one or another of the occupations included in that grade. His capability in this occupation is also taken account of, but in a different way, for his actual pay is based on the amount of his output and not (except indirectly) on his time rate. Thus the earnings of a competent and industrious electrician

[14] See *supra*, p. 53.

[15] For example, in the first national agreement for the iron and steel industry, concluded in 1908, the time rate specified for skilled non-production workers was 34 öre, and that for (adult) unskilled production workers 25 öre — a differential of 36 per cent, based on the lower figure. The corresponding rates in 1938 were 88 öre and 75 öre (17 per cent). (Sources: *Arbetsstatistik, A:5, Kollektivavtal*, vol. II, pp. 263–264; and *Överenskommelse mellan Järnbruksförbundet och Svenska Metallindustriarbetareförbundet för 1938*, pp. 1–2.) In the building industry, an even greater reduction in the skilled-unskilled time rate differential has occurred. Compare, e.g., *Arbetsstatistik A:5*, vol. II, pp. 354, 360 and the "Building Industry Agreement" for 1937 (concluded between the Swedish Master Builders' Association, on the one hand, and the Masons', Wood Construction Workers', and Laborers' and Factory Workers' Unions, on the other), p. 30.

may be 50 per cent or more, rather than a mere 12 per cent, above those of an average sweeper or yard laborer.

RAISES AND PROMOTIONS

Differences in *proficiency* among workers in a given occupation (as distinguished from mere length of time served) are of relatively minor significance as a wage determinant in Swedish industry. A majority of the agreements do, indeed, provide that workers of "unusual ability and diligence" (as judged, usually, by the employer) shall be accorded higher ratings than the minimum or time wages specified. But the only lines in which this clause is applied at all extensively are the industries manufacturing highly technical products, where it is possible for exceptional workers to demonstrate their superiority. In such routinized occupations as spinning, weaving, and paper making, the quality of work of even the most proficient operative is scarcely distinguishable from that of the average.

Closely allied to the question of higher ratings is that of *promotions* — the shifting of workers from their present jobs to others requiring greater skill or responsibility. However, provisions relating to this aspect of the employment problem are extremely rare in the fabrication industries. As a matter of fact, in many of the routine production lines the question of promotions is a rather empty issue, the number of "higher" jobs to which regular production workers might be shifted being very small. Even in occupations where special skill is important, the possibilities of advancement are usually so slight as to be almost negligible. After a wage earner has once passed the apprentice or "learner" stage, he is a full-fledged planer operator, or drop forger, or carpenter, and beyond this it is difficult to go. He may, of course, be made a foreman, but this contingency is seldom, if ever, dealt with in the agreements, and in practice it is left to the employer's discretion.[16]

The only major industry in which promotions are con-

[16] By the terms of a large number of agreements only "working" foremen are permitted to belong to the workers' unions.

sidered pertinent subject matter for collective bargaining is railroad transportation. The national agreement for the privately owned railway companies contains rather elaborate provisions specifying the conditions for promotion from a given position in the "traffic personnel" division to the next higher position, and from the repair shops to the traffic force. The factor which figures most prominently in these provisions is length of service.[17]

OTHER BASES OF PAYMENT

Up to this point we have been dealing exclusively with wages in the narrowest sense — i.e., payment reckoned by the hour or by the amount of work done. The industries in which one or the other of these two methods of compensation prevails employ by far the larger proportion of the country's worker population.[18] However, there are a number of lines of activity in which the workers are salaried employees rather than wage earners — that is, the unit of time used as the basis of payment is the week, month, or year. The more important of these industries and occupations, together with the time base predominant in each, are listed below. In all, they account for somewhat less than 20 per cent of the total of gainfully occupied workers.

Industry or Occupation	*Basis of Reckoning Payment*
Printing	Week
Baking	Week
Merchandising (wholesale and retail trade)	Week or month
Water transportation	Month
Railroad traffic personnel (conductors, station attendants, etc.)	Year
Agricultural workers	Year

It is obvious that none of these lines, with the possible exception of printing and baking, are well adapted to either

[17] Cf. *Landsorganisationens Verksamhetsberättelse* for 1930, p. 91.

[18] We are assuming here, as previously, that independent farmers are not included in the category "worker population."

piecework or work by the hour. Aside from this, the methods of establishing wage scales are not greatly different from those used in the more strictly "wage work" industries. Especially is this true as regards the fixing of differentials among grades and kinds of workers. In wholesale and retail trade, for example, sex, age, and responsibility of position are the chief determining factors. For steamship employees, it is position or degree of skill and length of service, while for railroad traffic workers the period of employment with the particular company counts far more heavily than other considerations. In agriculture, responsibility — with, of course, a certain concomitant degree of skill — is almost the sole criterion. Here, as in many of the fabrication industries, the various kinds of workers are graded — overseers comprising the highest grade; tractor, truck, and milking machine operators, blacksmiths, etc., the next lower; and so on down to the ordinary farm hands.

One type of compensation which figures prominently in the agricultural workers' wage system is payment in *goods* (food, fuel, the use of arable land, and living quarters). The provisions in the agricultural agreements regarding such payments are, of necessity, quite detailed and comprehensive, since they constitute the major part of the average farm worker's income. In the main, the national agreement [19] stipulates the *kinds* of commodities and services that are to be included, while those for the individual provinces specify the minimum amount of each. Thus according to the central document, each *statare* (farm servant living on the employer's property) is entitled to a dwelling place,[20] storage room for grain, potatoes and wood, a truck garden, a potato garden, a laundry, and shelters for swine and poultry. His wages also include a "sufficient amount" of milk, grain, and firewood. In the provincial agreement for Uppland it is specified that the (yearly) *stat* of each farm worker shall

[19] Reproduced in *Landsorganisationens Verksamhetsberättelse* for 1936, pp. 166–176.

[20] "Not less than 35 square meters in floor space." This is the only quantitative specification in the national agreement.

consist of 500 kilograms of rye, 400 of wheat, 200 of barley, and 200 of mixed grain; 1460 liters of milk; 3 ares of garden land and 15 ares for potatoes; and firewood "according to needs." [21]

The only other activity in which this type of payment is of major importance is maritime transportation, in which free food and living quarters are provided for all "traveling personnel." As for the fabrication industries, only those which are located predominantly in rural districts (e.g., sawmills, pulp, and paper) pay wages in nonmonetary form to any appreciable extent today, and even here the practice is gradually being done away with. Aside from fuel, the item most frequently encountered is the use of company-owned dwellings or barracks. In iron and steel, which is still in part a rural industry, the "company house" is definitely passing out of the picture. The sentiment among workers and employers is that this patriarchal institution is ill suited to present-day conditions. Indeed, many employers are now actively encouraging their workers to build their own homes, by helping them to secure credit at low rates of interest and in various other ways.

UNION AND EMPLOYER WAGE POLICIES

The foregoing discussion of the wage provisions found in the agreements naturally raises the question as to the part played by the respective parties to the wage contract in establishing them. In most cases they are the result of several decades of negotiation and compromise, and for this reason it is often difficult to ascertain whether, in any given instance, the union or the employers' association has been the aggressor. However, one or two general policies may be singled out.

The classification of workers into wage groups according to age and experience came about chiefly through employer initiative. From the very start, the employers held to the view that time rates should be based primarily on the skill

[21] *Kollektivt Löneavtal mellan Upplands Lantarbetsgivareförening och Upplands Distrikt av Svenska Lantarbetareförbundet* (Örebro, 1937).

and ability of each individual worker. But the unions were just as emphatic in their opposition to the idea, and in the end the employers had no choice but to make some sort of concession. The age and experience clauses were, in large part, the result of this compromise. The practice of ranking workers of different occupations in successive wage grades is quite as definitely traceable to union initiative. Without it, it is doubtful if the more highly skilled workers would have been willing to relinquish their craft organizations in favor of industrial unionism.

But these questions, however vital in the past, are of only secondary importance today, for the classifications and time rate differentials are by now practically permanent features of the agreement structure. However, there are certain union and employer policies regarding the *general level* or wages to be striven for, which still play an active part in the bargaining process.

On the worker side, two distinct and to some extent opposing views are prevalent. In most of the industries manufacturing uniform competitive products, the national unions follow what may be called the "leveling" principle (*nivelleringsprincipen*). The central aim of this policy is to make wage rates for similar work and like age and experience classes the same in all plants throughout a given industry. So far as it affects the nationally organized enterprises in these industries, this policy is of only nominal importance, because the members of the employers' associations are themselves strongly in favor of it. In the relations between the unions and the *unorganized* employers, however, the leveling principle takes on considerable significance, since by demanding that all of these latter pay the "national agreement rate," the unions are enabled to eliminate all possibilities of nibbling at wages.

Under the rules of the Swedish Employers' Federation, each member of a constituent employers' association must pay dues and insurance fees totaling approximately one öre per hour for each worker in his employ. If the unorganized employers (usually small-scale producers, operating on narrow margins of profit) accept the national agreement rate and remain outside the S. E. F., their total wage cost per worker is, therefore, about 1 per cent less than that of the organized employers in the same line. They can scarcely fail to see the wisdom of choosing this course, since if they try to pay less, the powerful national unions can effectively (and for most purposes permanently) shut off their labor supply.[22]

In certain industries where there is little direct competition, the unions adhere to a policy of "maximization" — i.e., they try to secure the highest wage which the relative bargaining strength of the parties and the employer's cost-profit situation will allow. Machinery manufacturing, the most important of these, is in reality not a single industry but a congeries of (more or less) non-competing industries, with comparatively few enterprises in each line. In consequence, the nature of the work also varies greatly from plant to plant, and it becomes impracticable to try to establish uniform wage scales on a national basis.

Maximizing is also practiced by the Railroad Workers' Union in their dealings with the private railway companies. Here, in addition to employer efficiency, the geographical factor enters in, for each company operates in its own exclusive territory and competition is almost nonexistent. It is in the iron ore industry, however, that the application of the principle is most strikingly demonstrated. The average wage in the export mines of northern Norrland is nearly twice as high as that paid in the mines of middle Sweden, which supply the domestic iron and steel industry. The continuance of this situation is ascribable partly to the great difference in the richness of the ore, partly to differences in the cost of living, and partly to the fact that many iron miners are unwilling to put up with the rigors of the Arctic winter, even at considerably higher real wages.

The employers' associations also have a number of fairly well-defined wage-making policies. They are, of course,

[22] The effects of industry-wide wage scales on *relatively inefficient* concerns are discussed in Chapter XVI (pp. 284–287).

primarily interested in keeping wages at the lowest level that is consistent with productive efficiency, and in general the methods which they use in pursuing this objective do not differ greatly from those followed by organized business-men in the larger industrial countries. In one respect, however, they have made a rather radical departure from "accepted" practice — in their approach to the problem of adapting wage rates to the swings in the business cycle. They have come to believe — in fact, have demonstrated in practice — that there is more to be gained by allowing wages to remain at a relatively high level in times of depression than by forcing them to keep pace with the fall in the selling prices of their products. This wage policy of the organized Swedish employers will be dealt with more fully in Chapter XVIII.

CHAPTER VII

THE COST OF LIVING AS A WAGE DETERMINANT

In most countries, especially those in which competition among the sellers still prevails in the labor market, the quantity of product or service produced by the individual worker is by long odds the chief determinant of wages. This holds whether payment is made according to results or per unit of time, for in the latter case it is the most productive workers who usually get the highest hourly rates. In Sweden, however, wage earner productivity shares importance with another factor — the worker's needs as a consumer. To be sure, this criterion is considered to some extent in Great Britain, the United States, and the other major capitalistic nations, but it is for the most part a haphazard, trial-and-error process, whereas in Sweden the thing is done more thoroughly and systematically.

The basis of this second wage determinant is the relatively high level of commodity prices in the larger cities as compared with the rural areas, and in the northern as compared with the southern provinces. The adjustment is usually accomplished by dividing the localities within which a given industry operates into a number of groups — so as to give approximately equal differences in living costs from group to group — and by establishing proportionate wage rate differentials between adjacent groups.

DEVELOPMENT OF GEOGRAPHICAL WAGE RATE DIFFERENTIALS

The practice originated shortly after the turn of the century, when the first national agreements were being negotiated. The need of adapting wages to local living conditions was by no means new then, but inasmuch as only the workers had been organized nationally prior to that time, there had been no available way of effecting the adjustment. It was in the printing industry that the cost-of-living wage scale was first applied. In the fall of 1903 a negotiating committee consisting of employers and union representatives drew up a plan whereby the 129 *tryckorter* (communities with printing establishments) in the kingdom were divided into six groups. The quarterly incomes of workers in the two "highest-cost" groups were to be increased by 15 per cent over a certain basic rate, those in the next two by 10 per cent, and those in the fifth by 5 per cent. The lowest group was to be left "uncompensated." This arrangement was incorporated in the printing trades national agreement, concluded at the beginning of 1904.

Almost simultaneously with the printers' committee, the negotiators in the great machinery trades lockout [1] presented a similar proposal. However, it was not until 1905 that this conflict was settled and the cost-of-living principle introduced into the machinery agreement. Only three groups were set up in this industry, as against six in printing, and instead of percentage additions to quarterly income, the scheme applied the wage differentials to the minimum time rates.[2] It is not apparent from the records whether these two committees were in communication with each other, but from the similarities in their respective allocation of various localities it seems likely that they were.

The only statistics which these first wage adjusters had to go by in determining the locality groupings were the so-called *markegångssättningar* — reports made yearly by local officials to county authorities regarding the average prices of certain commodities. However, these data were rather meager, and the committeemen undoubtedly had to rely a good deal on hearsay and estimates. The machinery trades committee, in particular, averred in its proposal that "it would not be possible to base the minimum wage rates exclusively on cost-of-living levels, but that . . . account

[1] See Chapter IV, pp. 68–69.

[2] This idea was also adopted by the printing trades in 1909 when the first agreement expired.

should also be taken of existing wage differences among the several localities."

Most of the other privately owned industries which incorporated this *behovsprincip* in their national agreements during the first decade of the century followed the same empirical approach as the machinery trades. When the idea was adopted by the state-owned railways in 1908, an even more arbitrary method of grouping was used, in that all communities with more than 15,000 population, together with all those north of the Dal River, were designated as "high cost" localities (*dyrorter*), and all others "low cost." As early as 1906, however, the State Board of Trade (*Kommerskollegium*) had begun to gather commodity price and house rent data from various sections of the country, and in 1909 this body devised a scheme of differentials for postal and telegraph workers — the first one to be based entirely on official statistics.[3]

When the Social Board (*Socialstyrelsen*) was established in 1912, it took over the handling of social statistics from the *Kommerskollegium*. In 1914 the board made a thorough investigation of living costs in Sweden and using this as a basis published, two years later, the first official "classification of localities by cost of living" (*dyrortsgruppering*). The first step in establishing this classification was to compute an average cost of living for the whole country and express the cost level for each of the 3500-odd localities as a percentage or "index" of this average. These indices were then arranged in an ascending series. Finally they were divided into seven groups, with approximately equal differences between the "mean indices" for each adjacent pair of groups. The scheme is represented on the following page (figures as of 1935 revision).

Each of the five middle groups, it will be noted, represents approximately a 6 per cent step, while for the two end groups the spread is considerably wider. The mean of Group G lies some 56 per cent above that of Group A. The asymmetry

[3] This information is contained in a special report furnished by the Royal Social Board at the writer's request.

of this arrangement with respect to 1000 (i.e., with the national average) is due to the extreme skewness of the series — that is, the localities below 1000 are "bunched," whereas those above are scattered.

Soon after its publication, the negotiating bodies in both the private and publicly owned industries began to take

GEOGRAPHICAL COST-OF-LIVING INDICES FOR SWEDEN

Locality Group	Indices	
	Limits	Mean Index
A	up to 930	870
B	931– 990	960
C	991–1050	1020
D	1051–1110	1080
E	1111–1170	1140
F	1171–1230	1200
G	1231 and over	1360

Source: Socialstyrelsen, *Lönestatistisk Arsbok för Sverige*, 1936, p. 70.

the Social Board's *dyrortsgruppering* as the basis of the cost-of-living differential schemes in their national agreements, a practice which has continued ever since. A new investigation is made by the board every five years, for the purpose of reallocating those communities whose price levels — relative to the national average — have changed appreciably in the interim, and these shifts are usually, though not always, followed in the wage adjustment schedules.

GEOGRAPHICAL LIVING-COST GRADATIONS IN PRACTICE

Except in comparatively few cases, the locality groupings in the national agreements do not adhere strictly to the Social Board's classification. More frequently they are adaptations of it, designed to suit the needs of the particular industry. In general, it may be said that for the industries whose individual establishments are spread fairly evenly throughout the country — e.g., building construction, wood products, printing, and garment making — the groups are approximately the same in number and makeup as in the official scheme, whereas for such relatively localized lines as textiles, pulp, and paper, the number is smaller.[4] Indeed, in certain of the more highly localized branches of activity — notably sawmills and iron and steel — the agreements contain no groupings or differentials at all. Some idea of the wide variation in practice among the major industries, as regards the grouping of localities and wage rate differentials, may be gained from the accompanying table.

Cost-of-living Differentials in Selected National Agreements

Industry	Number of Locality Groups	Total Differential (Lowest to Highest Group) as Per Cent of Lowest Time Rate
Machinery	3	23
Building Materials	5	27
Wood Products	8	47
Wood Pulp	5	18
Paper	5	19
Textiles	5	22
Ready-made Clothing	6	32
Printing	8	37
Shoe Manufacturing	4	17
Slaughtering and Meat Packing	3	12
Building Construction	9	38
Electrical Installation	4	29
Railroad Repair Shops (State-owned railways)	7	41

Sources: Latest agreements for industries listed. (Most of these are reproduced in *Landsorganisationens Verksamhetsberättelse* for years 1933–1937, inclusive.)

It will be observed that the scattered industries, besides having the largest number of groups, also show the widest total spread in wage differentials. Moreover, the more localized the industry, the narrower the spread becomes. Thus wood pulp, with establishments mainly in rural areas, shows a total differential of 18 per cent, as against 38 per cent for building construction. It should also be mentioned that for those industries which operate to any extent in the larger cities, the Stockholm metropolitan area is practically always designated — by itself — as the highest-cost "group," this being the case in the Social Board's classification as well.

[4] The rule is not universal, however — witness machinery manufacturing, a fairly scattered industry, with only three groups.

As regards living costs, Stockholm is in a class quite apart from the rest of the kingdom.

In the official government wage statistics, the average yearly wage incomes (for all industries taken together) are broken down according to cost-of-living groups, and this affords a means of making a rough comparison between the differentials specified in the national agreements and the actual differences in wages paid. However, in order to make such a comparison even approximately valid we must confine our estimate of a "representative" time rate differential to those industries which extend over as wide (or nearly as wide) an area as the income statistics — the entire country. Of the industries listed in the above table, the only ones meeting this requirement are wood products, clothing, printing, building construction, and railroad repair shops. The average of the total differentials for these five industries is 39 per cent.

The average earnings of male workers in the several locality groups for 1936 are reproduced below (data from *Lönestatistisk Årsbok för Sverige*, 1936, p. 70).

Locality Group	Average Wage Income (*in kronor*)
A	2126
B	2417
C	2601
D	2749
E	2940
F	2951
G	3687

The total differential between groups A and G is 73 per cent — a considerably higher figure than our estimate of a representative time rate differential. However, a large part of this spread is accounted for by the exceptionally high income shown for Group G, which in turn is due to the concentration of several highly paid occupations in Stockholm. If the highest group is omitted from the reckoning of both the income spread and the time rate differential, the figures become 38 per cent and 33 per cent. It is safe to conclude, therefore, that the spread in actual earnings is not far out of line with the cost-of-living adjustment scheme in the national agreements.

INCIDENCE OF THE COST-OF-LIVING DIFFERENTIALS

Oddly enough, the question of making adjustments for variations in the prices of necessaries from place to place has never been a source of serious controversy between workers and employers in Sweden. The prevailing view on both sides appears to be that this factor is so real and definite that, of necessity, some allowance must be made for it.

To the observer with American experience as a background, this will hardly seem an adequate explanation. How, it will be asked, is it possible to keep workers in a rural community only a few miles from Stockholm satisfied with wages that may be 30 per cent lower than those paid for the same kind of work in the capital? And equally important, how is it that employers in the "dearer" localities are willing to put up with high wages in the face of the ever-present consideration of selling price minus costs?

Let us take these questions in the reverse order. To begin with, there is little point in discussing the question of inequitable distribution of wage costs in relation to Swedish industry as a whole, since it presents quite different aspects in different industries. It is mainly in the export industries, and in those home industries which compete with foreign-made goods, that it is of first-rank importance. In the "protected" and "inherently home market" industries the problem is not unduly serious, owing to the infrequent occurrence of direct intersectional competition. In the former type of activity, the goods are in most instances produced within a particular region. Hence it is only necessary to establish small cost-of-living differentials, and the burden on the employers in the dearer localities is correspondingly small.[5] In the latter type (e.g., inland transportation, the building trades, and most kinds of building materials), there is relatively little difficulty involved in using the full cost-

[5] E.g., slaughtering and meat packing. Here only three cost-of-living groups are distinguished; and the total spread in time rates is only 12 per cent.

of-living spread in the wage differentials, since the employers with the higher wage costs are able to pass a substantial part of the margin on to the buyers of their products.

The principal export and "unprotected" home market industries are logging, sawmills, wood pulp, paper, iron and steel, machinery, and textiles. In the national agreements for logging, sawmills, and iron and steel, the living cost differential principle is not applied at all, the two first named industries being located chiefly in the outlying districts of the north, the latter in the *Bergslagen* counties of middle Sweden. The machinery trades agreement specifies three groups of localities, with a total time rate spread of 23 per cent. However, in this "industry" there is comparatively little direct competition, owing to the great diversity of products from plant to plant. In addition, there are better possibilities of deviating from the agreement specifications here than elsewhere, because of the flexibility allowed in setting piece rates.[6]

This leaves wood pulp, paper, and textiles as the principal lines in which the application of geographical wage differentials places more or less of a burden on firms located in sections with higher living costs. However, it should be noted, that all three of these industries are semilocalized (from the cost-of-living standpoint), and that the time rate spreads — 18, 19, and 22 per cent — are correspondingly narrow. In the main, the firms in the higher-cost localities are also the largest and most highly modernized,[7] hence the most efficient as productive establishments. Thus they can "afford" to pay higher wages than those in the lower groups. Strange as it may seem, the employers in the "dearer" localities agree that this is a valid reason for the existence of the cost-of-living differentials.[8] It appears likely, however, that

[6] See Chapter XIV.

[7] This is distinctly the case in pulp and textiles; but it cannot be said to be true of the paper industry, except to a minor degree. Information from *Svenska Arbetsgivareföreningens Kalender, 1937* (S. E. F. Directory for 1937), and from various employer-association officials.

[8] According to Administrative Director Gustaf Söderlund of the S. E. F.,

balance-of-power considerations have had a good deal more to do with their acceptance of it. For one thing, the consensus of worker sentiment is in favor of retaining the scheme. Furthermore these employers need the *organizational* support of the others in order to maintain parity in bargaining strength with the powerful union movement.[9]

These facts explain, in part at least, the absence of any strong opposition to *dyrortsreglering* from the employer side. As to the attitude of the *workers* in the *low-cost areas*, it is more difficult to make any accurate appraisal. Local unions often complain that the arrangement discriminates unfairly against them. But the cause of the dissatisfaction usually is that the town or district in question lies near the *upper edge* of a particular group, rather than in the lower groups generally. Complaints of this type are, in fact, the most common source of trouble connected with the cost-of-living adjustment practice at the present time, and it is frequently necessary to institute special negotiations, with representatives of the central organizations present, in order to effect a satisfactory settlement.

The continuance of a favorable union attitude toward this wage differential device is undoubtedly attributable in large measure to the fact that it has the support of the top men in the national unions.[10] The *förbund*, rather than the local, is the significant unit of worker organization in Sweden, and the *förbundsledare* not only have wide decision-making powers but also exercise a considerable influence over the individual members. With the purely pecuniary sentiment among the rank and file about equally divided, the power and influence of the national union leaders is sufficient to

---

and several other employer-association leaders whom the writer questioned on this point.

[9] Some of the other aspects of the incidence of national collective bargaining in industries where efficiency varies widely from plant to plant are discussed in Chapter XVI.

[10] A number of national union officials expressed to the writer the belief that wage scales graduated according to living-cost variations give the most equitable *overall* results, while not denying that they work injustice and even hardship in particular instances.

make the balance of effective opinion strongly in favor of retaining the living-cost differentials in the national agreement wage scales.[11]

OTHER WAGE PROVISIONS BASED ON NEEDS

Besides compensation for geographical differences in living costs, there are two other, less commonly used wage adjustment devices which take account of the worker's status as a consumer: the so-called "cold region compensation" (*kallortstillägg*), and correction for price level changes over time (*dyrtidstillägg*). The first of these is in effect only in the state-owned public utilities — the postal, telegraph, telephone, electric power, and railway systems. It is intended to compensate for the inconvenience and hardship incident to living in the Arctic and sub-Arctic regions of northern Sweden. The compensation scheme consists of a classification of the stations, power plants, etc. of the north into six groups, with an "extra allowance" which rises with the increasing coldness and remoteness of the respective groups.

The second device was used widely during the war of 1914–1918 as a means of adjusting wages to the rapid rise in commodity prices which occurred at that time. In a number of cases the agreements explicitly stated that the wage changes should be regulated by the Social Board's national cost-of-living index, and it appears that some such statistical measuring rod was usually relied upon even where specific

[11] Despite the absence of any articulate general opposition to the cost-of-living differential scheme among the rural workers, there is no question but that it tends to keep their *standard* of living at a lower level than that prevailing in the cities. From this standpoint the regimen on which the Social Board's geographical index is based is inequitable, in that it comprises mainly "subsistence goods" (e.g., bread, milk, houseroom), the prices of which are much higher in urban than in rural communities. Such semi-necessities as bicycles, central heating and sanitary conveniences, which cost at least as much in the country as in the city, are not included. A government commission is at present engaged in revising the index so as to make it conform more nearly to actual living standards. Professor Alf Johansson, a member of the commission, estimates that after the revision is completed, the spread between the lowest and highest locality-group indices will be reduced from its present figure of 56 per cent to approximately 35 per cent.

stipulations were absent. It was the employers who took the initiative in introducing this scheme, principally as a "tactical measure to facilitate wage reductions in the event of an ensuing deflation." [12]

While this practice was largely discontinued after the war, modifications of it are still used in a few lines, principally the government service occupations. For example, Section 24 of the agreement for repair shops in the state-owned railway system provides that "if, during the life of the agreement, the Social Board's index rises to 160 or higher, the workers shall receive additional payment of one öre per hour."

An important adjunct to the wartime *dyrtidstillägg* was the "family allowance," according to which workers with families were paid a certain sum per month for each dependent, in addition to their regular wages. The use of this device at the present time is confined mainly to the textile industry and to state-owned enterprises.

[12] *Kollektivavtal vid Årsskiftet 1920/1921*, vol. I, p. 33.

CHAPTER VIII

THE PIECEWORK SYSTEM

ONE OF THE OUTSTANDING features of wage-making practice in Sweden is the unusually widespread use of piecework. In Great Britain and the United States, the question of whether payment by results is superior to the time wage is still considered a debatable one, but in Sweden it is and has been for years the accepted rule that piecework shall be utilized wherever it is reasonably possible to do so. It seems worth while, therefore, to examine in some detail the evolution and present status of this method of payment as an integral part of the Swedish collective bargaining system.

HISTORICAL: FROM DICTATED TO BARGAINED PIECE RATES

The "productivity wage" was known in Sweden long before the present industrial era. Styrman tells of a government ordinance issued in 1637 to the effect that "any hammersmith who could forge more than 18 *skeppund* of iron per week should be paid 8 öre for each extra *skeppund* produced." [1] However, it was not until the sixties and seventies of the last century, when the country began to industrialize in earnest, that the method came to be at all widely applied. The manner of its application at that time was wholly along familiar lines. Since the workers were as yet unorganized, the employers were able to dictate the rates. Revisions were frequent and — since more efficient methods of production were continually being introduced — usually in the downward direction. Hence, although the volume of the average wage earner's output rose steadily, his total earnings stood still or declined.

This *slumpackord*, as it was called, soon came to be cordially hated by the workers everywhere, and their an-

[1] *Verkstadsföreningen*, p. 277.

tagonism toward it was undoubtedly one of the strongest forces impelling the organization movement which gathered headway in the middle 'eighties. Thus the first Scandinavian Workers' Congress, which met in Gothenburg in 1886, strongly declared itself against piecework, and the resolution was reiterated by the second Congress, held in Copenhagen two years later.[2] As the unions themselves increased in size and strength, the workers' opposition became more and more emphatic. During the nineties, most of the national organizations introduced clauses into their by-laws condemning piecework in all its forms. What is more to the point, they began to present demands for its abolition, and in some instances the employers were obliged to accede to these demands.[3]

Aside from their hostility to the particular rate-setting methods employed, the unionists raised a number of objections to piecework in general. Among other things, they contended that by driving the intensity of the worker's efforts up to an unnatural pitch, it brought about a reduction in the quality of the work, injury to the worker's health, and a rise in the number of accidents; and that by giving the more avaricious individuals an incentive to work long hours, it resulted in maldistribution of jobs and unemployment.[4]

It was hardly to be expected that these considerations would count very strongly with the employers. They held to the belief that the average worker is naturally inclined to shirk, and that the only way to induce him to work at a reasonable speed is to make his reward dependent on the amount of his output. As they, in turn, became organized and succeeded in regaining some of their lost bargaining strength, the employers therefore countered with demands that payment by results be retained or restored. But they did not make the mistake, so common with American em-

[2] Landsorganisationen, *Fackföreningerörelsen i Sverige, Norge, Danmark, Tyskland, England och Frankrike* (Stockholm, 1912), vol. I, p. 63.

[3] See, e.g., *Statens Offentliga Utredningar, 1938:10* (*Byggnadsindustrin i Sverige*) (Stockholm, 1938), p. 364.

[4] *Fackföreningsrörelsen i Sverige*, etc., vol. I, pp. 111–113.

ployers, of refusing to budge from an established position. Rather, they took the stand that if the unions' voluntary acceptance of the advantageous features of piecework could be obtained in return for reasonable concessions on less essential points, such concessions were well worth making.

The compromises were effected in various ways, but in most cases they centered around two principal points: according the workers a voice in the setting of rates, and giving them some measure of insurance against arbitrary reductions. For example, the Western Section of the Machine Industry Association agreed to the inclusion of the following provisions in its contract with the molders of Gothenburg, concluded in the summer of 1903.

> The piecework price shall be determined, wherever possible, by agreement between the worker and his superior, before the work is started; and it shall be so calculated as to give the worker an "overage" (*överskott*) of at least 25 per cent above the wage he would receive if he were on time work. Piece rates shall on no condition be set lower than the level which corresponds to the worker's time rate earnings.[5]

A similar clause was incorporated in the national agreement for the machinery industry, concluded in 1905. In a number of other industries — notably iron and steel, printing, textiles, and shoe manufacturing — the compromise consisted in establishing "fixed" rate schedules, arrived at through central negotiations and applicable during the life of the main agreement.[6] Long-term price lists, centrally determined, were the most logical solution in these industries, owing to the relatively high degree of uniformity of their products — both over time and from plant to plant. In the machinery trades, on the other hand, the extreme heterogeneity of the products made such an arrangement practically impossible.

[5] Styrman, *op. cit.*, p. 103.

[6] In some cases where the agreements were to run for more than a year, it was provided that the rate schedule might be terminated at the end of the first year, at the option of either party.

Of the major industries, the machinery trades was the only one which granted the workers the guarantee of time rate earnings on *all* piecework. However, a modified form of "insured piecework" was adopted in a number of other manufacturing lines. Thus the iron and steel agreement, concluded in 1908, provided that "on all piecework for which fixed piece rate lists have not been established (such as when new kinds of work, new methods, or new machines are introduced), the workers shall be guaranteed their time rate." [7]

The efficacy of compromise in settling labor disputes was amply demonstrated in this instance. The introduction of bilateral rate setting and the guarantee feature afforded the workers for the first time a real and dependable incentive to work harder. Moreover, the increased use of piecework enabled the employers to cut down on supervision, which not only reduced their costs, but also improved the "shop spirit"; for Swedish wage earners have a strong dislike for authority, and much prefer driving themselves to being driven by bosses. Finally, when the new arrangement had once been given a reasonable trial in two or three industries, it became apparent that piece scales were no more difficult to adjust through collective bargaining than hourly wages.

As a result, the unionists' attitude toward piecework underwent a marked change during the first decade of the present century — from open hostility to a quite general acceptance of the idea. By 1910 the clauses condemning it had been stricken from the by-laws of all the national unions. A few even went so far as to recommend it specifically, in preference to time work.

Since then, the method has been extended to a wider and wider range of occupations, until today it is the predominant practice in all the major fabrication industries, and in a number of service industries besides. Even building construction work, which is regarded as inherently a timework occupation in most countries, is in large part paid for according to results in Sweden. It is of interest to note that in

[7] Cf. *Fackföreningsrörelsen i Sverige*, etc., vol. I, p. 113.

this industry the strongest advocacy of piecework comes from the union side.[8]

EXTENSIVE USE OF PIECEWORK

Aside from the rate schedules, the collective agreements usually contain a separate section devoted to piecework, in which the general rules of productivity wage making are set forth. Among these rules, the most common is the provision that "piecework shall be applied wherever possible." This stipulation, or its equivalent, occurs in no less than twenty-eight national agreements, the only important exceptions in the manufacturing industries being printing, bookbinding, food products, tanneries, and stone cutting. The significance of this clause depends, to a considerable extent, on whether the phrase "wherever possible" is given a broad or narrow interpretation. Nevertheless, it is evident that in practically all the industries in which the volume of product or services is at all readily measured, the parties to the employment bargain are agreed as to the desirability of gauging wages by the amount of output.

The extent to which piecework is actually used is indicated in the table on the following page, compiled from official government statistical sources. The figures for "gainfully occupied workers" afford a measure of the relative importance of the several industries, although it should be noted that some of the items represent combinations of a number of industries rather than single lines. The figures in column 2 represent the ratio:

$$\frac{\text{Hours worked on piecework}}{\text{Hours of wage work } \textit{of all kinds}}$$

In one sense this is an understatement, since the denominator in the ratio includes not only production work but all maintenance, repairing, transportation, storekeeping, services of watchmen, and other "overhead," much of which is by its very nature unadapted to the productivity method of payment. The available evidence indicates that this

[8] *Statens Offentliga Utredningar, 1938:10,* pp. 361, 363.

"inherently non-piece wage work" comprises, on the average, at least 10 per cent of the total, in point of hours consumed. Therefore, in order to give an idea of the extent to which the *possibilities* of applying piecework are utilized, a set of "adjusted" percentages is shown in column 3, the adjust-

UTILIZATION OF PIECEWORK IN PRINCIPAL SWEDISH INDUSTRIES, 1936

Predominantly Piecework Industries	Total Gainfully Occupied Wage Earners [a]	Ratio of Piecework Hours to Total Hours Worked (*in per cent*)	
		Unadjusted	Adjusted [b]
Mining	8,500	72	80
Iron and Steel Production	24,100	76	84
Metal Products (non-machinery)	34,200	52	58
Machinery Manufacturing and Repairing	88,800	56	62
Quarrying and Stone Cutting	8,400	53	59
Building Materials and Ceramics	13,600	48	53
Logging	80,000 [c]	..	100 [d]
Sawmills	35,600	58	64
Wood Pulp	18,200	60	67
Paper	17,100	75	83
Textiles	48,300	52	58
Clothing	24,800	48	53
Leather, Shoes, and Leather Products	17,000	48	53
Building Construction	53,000 [e]	60 [f]	67
Dockwork	13,000	81	90
Total	484,600	Average 60	Average 69

Sources: *Lönestatistisk Årsbok för Sverige*, 1936; *Statens Offentliga Utredningar, 1938:10*; *Statistisk Årsbok*, 1935.

[a] As of 1935.
[b] Unadjusted figures ÷ .90.
[c] Estimate of full-time logging workers.
[d] "Logging work (in Sweden) is practically exclusively a piece-wage occupation." *Lönestatistisk Årsbok för Sverige*, 1936, p. 25.
[e] Includes carpenters, bricklayers, plasterers, pipe fitters, and electricians.
[f] Average for above occupations, as of 1935. The piecework ratio for *building laborers*, as of the same year, was approximately 27 per cent. *Statens Offentliga Utredningar, 1938:10*, p. 366.

ment consisting of dividing the official "percentage piecework" figures in column 2 by .90 (i.e., 1.00 minus .10).

Even without taking account of this factor, it is evident that piecework has a comfortable margin over timework, at least in the manufacturing industries. And when the allowance is made, we obtain an overall average ratio for the "predominantly piecework" industries of 69 per cent. If one considers further that there are only three production industries — food processing, wood products, and printing and engraving[9] in which less than 50 per cent of the wage work is paid for by results, it is clear that the preference for piecework, in practice as well as in principle, is very strong.

In the remaining major occupations — merchandising, land and water transportation, hotels and restaurants, public utilities, and agriculture — it would obviously be extremely difficult to apply the productivity method. However, even these are by no means exclusively time work industries. For example, the pay of taxi drivers and store clerks frequently comprises a basic weekly wage plus an additional sum proportioned to the amount of "intake" during the week. This bears a close resemblance to the "modified incentive" devices used in certain lines of manufacturing.

METHODS OF SETTING PIECE WAGES

Let us turn now to the question of how piece wages are determined. Although no two industries follow exactly the same practice, it is possible to divide the various schemes into two main categories and six classes, arranged and designated as follows:

- I. Straight piecework
  1. Simple fixed rate schedules
  2. The group system
  3. The building trades method
  4. "Temporary" or individual job rates
- II. Modified incentive methods
  5. The premium plan
  6. Combination of time and piece rates

So far as the process of wage reckoning is concerned, the first method is not essentially different from "ordinary piecework" as we know it in the United States. Weavers are paid so many öre per meter for each kind and width of cloth, iron miners so many kronor per ton of ore, woodcutters so much per unit volume, etc. What chiefly distinguishes the

[9] The aggregate number of wage earners in these three industries is approximately 100,000.

Swedish practice is the fact that the rates are fixed, by agreement and for relatively long periods of time.

The way in which simple piece rates are established for a whole industry in a single document may be illustrated by the following excerpt from the clothing workers' national agreement. (The figures are in kronor.)

PIECE RATES FOR TROUSERS

COST-OF-LIVING GROUP	I		II		III		IV	
Grade of Cloth [a]	1	2	1	2	1	2	1	2
Trousers of black worsted, black foule, etc.	7.50	...	7.15	...	6.75	...	6.35	...
Ditto, other fabrics	6.50	5.00	6.20	4.75	5.85	4.50	5.50	4.25
English riding breeches	15.00	...	14.25	...	13.50	...	12.75	...
Ditto, of cheviot, manchester, and similar fabrics	...	10.30	...	9.75	...	9.25	...	8.75
Riding breeches, ordinary	11.25	8.50	10.70	8.10	10.10	7.65	9.60	7.25
Sport trousers, with band and buckles	6.50	5.00	6.20	4.75	5.85	4.50	5.50	4.25
Ditto, with "slits," up to 3 buttonholes	7.50	5.65	7.15	5.40	6.75	5.10	6.40	4.80

Source: *Kollektivavtal vid Årsskiftet 1920/1921*, vol. II, p. 122.

[a] Grade 1 includes all "prime" (high quality) fabrics; Grade 2, those of lower quality.

Closely allied to the simple fixed-schedule method is the *group piecework scheme*, by which all the workers engaged in making a product as a team are accorded a lump sum per piece or unit of measure produced and the proceeds divided among the individual members according to some prescribed arrangement. The schedules containing rates and bases of division are usually drawn up through negotiations between the local union and the individual employer, although in most industries employing this device the decisions reached at the national conferences determine what rates the local negotiators are to agree on.

Lumber production (sawmills) may be taken as fairly typical of the preponderantly group piecework industries. Here a certain base price is paid for sawing various dimensions of boards, planks, etc., each of the several participants in the process receiving a percentage of this, in proportion to skill and responsibility. Head sawyers, edge sawyers, and measurers get the largest proportions; after which come sawyers' helpers, "back drawers," and so on down to the unskilled "timber heavers." [10]

So far as its contractual framework is concerned, the *building trades method* is very similar to those described above. Fixed rate lists, usually operative for a year or more, are used in all the building occupations. Thus building laborers are paid per unit volume excavated or per thousand of brick carried; carpenters and bricklayers, per unit area of structure erected; electricians, per meter of each size of cable or conduit run, etc.

As to the mode of its application, this scheme is mainly, though by no means entirely, based on the group payment principle. In masonry, wood construction, electrical installation and painting, team piecework is the rule; whereas in pipe fitting work, and in the various unskilled occupations, each individual usually works "on his own."

However, there are two important distinctions which put the building trades schedules in a class by themselves. In the first place, they are much more detailed and elaborate than those used in manufacturing — a feature necessitated by the varied character of the work. An attempt is made to classify every kind of job that may arise, and establish a price for it. The second distinction lies in the fact that the magnitude of each kind of work on a given piece of construction cannot ordinarily be ascertained from the superficial data available at the start. This difficulty is surmounted by having the work "measured" and the piecework earnings computed by expert surveyors (*ackordsmätare*). Both the unions and the contractors' associations employ such surveyors, and any differences in their respective appraisals are ironed out through negotiation and compromise.

It must be obvious that payment by results is a troublesome method to apply in this industry, especially since no two pieces of construction work are ever exactly alike. Never-

[10] *Kollektivavtal vid Årsskiftet 1920/1921*, vol. II, p. 51.

theless, the majority of both employers and workers prefer it to time work, and the indications are that it will remain the predominant wage-making scheme for some years to come.[11]

The fourth class of piecework, which we have termed the "temporary" or individual job method, is found chiefly in the machinery industry.[12] In this scheme the period of validity of a given rate is not an explicit, contractually determined time interval, as in the case of fixed rate schedules; rather it coincides with the duration of the particular job or lot of work to which the rate is applied. Indeed, most temporary rates are not established through collective contract making, in the ordinary sense of the term, but through bargaining between the employer (or his representative) and the individual worker. Ordinarily, collective negotiations are instituted only when a worker refuses to accept a profferred rate and "appeals" the case to his local union, in accordance with the "disputes clause" in the national agreement.

This device is designed primarily to afford flexibility in rate making in the more highly diversified and shifting lines of production — e.g., machine tool and electrical machinery plants. In point of fact, however, temporary piece rates are also widely used in many metal products factories where the articles produced and the productive operations are both uniform and continuous. The problems incident to this practice will be discussed in a subsequent chapter, under the heading "Wage Bargaining in the Machinery Industry." [13]

COMBINATIONS OF TIMEWORK AND PIECEWORK

In a number of industries, straight piecework is used only for certain of the production operations, while others are paid for according to some form of "modified" incentive scheme. Although the particular devices of this latter sort

[11] The makeup and functioning of the building-trades piecework system is discussed more fully in Chapter XIII.

[12] It is also fairly common in the iron and steel industry, and in furniture manufacturing. Cf. *Kollektivavtal vid Årsskiftet 1920/1921*, vol. I, p. 81.

[13] Chapter XIV, pp. 241–245.

vary considerably from industry to industry, all are essentially compromises between time work and piecework.

When the modified incentive idea was first introduced in the early years of the present century, it was widely hailed as a means of remedying some of the defects of "pure" piecework. Its proponents claimed that under it the stimulus to greater effort was preserved, but not to the extent where it caused slackness in maintaining quality. They also held that the inequities in earnings among piece workers, due to faulty or inadequate appraisal of time requirements, would be reduced — an important factor in keeping the workers satisfied.

However, in neither of these respects has the method come up to expectations. Regarding the second point especially, it has been found that, as a means of ironing out inequalities in earnings, accurate and thoroughgoing investigations of time requirements are far superior to any modification of the piecework idea. With the introduction of scientific time study technique, the use of modified incentive schemes has diminished considerably.[14]

Most prominent among those still in force, perhaps, is the so-called "premium plan," utilized in the state-monopolized tobacco and cigarette industry, in the railroad shops, and for certain kinds of high quality work in the machinery industry. It consists essentially in establishing a "normal time" for the performance of a given task. If the worker requires this period (or longer) to do the work, he is paid according to his regular time rate. If he completes it in less time, his hourly rate of pay is increased in proportion to the time saved.[15]

[14] Time and motion studies play an important part in wage-making procedure in machinery, iron and steel, and a number of other major industries. Herr Styrman, in his book on the Machine Industry Association, gives an illuminating account of the development and present-day use of the time-study technique in Swedish machinery plants. See *Verkstadsföreningen*, pp. 279–282.

[15] This is the Rowan plan, developed in England during the late nineties. It is the only premium system that is at all widely applied in Sweden, whereas in England and the United States a number of other schemes — e.g., Taylor's,

Another, somewhat simpler form of modified incentive scheme is the "combination time and ton wage method," used extensively in the pulp and paper industries. Under this setup, the major part of the worker's wage is reckoned on a straight time basis; the remainder, which ordinarily comprises about one fourth of the total wage, is paid in proportion to the number of tons produced, at a price per ton which rises with the volume of production.[16]

Although most Swedish employers now prefer straight piecework to the "compromise" method, the pulp makers and paper manufacturers believe that the latter is better suited to their particular type of production. In these two industries, setting the speed of the machinery is for the most part a function of management; hence the degree of the worker's control over his output is relatively small. However, the "fractional piece wage" does give him an incentive to keep his machine constantly supplied with material and to adjust or repair it promptly when anything goes wrong.[17]

OTHER ASPECTS OF BARGAINED PIECE WAGES

It will be noted that the modified incentive plans, besides effecting a compromise between piecework and time work, have the additional feature of establishing a lower limit to the worker's income.[18] In this respect they are closely related to the guaranteed time rate, referred to earlier in the present chapter. Since its first appearance in the early years of the century, this latter form of "pay insurance" has been considerably extended. The following tabulation

---

Gantt's, the "standard hour" system, etc. — are also used to a considerable extent. Cf. National Industrial Conference Board, *Systems of Wage Payment*, chapters iii and iv.

[16] Cf. *Kollektivavtal vid Årsskiftet 1920/1921*, vol. I, p. 84, and vol. II, p. 64.

[17] Interview with Herr Albin Ahlin, executive director of the Swedish Paper-mill Association (*Sveriges Pappersbruksförbund*), August 15, 1938.

[18] Sometimes this lower limit is determined by the minimum time rates as specified in the national agreements, but more often it is based on the individual worker's "regular" time rate, which is customarily higher than the minimum rate. Cf. Chapter XIV (pp. 235–236).

shows the extent to which the worker's regular time rate is guaranteed in the principal piecework industries and occupations, as provided in the national agreements.

It should be added that although the agreement for textiles contains no specific guarantee stipulations, a limited guarantee is effected in this industry in another way. The agreement provides that when new methods or machines are introduced, piecework shall be discontinued until the proper time studies have been made and new piece rates worked out. During the interim the affected workers are paid on the basis of their regular time rates plus 10 per cent. Similar practices are in effect in a number of the other industries listed in column 3 of the table — notably paper, pulp, and clothing. When these facts are taken into consideration, it becomes evident that a large majority of the workers in the fabrication industries enjoy at least some measure of insurance against the vagaries of the piecework system.

USE OF GUARANTEED TIME RATES IN SWEDISH INDUSTRIES

Time-rate Wage Guaranteed		Time-rate Wage not Guaranteed
On All, or Nearly All, Piece Payment Work	Only in Cases Where Fixed Piece Rate Schedules do not Exist	
Machinery trades [a]	Iron and steel production, and metal products	Mining
Municipal works (highway and construction workers)	Building materials	Quarrying and stonecutting
Telephone and telegraph (linemen and shop workers)	Wood products	Glass and glassware
State railway repair shops	Railroad track and construction workers (state and private)	Logging
Plumbers	Bricklayers	Sawmills
Electricians	Carpenters	Wood pulp
	Building laborers	Paper
	Painters	Textiles
		Clothing
		Dockworkers

[a] The "guarantee provision" in the machinery-trades agreement now contains the supplementary clause "except where fixed schedules exist." Since, however, most rates in the machinery industry are temporary, the guaranteed time rate was still applicable to most of the industry, even after the addition of this clause.

Most of the fixed piece rate schedules have a life of one year, with a required termination notice period of from one to three months. When these schedules were first introduced, they usually remained in force for the same period as the agreements proper. As the duration of the latter was increased to two or more years, it became apparent that the period of the piece wage contracts could not be similarly extended without inflicting hardships on one or the other party, depending on whether prices and business activity moved up or down during the interval. The one-year period thus represents a sort of empirical optimum, established after considerable trial and error over several decades.

In addition, practically all the national agreements provide that upon the introduction of improvements in the productive setup — whether as new machines, processes, arrangements, or in any other form — the affected piece rates may be terminated immediately, by either party.[19] The new rates are customarily determined through the regular "adjustment machinery" channels — i.e., between the individual worker and his superior or between the local organizations, with the right of appeal to the higher organizational units in the event of failure to agree. During the change-over interval the workers are paid either at certain time rates, as described above for textiles, or on the basis of their earlier piecework earnings.

WHY PIECEWORK IS PREFERRED

In conclusion, it is worth reëmphasizing that both the employers and the unions prefer piecework to time work as a method of determining wages. The consensus of opinion among the former is that the productivity wage has done more than anything else to keep the cost per unit of product down in the face of a continually rising wage level.[20] On the worker side the approval is a more passive one, for the unionists are not anxious to have the incentive idea "work" too well, lest it result in inordinately wide differences in earnings among workers in the same occupation and hence

[19] A few agreements specify a short notice period — usually a week.

[20] Cf. von Sydow, *op. cit.*, p. 15.

undermine union solidarity.[21] Nevertheless, the principle of piecework is quite generally accepted by the organized wage earners in Sweden, and outspoken opposition to it is practically unknown.

There can be no doubt, at any rate, that payment by results is far more prevalent in Sweden than in the United States. One important reason for this lies in the difference in pattern of industrial organization in the two countries. The average Swedish manufacturing plant, while fully modernized so far as equipment and processes are concerned, is smaller and less highly integrated than the typical American plant. There must, of course, be a great deal of specialization and division of labor, but the "continuous production" type of factory organization, with its intimate linking up of the operations necessary to the making of a product, is relatively rare. And obviously the possibilities of applying the incentive idea are much better where the activities of the several contributors to a productive process are kept separate than where they are controlled by the speed of an assembly line.

Another reason is that the Swedish piecework system has been built up simultaneously with, and within the framework of, the collective bargaining institution itself. Both parties to the wage contract have participated in its development and application, whereas in the United States the power of decision, both as to establishing methods and setting rates, has usually been exercised by the employers alone. As a result of their participation the Swedish wage earners are insured, through their collective agreements, against being arbitrarily deprived of the fruits of their efforts. The ma-

[21] A number of employers whom the writer interviewed conceded that there is considerable "withholding of effort" on the part of the faster workers — a phenomenon which they attributed largely to union influence. An official of the Metal Workers' Union asserted that the faster workers often help the slower ones increase their earnings. In the building trades, differences in earnings are prevented from becoming too wide through the use of the "gang piecework" scheme, whereby the piecework proceeds for each gang are distributed in proportion to the time rates of the individual members. See Chapter XIII, pp. 219 ff.

jority of American pieceworkers, on the other hand, are still without any dependable insurance of this kind. It would seem, therefore, that the attitude of workers toward the incentive wage idea is in large measure a function of the degree of *security* afforded them under the particular method by which it is applied.

PART THREE

THE AGREEMENT MAKING PROCESS

CHAPTER IX

NEGOTIATION [1]

IN THE FOREGOING chapters we have been concerned primarily with the collective agreements — the written documents which constitute the framework of the Swedish bargaining system. We now turn our attention to the implementing machinery, which is no less essential to the system's proper functioning. This machinery consists of well-tried methods of negotiating, interpreting, and enforcing agreements; of supplementary devices for settling questions not adequately covered by them; and, not least, of laws and governmental agencies through which the state exercises an important influence over the whole process.

PROCEDURE PRIOR TO NEGOTIATION

Let us examine first the *negotiating procedure*. This term may be taken to include both the making (and revising) of agreements and the settlement of intra-agreement-period disputes, but in the present chapter only the former will be dealt with.[2]

It will be recalled that practically all the national agreements contain the so-called "termination clause." According to this provision, when one of the parties desires a revision of the terms of employment, it must notify the other

[1] The following trade-union, employer association, and government officials have been especially helpful in supplying information for this chapter: Knut Larsson, Secretary of the Wood Products Union; Gustaf Söderlund, Administrative Director of the Swedish Employers' Federation; Frithiof Söderbäck, Director of the S. E. F.'s "General Branch"; Olle Ekblom, formerly State Mediator in the second district, and now Governor of Jönköping County; and Carl Christian Schmidt, Secretary of the National Mediation Service.

[2] The procedure followed in adjusting interpretational disputes and "grievances" is described in Chapter XII.

party of its intention to terminate at least three months before the termination is to become effective, and must accompany the notice with a proposal for a new contract.

Except in rare cases, the procedure subsequent to this stage is not determined by contractual prescription, and theoretically the parties are free to adopt a different method each time an agreement is terminated, or to discontinue the relationship permanently.[3] Actually, the process of negotiating and concluding new agreements is almost as much of an institution as the collective contract itself. By a series of trial-and-error experiments extending over nearly four decades, the national unions and employers' associations have developed a body of workable and mutually acceptable practices for carrying on collective negotiations, and these unwritten rules are adhered to just as closely as though they were incorporated in legally enforceable covenants or in the law of the land.

What is more, the practices followed are essentially the same in all industries operating under national agreements.[4] For present purposes this is a fortunate circumstance, since it enables one to present a fairly accurate general picture of Swedish agreement-making procedure by describing a single sequence of dealings between the employers' and workers' organizations. In our description of a typical negotiation sequence, we shall suppose it is the union which takes the initiative. The main course of events is not substantially different when the employers' association is the aggressor party.

[3] The major exceptions are found in municipal works and privately owned railway transportation. In each of these two branches of activity a national "negotiation-procedure contract" is concluded, which runs for a longer period than the main agreement. These documents, besides stating how and by whom the new agreement is to be concluded, also provide that in the event of failure to agree, the case must be referred to a board of arbitration for definitive settlement if *either* party so requests.

[4] This uniformity is due in large measure to the centralizing influence of the Employers' Federation. All of the national agreement conferences to which constituent associations of the S. E. F. are parties are held in the Federation's office building in Stockholm, in a suite of rooms designed especially for the purpose.

Prior to the filing of the termination notice, there must have been a decision to terminate, which is in itself a matter of no small moment. The executive board of a national union may decide, on its own initiative, whether or not to terminate the union's agreement or it may submit the question to an "agreement convention" (*avtalskonferens*) composed of delegates chosen representatively from the locals. If the decision is in favor of termination, each local submits a list of the changes in the terms of employment (wage increases, better overtime percentages, etc.) desired by the majority of its members. With these lists as a basis, the executive board draws up a proposal for a new agreement.[5] The proposal must be approved by the agreement convention (which is always convened, even though the board decides the question of termination), after which it is communicated to the employers' association along with the termination notice.

Finally, the convention selects a negotiating committee, which ordinarily comprises three members of the executive board and five or six delegates from the locals, chosen so that the several districts or geographical sections have approximately equal representation. An executive of the Federation of Trade Unions is also included on the committee as an *ex-officio* member.

Upon receipt of the union's notice and proposal, the employers' association prepares a counterproposal and selects its own negotiating committee — consisting of the executive director and his principal assistants, one or two officials of the S. E. F., and several member employers. After the association has acknowledged receipt of the decision to terminate and communicated its counterproposal to the union, a date is set for the negotiations to begin.

Termination from the employer side is a less elaborate process than union termination, and is characterized by considerably greater centralization of the decision-making power. Despite the fact that the by-laws of most employers'

[5] In the case of a drive for higher wages, the increases demanded usually represent some sort of average of the figures submitted by the locals.

associations specify the submission of the question to the member firms, in practice both the decision to terminate and the formulation of demands for the future agreement are usually left to the discretion of the association executives. However, it should be remembered that in deciding on a particular course, these officials must always act in collaboration with, and with the approval of, the leaders of the Employers' Federation.[6]

MAKING THE NEW AGREEMENT

When the issues at stake are not considered to be unduly serious, the two delegations meet and begin their negotiations without any outside assistance. If questions of larger importance are involved — for example, major wage changes — the negotiators usually agree beforehand to call in one of the state mediators[7] to direct the proceedings. At this stage the mediator is *hired* by the parties, who share the cost on an equal basis. In what follows, we shall be assuming that our illustrative case is one of these more serious occasions.

The first phase of the actual negotiating consists of a regular round table meeting of the delegations, at which each side presents its demands — ordinarily the same as those contained in the original proposal and counterproposal. These demands are then discussed, the whole procedure customarily extending over two or three days. Little in the way of concrete settlement of differences is accomplished at this stage, but it gives the mediator an opportunity to ascertain the degree of difference in viewpoint on the various issues.

Next the two delegations convene in separate rooms, and the mediator shuttles back and forth from one to the other, trying to induce each side to give some ground on the disputed points.[8] Obviously he can now express to each party,

[6] See *supra*, p. 30.

[7] The makeup and functioning of the National Mediation Service are described in Chapter XI.

[8] In cases where the differences are unusually wide, or where there is

much more strongly than at the joint conference, his beliefs as to the concessions it can afford to make. If he is able to obtain something approaching a meeting of the minds on the major questions, he draws up a compromise proposal which he presents to the delegations (now convened in joint session again) for their approval or rejection. This process may be repeated several times before a compromise is reached which both sides are willing to sign, or before the mediator is convinced that further efforts are useless. In the latter event, the mediator declares the proceedings broken down, and the parties are free to take more drastic measures, if they see fit to do so.

In the early days of the bargaining system's development, stoppages of work frequently began at this point. The aggressor party usually initiated the stoppage — i.e., if times were prosperous the workers struck, if dull, the employers declared a lockout. For at least twenty years past, however, it has been the almost unvarying practice, on both sides, to refrain from taking coercive action pending the outcome of the second ("officially mediated") series of bargaining conferences.

When the original negotiations break down, the government practically always intervenes by appointing a mediation commission to make a further attempt at reconciliation. (As we have noted, state participation in the previous stage is unofficial.) The commission, of which the original mediator is ordinarily made a member, usually allows a week or two to elapse, in order to give the bruised feelings a chance to heal, and then calls the parties together again. After "feeling out" the sentiment among the opposing delegates, the commissioners prepare a new compromise proposal, which is laid before the joint negotiating conference. It is tacitly understood that the government agents shall continue their efforts until an agreement is reached; and nowadays they always do, although it often takes them sev-

considerable ill feeling between the parties, he may confer with only one or two of the most responsible men on either side. Any agreement effected with such a subcommittee must, however, be approved by the larger delegation.

eral months to devise a proposal which meets the approval of both delegations.

The part played by the Employers' Federation and the Federation of Trade Unions in the settlement of disputes incident to the negotiation of national agreements deserves special mention. When the lines of interest are sharply drawn, it is usually the representatives of the central organizations who take the more conciliatory attitude. At all events, this has been the case in the recent past. Herr Söderlund, the present director of the S. E. F., is a strong advocate of "peace even at a price," despite considerable opposition from prominent individual employers who hold other views. Similarly, the top executives of the S. F. T. U. — especially the chairman, August Lindberg — are the most outspoken champions of peaceful settlement on the union side.

This situation often results in a kind of "unilateral mediation" at the national agreement negotiations, with the representatives of the central organizations — in the role of mediators — trying to induce their fellow delegates to give ground to the other side. According to one government official [9] who has witnessed many hard-fought verbal battles in the labor arena, this is frequently the most difficult and crucial part of the whole proceeding.

THE BALLOTING PRACTICE

Even when the negotiating groups have accepted and signed the mediator's compromise proposal, the new agreement is still not actually concluded, but merely "approved" (*godkänd*). To be sure, the employer delegates are empowered to accept or reject unequivocally any agreements which they negotiate, for all the constituent firms of the association concerned; hence their signatures may be considered a *potential* conclusion of the contract. However, the powers of the workers' representatives extend only to the point of tentative approval. The proposed agreement must then be submitted to a vote of the rank and file, and in the great

[9] Governor (formerly State Mediator) Olle Ekblom.

majority of cases this vote is the deciding factor.[10] Occasionally, it is true, one finds a board or individual leader courageous enough to close a contract despite an adverse vote. For example, this happened in the sawmill industry in 1936. After being apprised that a majority of the members participating in the poll had voted to reject, the president of the Sawmill Workers' Union decided on his own responsibility to change the basis of reckoning from total participants to total *membership*. When referred to this larger base, the total of no-votes fell considerably short of a majority, and on the strength of this "mandate" the agreement was duly concluded.[11] But cases of this sort are of rare occurrence. Most of the union leaders are too keenly aware of the strong "democracy consciousness" prevalent among their constituents to risk such a course of action, realizing that it might cost them their jobs at the next election.

The employers have always protested strenuously against the balloting practice. They maintain that the situation at the stage of approval is a fair one for all concerned. The negotiators on both sides have made approximately equal concessions in the interests of preventing a breakdown (or of restoring peace). If the workers then reject the approved pact, they (the employers) are put at a disadvantage, for they must now make further concessions or a peaceful settlement becomes impossible. They have therefore repeatedly urged the unions to discard the voting feature and institute a more centralized method of delegating responsibility.

There is no denying that the employers' case here is a strong one. During the weeks of parleying preceding the approval stage, the conferees on both sides become thoroughly acquainted with the issues at stake and bring their best faculties of diplomacy and judgment to bear on the situation.

[10] In most unions a bare majority is sufficient either to uphold or reject the negotiated pact, but in a few cases (e.g., the paper workers) the union by-laws specify that a two-thirds adverse majority must be obtained in order to constitute rejection.

[11] It is worth noting, in this connection, that in Denmark and Norway the negotiating parties are required by law to calculate the results of agreement balloting on the basis of total membership.

The majority of union members, on the other hand, are not well informed either as to the problems involved or the efforts made to solve them. Moreover, they usually have only a few hours' notice before the voting begins. Yet their decision is final.

In the past, the importunings of the employers have met with little success. The rank and file have objected strongly to giving up any of their democratic prerogatives. However, the leaders have realized for some time that the present arrangement is not a happy one, and recently the executive committee of the S. F. T. U. drew up a reform plan, the main proposal of which was that the union negotiators be given full power to close contracts. The democratic power of refusal would be retained, but in modified form. It would be exercised by a body of elected representatives instead of the individual members directly. The negotiators would keep in contact with these representatives during the parleys, and would not commit the union in any way unless they were sure that a majority of them favored it. This scheme has already been adopted by the Metal Workers' Union, and was successfully used for the first time in the agreement negotiations with the Iron Masters' Association, which took place in the fall of 1937.[12] The plan meets most of the employers' objections and, in view of the metal workers' experience, the chances are better than even that the other unions will ratify it in the near future.

AGREEMENT MAKING WITHOUT TERMINATION

Among the recent innovations in the sphere of agreement making may also be mentioned the so-called *förhandsförhandlingar*, or "pretermination negotiations." For years the

[12] See *Fackföreningsrörelsen* (official journal of the S. F. T. U.), 1937, No. 46, p. 456. The body of representatives to which the union negotiators were responsible in this case was the "agreement convention"—i.e., the group chosen earlier to decide on the question of termination. It is probable that the other national unions, if and when they adopt the idea, will make a similar use of their conventions. It would seem to be the most logical choice, since these bodies usually comprise at least one representative from each constituent local.

termination of agreements has been a source of considerable uncertainty, and even pecuniary loss, to the managers of Swedish industry, especially those producing for export. Because, in the past, agreement conferences have frequently broken down and eventuated in stoppages, foreign customers of Swedish manufacturing firms have come to regard the termination of national labor contracts as a sort of warning that deliveries in the near future may be seriously delayed. At such times, many of these customers have shifted their purchasing to other countries or have refrained from buying altogether.

The new scheme, sponsored by the S. E. F. and its constituent associations, is designed to prevent such interruptions from occurring. Under it, the heads of the respective organizations would meet some time before the stipulated termination date and work out an approximate understanding regarding the important current issues. Neither side would give notice of termination; instead negotiations would be instituted — on an informal basis and without the intervention of the state — to establish in exact terms the changes to be made. The result would be not a new contract, as heretofore, but a revision of the old one, which would continue in force during the proceedings.[13] As a precautionary measure (to meet the possibility of the negotiators not being able to agree) a new termination date would be set, from a month to two months later than that originally specified.

As in the case of the "modified" balloting device, credit for making the first large-scale attempt to introduce the pre-termination idea goes to the iron and steel industry. The metal workers and the iron masters began their negotiations early in October, 1937, after agreeing to postpone the termination date to November 15. Three days before the dead-

[13] Wage adjustments comprise the majority of agreement changes which come to question today, most of the other terms of employment being established on a permanent or semipermanent basis. It is therefore considerably easier now than formerly to effect a revision and dispense with writing a new agreement.

line date a settlement was reached, the union gaining an increase in both time and piece rates of approximately 8 per cent. Because of the smoothness and dispatch with which the revision of the iron and steel agreement was carried through, it has been hailed by employers and unionists alike as an auspicious start in the movement to reform Swedish negotiating practice.[14]

BARGAINING IN GOVERNMENT SERVICE

The bargaining methods we have described are not confined to private industry. Substantially the same procedure is followed in a number of fields of government activity, such as municipal works, the repair shops of the state-owned railways, and the telegraph and telephone systems. However, certain classes of government employees are considered to be above the level of mere wage earners, in that their positions carry greater responsibility and are closely related to the continuous functioning of essential services. Such workers are not accorded the right of sharing directly in determination of their wages and working conditions through negotiations with the state authorities. Instead, their terms of employment are worked out through the national legislative process.

The railroad traffic personnel (conductors, engineers, station attendants, etc.) constitutes one such class. From time to time, the State Railways Executive Board (*Järnvägsstyrëlsen*) makes proposals for changes in and additions to the code of rules governing the traffic workers' salaries and submits them to Parliament, which acts on them much as it does on regular legislation. However, the employees do have some voice in the matter, since members of the Railroad Workers' Union are usually invited to "assist" the board in drawing up the proposals.

LOCAL NEGOTIATION

Local negotiations vary considerably in procedural detail from place to place, but the general pattern followed is

[14] *Fackföreningsrörelsen*, 1937, No. 46, p. 456.

very similar to that of the national parleys — so far as agreement making is concerned, at any rate. There are two classes of local agreements: independent and supplementary. The former includes all contracts which do not operate under any national covenant — which means, in the main, contracts with unorganized employers. It should be remembered, however, that the presence of a strong national union often results in a close resemblance between these local instruments and the national agreement in the same industry.[15]

As the name implies, supplementary agreements are chiefly auxiliary in character. In certain industries — notably sawmills, paper, pulp, and machinery — only general working conditions and approximate wage rates are established in the central document, the determination of the exact terms of payment and rules applying to the particular workplace being left to the parties "on the ground." In negotiating both types of local contracts, the employer side is usually represented by a small group of executives (e.g., the manager, the superintendent, and one or two engineers), and the workers by a committee composed of the chairman and several elected representatives of the local union.

When negotiations concerning *independent* local agreements break down, the state mediator for the particular district usually intervenes. In settling local disputes, the mediators pursue substantially the same course as in national conflicts. In the event of disagreement in the making of *supplementary* agreements, recourse is had to the respective head organizations, either by calling in national representatives to carry on the local negotiations or by referring the disputed questions back to the central conference.[16]

In addition to this more or less formal and stereotyped process of local contract making, collective negotiating is used to settle a wide variety of petty grievances, differences of agreement interpretation, and other difficulties which arise at the individual workplace. However, most of these disputes

[15] See Chapter VI, pp. 113–114.

[16] Cf. *Statens Offentliga Utredningar, 1927:4* (*Utredningar till Belysande av Arbetsfredsgrågan*) (Stockholm, 1927), p. 129.

occur while the agreements are in force, hence are required to be handled by the methods prescribed in them. This phase of employer-employee relations, which we may term "bargaining within the agreement framework," will be examined in the fourth section of our study.

CHAPTER X

COLLECTIVE BARGAINING AND STOPPAGES OF WORK

DESPITE the steady progress of collective bargaining in Sweden, stoppages of work have been a very common occurrence in the annals of the country's industrial relations. Even today they are by no means unknown, although they occur much less frequently than formerly. Since the settlement (or avoidance) of stoppages is one of the primary purposes of collective worker-employer negotiations, it seems apropos at this point to give a brief account of how strikes and lockouts are conducted in Sweden, and of their relation to the functioning of the bargaining system.

THE EVOLUTION OF STRIKE POLICY

The first strikes, as noted earlier, were spontaneous group movements of unorganized workers. These practically always ended in failure. The strikers rarely had the means, either collectively or individually, of keeping themselves alive for more than a few days, and were soon driven back to work by force of necessity.

The establishment of local unions in the eighties, however, marks the beginning of a distinct change in this respect. These unions soon built up strike funds — small at the start, to be sure, but sufficient to keep their members in food for a period long enough to give the employers cause for serious concern. As a result, the workers began to appear occasionally in the win column.[1] And when, in the middle and late nineties, the locals banded together into national unions and pooled their strike funds, the number of worker victories increased rapidly. The strikes were still confined to individual workplaces or localities, and with the consolidation of resources, each central union was able to support a given

[1] See *supra*, p. 67.

group of striking workers much longer than any single individual local could have done.

The employers, it will be remembered, were still almost wholly unorganized at this time. Hence the unions in the better organized occupations, by "bearing down" on one or a few firms at a time, were able to wrest substantial concessions in the form of higher wages and better conditions. The resources of most of the individual employers singled out for attack were entirely inadequate to withstand a siege backed by the funds of an entire national organization of workers. They were, therefore, faced with the alternative of giving in to the workers' demands or going out of business. More often than not they gave in.

This lopsided situation lasted but a scant decade. For when the employers became nationally organized, they soon accumulated strike funds of their own, which made it possible for attacked member firms to fight back — that is, to put up a passive defense as strong as, and in some cases even stronger than, the workers' "passive aggression."

Despite this massing of forces on the other side, the unions did not abandon the policy of trying to keep their coercive activities localized. Although they could no longer overpower any individual (organized) concern by sheer force of economic strength, it was believed that a drive for better terms of employment could be prosecuted more effectively by concentrating the attack on a few employers than by spreading it over the whole of the opposing association's membership. Union funds would last longer, and the more long drawn out the siege — so it was argued — the greater the employers' embarrassment.

The principal change in strike strategy induced by the new situation was a more careful planning of the offensive. Whereas previously almost any concern might have been singled out, provided a substantial majority of the workers were organized, the unions now took pains to choose the most "vulnerable" ones — i.e., those which were in the midst of filling large "rush" orders or those whose financial condition was known to be unsound.

Whatever the advantages of this policy, it proved impossible for the unions, after the advent of the employers' organization, to realize them — for the very good reason that the latter refused to let the worker offensives remain localized. When a national union opened hostilities in a given plant or locality, the employers would usually reply by shutting down all the member plants within the affected industry, and on some occasions those in a number of related industries besides. In other words, the localization policy ceased to be a practicable type of strategy in union drives for better terms and became instead merely a method of inaugurating such drives.

Nevertheless, worker-initiated stoppages in Sweden have, on the whole, been confined within considerably narrower limits than those originated by the organized employers. Indeed, the only strike in the history of Swedish labor relations involving, in the first instance, more than one entire national union was the great conflict of 1909.[2] On this occasion, it will be remembered, the S. E. F. declared a lockout affecting five major industries, and the S. F. T. U. replied by calling out its entire membership, which included a majority of the workers in practically the entire field of manufacturing, mining, and construction.

The memory of this struggle and its disastrous outcome has undoubtedly had a good deal to do with the infrequent occurrence of sympathetic strikes in Sweden during the ensuing decades. An almost equally provocative situation arose in 1923, when four national unions were locked out simultaneously by the organized employers. But despite a considerable demand for another general strike among the rank and file, the S. F. T. U. leaders decided in favor of economic support of the locked-out unions by means of extra levies on the rest of the membership — and succeeded in getting their

[2] The "political strike" of 1902 was, to be sure, also more or less general in scope; but this trike was initiated by the Social-Democrats and not by the unions. Moreover, it was called as a means of demonstrating the strength of the demand for universal manhood suffrage, and hence was not really a strike at all, in the ordinary sense of the term.

decision approved. As it happened, the subsequent (government-initiated) negotiations worked out relatively advantageously for the workers. Since then there has never been any strong sentiment in favor of extending strikes beyond the confines of a single industry.

Besides the policy of keeping clear of interindustrial sympathetic strikes, there are several other features of the battle tactics followed by the national unions which deserve mention. Walkouts are the almost unvarying rule. Occasionally one hears of local strikes in the building industry in which the strikers continue to occupy the premises, but these instances are few and far between. Picketing, or "blockading" as the Swedes call it, is also a comparative rarity nowadays, except in such occupations as agriculture and retail trade, where the degree of worker organization is still comparatively low. Even here the blockading force seldom comprises more than two or three people, who usually spend their time distributing circulars or pamphlets.

In the early days, when only a minority of Swedish wage earners were organized, it would have been impossible to bring a strike to a successful issue without the aid of an effective picket line. There was practically always a sizable army of unemployed, hence potential strikebreakers were plentiful. The employers frequently took advantage of this situation and attempted, at least, to keep their plants open. In certain instances, they even went so far as to import strikebreakers from other countries. For example, we learn that in the conflict at the Arlöv wagon factory in 1901, the manager brought in a number of workers from Russia. With the aid of these and a somewhat larger number of native Swedish strikebreakers, he was able to carry on some sort of operations for practically a whole year.[3]

During the 1920's, however, the unions in most of the fabrication industries, as well as those in mining and trans-

[3] S. Hansson, *Svenska Träarbetareförbundets Historia, 1889–1923*, pp. 150–170. Despite this apparently successful move on the part of the manager, the Arlöv strike ended in a victory for the workers, all the strikers being reinstated, and all the strikebreakers dismissed.

portation, succeeded in increasing the proportion of organized workers within their respective fields to 80 and even 90 per cent. Since then blockades have become more a matter of form than necessity — where they are used at all. The advantages to be gained from active picketing would hardly repay the expenditure of time and effort involved, since it is almost inconceivable that anyone would attempt to hire out as a strikebreaker.[4]

ORGANIZED COUNTERATTACK: THE LARGE-SCALE LOCKOUT

The employers, on their side, almost never attempt to keep a plant open, once a strike has been called against it. They appreciate fully the impossibility of carrying on operations successfully when practically all the available experienced workers are able and willing to withhold their services. What is more, so far as the *organized* employers are concerned, there is seldom any incentive to continue operations. As already mentioned, the S. E. F.'s principal means of applying pressure is the large scale lockout, the use of which is obviously quite the antithesis of attempting to carry on business.

The sympathetic lockout weapon, as it has been developed by the Swedish employers' organizations, is used both for defensive and offensive purposes — in the one case, by expanding localized strikes into industry-wide shutdowns; in the other, by closing down one or more entire industries as an initial move. A few summary figures from the official government statistics on stoppages[5] will serve to give an idea of the great difference in scope between the employers' coercive activities and those of the national unions.

During the period 1903–1935 there were 6,901 strikes,

[4] By the same token, violence in strikes and lockouts is practically a thing of the past. Physical force has, in fact, never been much in evidence in labor conflicts in Sweden. Even in the great strike of 1909, when the feeling ran unusually high, it was a by-word that the strikers in Stockholm spent most of their time on the docks fishing.

[5] *Arbetsinställelser och Kollektivavtal samt Förlikningsmännens Verksamhet*, published yearly by the Social Board (*Socialstyrelsen*); prior to 1912, published by the Board of Trade (*Kommerskollegium*).

342 lockouts, and 483 "stoppages of mixed character." (The last named category comprises mainly conflicts which began as local strikes and were later "enlarged" into district or country-wide lockouts.) On the other hand, the average number of man-days lost per strike was only 5,600, whereas the corresponding figures for lockouts and "mixed conflicts" were 43,000 and 34,000. In other words, although the number of employer attacks and counterattacks was much smaller than the "purely" worker offensives, this was more than balanced by their extent and/or duration.

Not infrequently the mere threat of a major shutdown has caused the unions to modify their stand, or has led the government to take extraordinary measures to settle the dispute through mediation. During the postwar decade in particular the lockout weapon, either as threat or fact, was used more freely in Sweden than in any other country and, on the whole, with rather remarkable efficaciousness, considering that the workers' organizations grew much faster during this period than did those on the employer side. More often than not, to be sure, the state intervened, and the final outcome was decided through mediated bargaining; but the settlement was in many cases profoundly affected by the employers' high-powered pressure device.

A brief résumé of the major disputes of the 1920's will show how important a part the large-scale lockout has played in recent Swedish industrial relations history.[6] At the beginning of 1920 the Metal Workers' Union set off strikes in a number of machinery plants, in an effort to obtain wage increases to compensate for the working time lost when the Forty-eight Hour Law went into effect. After an attempt to settle these disputes by a government mediation commission had failed, the S .E. F. counterattacked by declaring a lockout involving the entire membership of the Machine Industry and Iron Masters' Associations. More than a month elapsed before the mediators were able to bring about a meeting of the minds and put an end to the shutdown. In the settlement,

[6] Principal source: Olle Ekblom, "P.M. Beträffande Arbetsinställelser m.m. i Sverige" in *Statens Offentliga Utredningar, 1935:66, Bil. 21.*

the workers did get some compensation for the shortened work week, but it was considerably less than "full" compensation.[7] A little later in the same year, when the building trades unions demanded a wage increase, the Employers' Federation locked them out also, and this time it took more than eight months to put an end to the conflict. Here again — and despite the effectiveness of the lockout — the workers got a part of what they had demanded. It must be remembered, however, that the year 1920 was an unusually favorable one for the unions, being the crest year of the postwar boom in Swedish industry.

But if the employers made some concessions in the boom of 1920, they made none in the severe depression which followed in 1921–1922. In the latter year they shut out first the sawmill workers and a little later the pulp workers; and in each case they were able to force down wage rates by nearly a third. In fact, wage reductions of this order of magnitude were effected practically all along the line during these two years, albeit in most of the other industries it proved unnecessary to resort to the lockout weapon.

The lockouts incident to the wage movements of 1923 covered an even wider area. Almost simultaneously the organized plants in the iron and steel, sawmill, and pulp industries were closed down, and the building materials establishments somewhat later. In this struggle, the balance of power was to a considerable extent restored through financial support of the locked-out unions by the S. F. T. U., and when the differences had finally been cleared up the workers were somewhat better off in the matter of wages than before. But the increases were trifling as compared with the cuts of the preceding two years.

In 1925 the S. E. F. put into effect a lockout which in point of coverage dwarfed all its earlier activities in this sphere. A large number of agreements had been terminated at or near the first of the year, principally by unions demanding wage increases. In connection with these demands, local strikes had been called in a number of industries and occu-

[7] See Chapter V, pp. 90–91.

pations, including the iron and steel plants, paper mills, glassware establishments, and plumbing and electrical installation firms. On February 14, the Employers' Federation informed the union leaders that if the existing disputes were not settled by the twenty-fifth, the plants of all its members in the machinery, sawmill, pulp, paper, and textile industries would be shut down. A government mediation commission, appointed on the seventeenth, succeeded in persuading the employers to postpone the deadline date, in order that it might attempt to bring about a peaceable settlement. On March 2 the commission presented a compromise proposal, embodying in its main points a continuance of the status quo. This was accepted by both employers' and workers' representatives. However, when it was submitted to a vote of the union rank and file, most of its provisions were rejected, whereupon the S. E. F., on March 16, put the threatened "general lockout" into effect.

Despite this setback of its attempts to restore peace, the mediation commission continued its efforts to bring the parties on common ground. The prospects brightened considerably when the S. F. T. U. council met two days later and gave the union negotiating committee a vote of confidence. This afforded the latter body at least some measure of assurance that its repudiation by the rank and file would not be repeated. On March 28 the mediation commission finally succeeded in effecting a settlement, so that the lockout lasted only twelve days in all. It is worth noting, however, that the proposal as finally accepted still represented, in most essential particulars, a continuation of the status quo. The leaders of the S. E. F. could therefore say, with some justification, that their big lockout had been a success.

In the immediately ensuing years the organized employers availed themselves of the shutdown or shutdown threat on at least a half-dozen occasions — most of the time with (for them) quite satisfactory results. During the late twenties and early thirties, however, the S. E. F. modified its earlier militant policies considerably, and since then there has been a marked decrease in the number of lockouts. Nowadays local strikes are usually allowed to remain localized, instead of being spread out over whole industries as formerly; and the affected employers are enabled to fight back by means of adequate financial aid from the central organization.

According to one prominent S. E. F. official, the organized employers were led to adopt a less militant line of policy principally by the developments in the political sphere. They realized that large scale lockouts were exceedingly unpopular with the rapidly growing leftist portion of the electorate, and that if the Social-Democratic Party should come into power severe repressive measures might be forthcoming. Better to retreat voluntarily now, they reasoned, than to be forced to do so later.[8]

Nevertheless, the lockout weapon has by no means lost its potency, as the S. E. F. amply demonstrated early in 1934. The occasion was a nation-wide strike in the building trades, which had been called in April of the previous year in answer to an attempt by the employers to force through a sharp reduction in wages. After a number of efforts to settle the conflict through negotiations with the building unions had failed, the Employers' Federation at last carried the fight to the central workers' organization. It informed the Federation of Trade Unions that unless the building trades quarrel was satisfactorily settled, it (the S. E. F.) would shut down its members' plants in all the principal manufacturing industries. This ultimatum forced the S. F. T. U. leaders to bring extraordinary pressure to bear on the recalcitrant unions. The latter finally gave in, and within a few weeks a new agreement — embodying in many particulars the employers' demands — was signed.

COMPARISON OF SWEDISH AND AMERICAN EXPERIENCE

One of the chief arguments advanced in favor of collective bargaining is that it provides a cheap and practicable substitute for strikes and lockouts. The frequent occurrence of widespread stoppages in a country where practically all

[8] Interview, Director F. Söderbäck of the S. E. F.'s "General Branch," July 4, 1938.

employer-employee dealings are conducted collectively must, therefore, appear something of a paradox. In examining this aspect of Swedish industrial relations experience, it will be useful to make a rough comparison of the volume of stoppages in Sweden with corresponding data for the United States, where collective bargaining has been used only to a very minor extent. In the absence of adequate comparable statistics for the total of man-days of productive labor lost, one may take the annual *number of workers* involved in stoppages and express this as a ratio of the total of gainfully occupied persons.[9] The following table gives an idea of how

COMPARISON OF STATISTICS ON STOPPAGES OF WORK IN SWEDEN AND THE UNITED STATES, 1916–1937

Period	Average Annual Number of Workers Involved in Stoppages, as Percentage of Total Gainfully Occupied Persons	
	Sweden	United States
1916–1921	2.9	4.4
1922–1926	3.5	1.7
1927–1932	1.5	0.6
1933–1937	0.8	2.4
Average for entire interval 1916–1937	2.2	2.5

Sources: For Sweden, *Arbetsinställelser och Kollektivavtal samt Förlikningsmännens Verksamhet* (annual volumes), and *Statistisk Årsbok för Sverige*; for the United States, *Monthly Labor Review*, May 1938, and *Statistical Abstract of the United States*, 1938.

this ratio has varied in Sweden and the United States since 1916, the earliest year for which dependable data are available for the latter country.

The only general observation which these figures elicit is that the overall volume of stoppages in the two countries has been much the same. To be sure, marked differences have prevailed in particular periods. During the twenties, stoppages were considerably less numerous in the United States, whereas in the present decade the reverse has been true. But

[9] This basis is used rather than the total of "organizable workers" because no truly comparable figures are available for the latter. In Sweden, wage and small-salary earners (in all occupations) comprise about 80 per cent of the total of all gainfully occupied persons; and the proportion is not substantially different in the United States.

taking the interval 1916–1937 as a whole, it is evident that cessations of work have been very nearly as prevalent in Sweden as in this country.

One might be tempted to conclude from this that the extensive use of collective bargaining has not helped appreciably in fostering peaceful relations between wage earners and managers in Sweden. If one interprets "peaceful relations" as meaning merely a relatively infrequent occurrence of coercive actions, such a conclusion is entirely warranted — so far as the developmental stage of Swedish industrial relations is concerned, at any rate. Militancy — both in policy and practice — has been an outstanding characteristic of the workers' and employers' organizations from the very start, and both sides have insisted on keeping unimpaired the right to take drastic measures. Indeed, the very fact of widespread organization is itself a reason for the prevalence of strikes and lockouts. For when the protagonists on either side are banded together in large and well-disciplined common interest groups, the possibilities of inaugurating forceful collective action and carrying it to a successful issue are obviously much better than when no organizations exist.

But the number of stoppages alone by no means gives a true picture of the degree of peacefulness prevailing in a country's labor market. The manner in which the stoppages are conducted and the circumstances attending them must also be taken into account. And on this score it can be said with assurance that Sweden's record is by long odds the better one. Pitched battles between strikers and strikebreakers, armed intervention by police and military, wholesale eviction of striking workers from their homes, and the various other forms of violence so common in American labor conflicts are practically unknown in Sweden.

There is no question but that this absence of violence is closely associated with the extensive use of collective bargaining. For as the bargaining institution has developed and increased in scope through the years, departures from orderly and peaceable behavior in strikes and lockouts have become more and more of a rarity. In other words, the parties to the employment contract have learned to exercise, in the conduct of "open conflicts," the restraint and discipline acquired through experience at the conference table.

During the past decade, moreover, the frequency of stoppages has also diminished markedly, and there is good ground for believing that the arrival of the bargaining system at a stage of virtual maturity has been the main contributing factor. To this most recent episode in Sweden's strike-lockout history we shall return at a later point in the present chapter.

THE EFFECT OF BARGAINING ON STOPPAGES OF WORK

Turning now to a somewhat closer examination of the effect of collective bargaining on the *trend* of stoppages in Sweden, we may pose two pertinent questions: has it resulted in any shift in the *nature* of strikes and lockouts — i.e., in the kinds of disputes which lead to open conflicts? has it brought about any diminution in the number and severity of stoppages?

It will not, of course, be possible to establish any definitive cause-effect relationships in answer to either of these questions, since various other and perhaps equally significant factors have been acting on the situation simultaneously. For one thing, Sweden has been changing rapidly from predominantly agricultural to a predominantly industrial country, until today manufacturing and commerce are far ahead of farming. During the same period, moreover, the number of unionized workers has increased from a small fraction to a large majority of the gainfully employed population. Nevertheless, it seems worth while to examine briefly the official statistics on stoppages in the light of the progress that has been made in the art of bargaining.

Regarding the principal causes of strikes and lockouts there are, fortunately, fairly comprehensive data available in the annual publications of the Social Board and the Board of Trade, which extend back as far as 1903. These data have been summarized in the following table by dividing the interval 1903–1936 into four more or less logical periods and expressing the number of workers affected by stoppages due to various causes as percentages of the total number involved in stoppages of all kinds.

Wage disputes (demands for increases by the unions and for reductions by the employers) have been by far the most

CAUSES OF STOPPAGES [a]

	Number of Workers Affected (under each head) as Per Cent of Number Involved in *all* Stoppages						
Period	Wage Disputes	Hours of Work	Demand for Collective Agreements	Workers' Right to Organize	Hiring and Dismissal of Workers	Interpretation of Collective Agreements	Other Causes
1903–12 ...	64.8	2.0	4.2	2.3	7.2	7.8	11.7
1913–22 ...	84.1	2.6	5.3	0.3	3.8	0.6	3.3
1923–29 ...	80.6	5.2	6.0	0.1	3.1	0.4	4.6
1930–36 ...	84.1	0.3	5.7	0.3	2.9	0.2	6.5

Sources: *Statens Offentliga Utredningar, 1927:4*, pp. 42–43 (summary of statistics for years 1903–1922, as reported in annual publications of the Board of Trade and the Social Board); Socialstyrelsen, *Arbetsinställelser och Kollektivavtal samt Förlikningsmännens Verksamhet* (annual statistical series) for years 1923–1936.

[a] The term "cause" as used here signifies, for any given stoppage, *principal* cause. A particular strike or lockout may — and frequently does — involve several different issues.

common type of conflict throughout the entire interval. But they have been considerably more predominant in recent years than they were before the World War. In other words, stoppages caused by nonwage questions have become relatively fewer.[10] In particular, disputes over hiring and firing, the right to organize, and the interpretation of agreements have decreased markedly. This is what our appraisal of the development of collective bargaining would lead us to expect. For during the years under survey, many if not most of the nonwage problems have been settled on a permanent or semipermanent basis and have been incorporated in the agreements. On the other hand, very few criteria have been established for determining changes in the rate of payment

[10] The figure for wage disputes during 1913–1922 is obviously out of line with the trend. Wage strikes were unusually numerous during this period because of the maladjustments between wages and the cost of living occasioned by the great price inflation which took place during and immediately after the war.

— beyond the relative bargaining strength of the opposing parties on each separate occasion. Only within recent years has the uncompromising spirit on both sides regarding the level of wages shown any signs of abating.[11]

With respect to the question of whether the advance in bargaining has brought any diminution of stoppages, there is obviously little to be gained by examining the trend in the *absolute* frequency of strikes and lockouts. But if it could also be determined for any corresponding period how many disputes had been *settled*, whether by peaceable means throughout or after the occurrence of stoppages, the resultant correlation might be considerably more instructive. A rough approximation to this relationship may be obtained by comparing the total number of workers involved in open conflicts with the number covered by agreements *concluded* during the same time interval. These two sets of variables will not be strictly comparable, since the former includes, in addition to strikes and lockouts incident to the expiration and renewal of agreements, all other types of stoppages as well. However, these others are relatively few in number and of limited scope.

These data indicate that over most of the interval under survey the percentage of agreement negotiations resulting in stoppages has not only been relatively high, but also (for averages over periods of several years) fairly constant.[12] However, in 1929 the "stoppage ratio" decreased sharply, and except for a temporary rise in 1931, it has stayed at less than half its former value ever since.

Here again we find evidence of a development which our earlier analysis would lead us to expect. However, the drop in the frequency of stoppages has taken place much later than the shift in their nature, and with a suddenness that is

[11] See *infra*, pp. 300–303.

[12] Provided the figures for 1909 are left out of the reckoning. This seems admissible, since the big stoppage of that year was a nation-wide *sympathetic* strike, in which most of the participants disregarded *existing* agreements. Moreover, it is the only incident of its kind in the history of Swedish industrial relations.

difficult to explain. One would rather suppose that, as the parties to the collective employment contract gained experience in bargaining through the years, the number of strikes and lockouts would diminish *gradually*. Be that as it may,

COMPARISON OF STOPPAGES WITH AGREEMENTS CONCLUDED
(IN TERMS OF WORKER COVERAGE)

Year	Number of Workers Involved in Stoppages (*thousands*)	Number of Workers Covered by Agreements Concluded During Year (*thousands*)	Workers Involved in Stoppages as Percentage of Workers Covered by Agreements Concluded	Average for Period
1903–07, incl.	123	250[a]	49	
1908	40	136	33	41
1909	302	46	657	(figure for 1909 omitted)
1910	4	37	11	
1911	21	34	62	
1912	10	30	33	
1913	10	76	13	
1914	14	60	23	
1915	5	13	38	
1916	21	117	18	
1917	47	78	61	36
1918	61	118	52	
1919	81	204	40	
1920	139	260	53	
1921	50	185	27	
1922	76	280	27	
1923	103	213	48	
1924	24	120	20	
1925	146	225	65	
1926	53	76	70	43
1927	9	94	10	
1928	71	134	53	
1929	13	113	11	
1930	21	170	12	
1931	41	126	32	
1932	50	258	19	
1933	32	198	16	11
1934	14	140	10	
1935	17	172	10	
1936	3.5	342	1	
1937	31	454	7	

Sources: Kommerskollegium, *Arbetsstatistik F:1, F:2, F:3* (collective agreement statistics for years 1908, 1909, and 1910); *Arbetsstatistik E:1, E:2, E:3, E:4* (statistics on stoppages for years 1903–07, 1908, 1909, and 1910).

Socialstyrelsen, *Arbetsinställelser i Sverige*, for years 1911–1922, inclusive; *Kollektivavtal i Sverige*, for years 1911–1922, inclusive; *Arbetsinställelser och Kollektivavtal samt Förlikningsmännens Verksamhet*, for years 1923–36, inclusive.

[a] Estimated. The number of workers covered by agreements *in force* as of January 1, 1908, was 256,000. Most of these agreements had been concluded during the preceding five years.

we have the assurance of the leaders on both sides that the decrease in stoppages is not a result of external circumstances but rather of a conscious and voluntary abjuration of the use of coercive measures by their respective organizations. And the fact that peaceful conditions (comparatively speaking) have now prevailed for a full decade would appear to bear out their assertion.

CHAPTER XI

GOVERNMENT INTERVENTION: THE MEDIATION SERVICE

From what has been said about agreement making and the settlement of disputes, it is evident that the state mediators play a very vital part in the bargaining process. In order to round out our picture it will be necessary to describe in some detail the makeup and functioning of the branch of government service which centers around the activities of these official peacemakers.

DEVELOPMENT OF MEDIATION IN SWEDEN

As between mediation and arbitration in settling "interest disputes" (disputes concerning the making of new agreements), both the unions and the employers' associations have, for at least three decades favored mediation. Indeed, arbitration is almost never used for this purpose nowadays, except in a few minor industries such as municipal works and privately owned railways, and even here its use is for the most part permissive.[1]

Yet, peculiarly enough, arbitration was the first form of third-party intervention to be used to any extent in Swedish industrial relations. An exhaustive survey of early disputes, made by a parliamentary committee in 1899–1900, records ten instances of strikes and lockouts being settled by this means during the last two decades of the nineteenth century, as against only five by mediation, all of which occurred within the latter half of the period.[2] Of the former group, the Norberg miners' strike in 1891 and a strike of lumber

[1] It should be noted, however, that in *interpretational* disputes settlement of the disputed points by the Labor Court — a form of arbitration — is required by law. (See Chapter XV.)

[2] *Förliknings- och Skiljenämndskomiténs Betänkande* (Stockholm, 1901), pp. 28–36.

yard workers in Gävle in the same year were the most important. In each case, the calling in of troops by the local authorities appears to have had a chastening effect, for shortly afterwards the employers' and workers' representatives met and agreed to turn the disputed questions over to a board of arbitration, consisting of an equal number of members from each side and a neutral chairman. The verdict of the arbitrators was decidedly favorable to the workers in both instances. The principal early instance of mediation occurred in connection with a strike-lockout of cigar and tobacco workers in 1896, involving all the major establishments in Stockholm, Gothenburg, Malmö, and Linköping. The conference between representatives of the unions and the employers, and to some extent also the subsequent settlement of the dispute, was effected in this case through the efforts of leaders of the Social-Democratic Party.[3]

During this period the government took no official part, either in initiating the peace-making proceedings or in deciding the terms of settlement. More often than not, the initiative was taken by the parties themselves. In several instances, interested outsiders — e.g., a group of ship owners in a dockworkers' strike in 1896, and certain suppliers of construction materials in the Stockholm building trades lockout in 1900 — stepped in and helped bring about a meeting of the minds.

Nevertheless, there was strong evidence, even at this stage, that some government agent or group of agents would be the most appropriate go-between in interest disputes. Indeed, one might almost say there was a demand for it, for in no less than eight of the above-mentioned conflicts, public officials — either state or local — were chosen as the neutral party to guide the proceedings and (in the arbitration cases) cast the deciding vote. Regarding the miners' and lumber yard workers' strikes in particular, the parliamentary committee of 1899 expressed doubt that peaceful settlement could have been effected "had it not been for the energetic efforts

[3] T. Lindbom, *Tobaksarbetarnas Stockholmsavdelning, 1884–1934* (Stockholm, 1934), pp. 55-57.

of government officials and other prominent persons in bringing the parties together for rational discussion of the disputed questions." [4]

The first really large-scale clash between organizations of workers and employers in Sweden was the machinery trades dispute of 1903–1905, already referred to, and here again we find the parties turning to governmental circles for aid. At a meeting of employers and union representatives held on July 27, 1903, the conferees agreed to call off the industry-wide lockout and the antecedent local strikes then in progress. They then appointed a committee to design an agreement "for settling future disputes, so far as possible, by peaceful means." The man invited to head this bilateral committee as neutral chairman was Dr. Henning Elmquist, chief actuary of the State Board of Trade.

For nearly two years Dr. Elmquist, in his capacity as leader of this and several other similar bodies, struggled with the task of devising a written document which would be acceptable to both sides. But his efforts, successful on most points, foundered on the snag of minimum wage rates, and in June, 1905, the employers declared another industry-wide lockout. After this conflict had gone on for about five months, two members of the national cabinet finally arranged a conference between delegates of the parties. Again a government official became the neutral chairman — a provincial governor named Hugo Hamilton. The outcome of this group's efforts was the signing of the machinery trades national agreement,[5] which, as we have noted, provided the essential basis for most of the subsequent bargaining and agreement making in this and a number of other industries.

Although the public servants who assisted in settling this bitter and long-drawn-out dispute did so in an unofficial capacity, and at the behest of the disputants themselves, a movement had been under way for several years to establish a legally authorized "intervention agency," which would

[4] *Förliknings- och Skiljenämndskomiténs Betänkande*, p. 32.

[5] Many of the provisions of this document were based on the earlier proposals, formulated under the leadership of Dr. Elmquist.

enable the state to take the initiative in putting an end to industrial conflicts. In 1899, as a result of several motions in the Riksdag, the Government appointed the afore-mentioned parliamentary committee to investigate the subject and submit a legislative program. Early in 1901 the committee presented its report, which included a proposal for the setting up of a mediation service, its reasons therefor, and an account of both Swedish and foreign experience in this field of activity.

THE MEDIATION LAW OF 1906

The proposal was duly presented to the Riksdag in 1903, but failed of passage. In 1906 a new proposal was brought forward, differing from and complementing the original one in certain minor respects, and this time the Riksdag gave its consent. The law[6] provided for a division of the kingdom into seven geographical districts, for each of which an official mediator was to be appointed by the Government.

The essence of this statute is contained in Section 3, which specifies the duties of the mediators. It reads as follows:

> If within any mediator's territory, a dispute has arisen which has resulted or threatens to result in a serious stoppage of work, the said mediator shall, by a personal visit to the place where the dispute has taken place, or by some other means, thoroughly inform himself as to its nature and causes; request the disputants not to initiate, continue, or extend the scope of the stoppage (as the case may be) pending the settlement of the dispute; call the parties or their authorized agents to come and confer with each other at a determined time and place, and in his presence; and in the course of such conference (which he may arrange and conduct at his discretion) attempt to settle the conflict.

The law provides further that if the dispute extends over several districts, the Social Board may designate the mediator in *one* of the districts to handle the entire dispute (Section 1). In cases where "industrial peace is seriously

[6] *Lag Angående Medling i Arbetstvister* (*S. F. 113*). The currently effective version of this law, passed in 1920, is reproduced in A. Molin, *op. cit.*, pp. 233–241.

threatened," the government "may appoint expert and experienced persons acting as a special mediation commission to aid the mediator in settling the dispute or, if he is unable to lend his services, to act in his stead. Such office may also be delegated to a single person" (Section 12).

Section 8 of the law stipulates that if the mediator fails to bring about a settlement through mediation, he shall attempt to persuade the parties to resort to arbitration. He may aid in the selection of arbitrators and assist them with information, but may not himself become a member of the arbitrating body. In practice, this clause has little significance, since both the employers and the workers' organization in most industries are opposed to arbitration.

According to the literal interpretation of the law, mediation should be undertaken in all kinds of disputes. But the inclusion in Section 3 of the words "which has resulted or threatens to result in a *serious* stoppage of work" has from the very beginning limited the practical application of the law mainly to interest disputes. The establishment in 1928 of the Labor Court, for the express purpose of handling interpretational disputes (the only other kind which has any considerable significance today), merely served to make this limitation more complete.

It is noteworthy that although the mediator is required to call the parties together to confer with each other, nothing is said in the original statute about the parties being obligated to heed the call. When the law was revised (slightly) in 1920, a clause to this effect was added, but no punishment was provided for failure to comply. However, neither of these omissions has affected the course of events to any appreciable degree, since the parties — whether local or national unions, individual employers or large aggregations of them — practically always do heed the mediators' call.[7]

In 1931 a paragraph was added to Section 3 of the mediation law, which provides that even if the dispute "has not resulted nor threatened to result in a serious stoppage, the mediator shall call the parties into conference . . . if the

[7] *Statens Offentliga Utredningar, 1935:66*, p. 421.

desire for such conference is expressed by the employers or by an organization covering (*omfattande*) at least half of the affected workers." The purpose of this addition was to make it easier for the so-called *anställda* (i.e., such salaried employees as stenographers, bookkeepers, bank clerks, and salespeople), many of whom were still being denied the right to bargain, to enter into collective negotiations and obtain agreements with their employers.

Another addition — the so-called "stoppage notice period" (*varseltid*) clause — was made to Section 3 in 1935. The original law, which made no mandatory provision regarding the call to confer, made none as to heeding the mediator's request to refrain from calling strikes and lockouts either. However, the latter omission has been by far the more significant of the two, for on frequent occasions in the past the aggressor party has called a stoppage of work, even though there was no intention of refusing to enter into negotiations with the other side. The new clause was designed to cut down on the number of such occurrences and in general to reduce the economic loss occasioned by strikes and lockouts — the theory being that if the stoppage could be delayed until after the parties had actually begun to confer, the chances of its being prevented altogether would be greatly improved. It provides that "before a stoppage is undertaken, notice of (the aggressor party's) intention shall, in the absence of legitimate hindrance, be given to the other party as well as to the mediator (or, if the dispute involves several mediators' territories, one of the mediators) not later than seven days before the day when the stoppage is to begin. . . . The notice shall include a statement of the reasons for undertaking the stoppage." A fine of not more than 300 kronor is stipulated as punishment for breach of this provision.

It might have been expected that this legal limitation, amounting practically to prohibition of "lightning strikes," would have raised serious objections from the worker side. In point of fact, the only strongly adverse sentiment has come from the unions in the building trades, where walkouts, to be effective, must be as nearly instantaneous as possible. In the sphere of manufacturing — and despite the accepted union policy of calling strikes on the most vulnerable plants in the industry under attack — the introduction of an obligatory seven-day delay appears not to have seriously reduced the effectiveness of union aggression tactics. An average manufacturing plant, particularly one producing a highly fabricated product, cannot ordinarily "clean up" large outstanding orders in a week's time. Besides, the Swedish union leaders are well aware that these "vulnerable" plants are so only in a relative sense. The considerably increased strike and lockout benefits which the S. E. F. has been paying in recent years offset most of the loss incurred by the individual member employer.

THE MEDIATOR'S JOB

It will be apparent from the foregoing that the subject matter of the mediation law is of no great help to the mediator in his actual work of fostering industrial peace. It simply tells him that after he gets the parties together at a conference table, he must try to make them come to an understanding. Whether or not he succeeds in doing so must depend to a large extent on the man himself — his knowledge of the industry and the particular problems involved; his experience with similar situations in the past; and, not least, his tactfulness and other personal qualifications.

Because of this circumstance it is difficult, not to say impossible, to describe the activities and accomplishments of a *typical* state mediator. Each operates in a different district, with wide differences among the principal industries located therein. Each has his own methods, his own stock of knowledge, his own personal attributes; and no two achieve the same degree of success. Nevertheless, an attempt must be made to show what the mediators do and how well they do it.

In the two preceding chapters we have given some account of how the mediators assist in settling disputes of nation-wide scope — i.e., those which arise in connection with the making of new national agreements. After the "unofficially mediated" negotiations have broken down, such disputes are usually considered "cases where industrial peace is seriously threatened"; hence Section 12 of the law becomes operative. Under the law the government may appoint *any* expert and experienced persons to continue the work, but in practice the commissioners chosen are nearly always either present or former official mediators — men who have seen long service in this sphere of effort. Occasionally, when one of these nation-wide conflicts involves a relatively small industry, or when the task of reconciling the parties' demands is not considered too difficult, the government may appoint only one mediator, but in most cases it is a three-man commission which carries on the work.

Although the clearing up of these major conflicts by "specially appointed" mediators probably constitutes the principal function of the mediation service in point of economic and social importance, the work of the regular incumbents in settling smaller interest disputes within their own districts bulks considerably greater in total volume. Each year the problem of making or renewing local agreements arises in hundreds of workplaces and communities throughout the country. Most of the time the local bargainers manage to iron out their own differences, but the number of cases in which the initial negotiations break down is by no means small. During the past two decades, according to the annual reports of the Social Board, the mediators have intervened in, on the average, two hundred such disputes a year.

As one might surmise, instances of local mediation occur most frequently in those branches of industry in which a large proportion of the employers are unorganized — in other words, where the conditions of work are defined mainly in *independent* agreements. Transportation (exclusive of railroads), food processing, logging, and wood products are the principal industries in this class.[8] At the other end of the scale are textiles, paper, printing, and two or three other

[8] Merchandising (retail trade) is another line of business in which relatively few employers are organized, but here the proportion of organized workers is also comparatively small. That is to say, the majority of establishments in the industry have no agreements at all.

highly organized industries, in which the national agreements specify all or most of the terms of employment, including wage rates. Here the necessity for local mediation arises only on rare occasions. In sawmills, iron and steel, and machinery, where "supplementary" agreements are prevalent, the mediators sometimes intervene in disputes over local wage contracts. However, most cases of this sort are referred by the local disputants to their respective central organizations.

The "reported" cases of local interventions, referred to above, are those in which open conflicts either are imminent or have already broken out, and in which, consequently, more or less extended mediation proceedings are required. In addition, capable and experienced mediators often avert potential stoppages by a few well-chosen words of counsel to one side or the other, without having to resort to the usual tripartite negotiations. This informal but nonetheless important kind of peace-making may be illustrated by a concrete instance, related to the writer by an official of the Wood Products Union.

The workers in a newly opened woodworking factory in a country town had approached the owner with a request for a written contract, with wage rates on a level with those specified in the wood products national agreement. The employer, an ex-farmer who knew little about the workers' or employers' organizations, refused. The leaders of the local reported this to the national union officers in Stockholm, and after some discussion, it was decided that the situation called for coercive measures. In accordance with the law, the national secretary then informed both the employer and the mediator in the district, by mail, that in seven days' time the plant would be blockaded.

A day or two later, the mediator, who probably surmised at once what the real difficulty was, paid the employer a visit and explained to him carefully how the land lay. The latter was astute enough to realize that he could not hope to combat a powerful national union comprising most of the available labor force, and soon retracted his refusal.

The methods by which local interest disputes are ironed

out do not differ greatly from those employed in the larger conflicts. The mediator's essential task, in the one case as in the other, is to persuade both sides to give some ground on the disputed points, at the same time taking care to apprise each party of the concessions the other has made or is willing to make. However, the time required to clear up the average local quarrel is considerably shorter — mainly because the issues at stake are less complex, and the aggregate gains and losses involved much smaller, than in disputes over national agreements.

MEDIATED DISPUTES SETTLED WITHOUT STOPPAGE, 1922–1937

Period	Number of Mediated Disputes With no Stoppage Prior to Intervention	Number Settled Without Occurrence of Stoppage	Percentage of "Successful Mediation"
1922–1925	450	390	87
1925–1929	369	322	87
1930–1933	556	514	93
1934–1937	760	730	96

Sources: Socialstyrelsen, *Arbetsinställelser och Kollektivavtal samt Förlikningsmännens Verksamhet*, for years 1923–1937; *Statens Förlikningsmännens Verksamhet*, for 1922.

RESULTS OF MEDIATION

With the foregoing description of the mediation service in mind, we shall now make an appraisal of its usefulness in expediting peaceable and fruitful collective bargaining. In this connection, it may be helpful to present a few summary figures of the "business" handled by the mediators during the past fifteen years.

In the first column of the table above, the mediated disputes in which no stoppage occurred *prior* to intervention are summarized by four-year periods. Column 2 shows the number settled without any stoppage occurring; in column 3 these cases of "successful intervention" are expressed in per cent of the totals in column 1.[9]

Despite the absence of an objective basis of comparison

[9] It will be noted that the difference between Columns 1 and 2 represents the number of disputes in which stoppages occurred *subsequent* to intervention by the mediators.

(e.g., with corresponding experience in some other country), it can hardly be denied that this record of stoppage avoidance in mediated disputes is a commendable one. Moreover, the performance in recent years shows a distinct improvement over that of the earlier periods. However, it should be noted that the mediators have been considerably less successful in preventing stoppages in national than in local disputes.

A somewhat different view of the mediator's activities may be obtained by taking the total of *all* mediated disputes

DISPUTES SETTLED THROUGH MEDIATION, 1922–1937

Period	Total Number of Mediated Disputes	Settlement Effected Through Mediation [a]	Percentage Settled Through Mediation
1922–25	822	685	83
1926–29	684	564	83
1930–33	848	672	79
1934–37	896	813	90

Sources: Same as for preceding table.

[a] Either with or without occurrence of stoppage subsequent to intervention. Cases in which final settlement was effected between parties themselves (without mediation) *excluded* in both columns. The difference between columns 1 and 2 represents the number of cases in which no settlement had been reached *by the end of a given year.*

(those in which stoppages occurred prior to intervention, as well as those in which they did not) and setting over against this total the number of cases in which settlement was affected through or with the mediator's efforts.

Here again the record of successful mediation seems impressive, when examined in the light of difficulties ordinarily involved in bridging the gap between employer and worker viewpoints. Indeed the above percentages understate the actual performance, since they represent only the proportion of disputes settled by the end of each particular year. A closer perusal of the Social Board's reports reveals the fact that nearly 35 per cent of the conflicts *not* so settled were cleared up during the following year.[10] If allowance

[10] The proportion of local "unsettled" conflicts disposed of in this way was about 30 per cent; for *national* conflicts the corresponding figure was practically 100 per cent.

is made for these delayed settlements, each of the figures for "per cent settled" becomes approximately four units higher.

Of course, it is not unlikely that most or all of these "settled" disputes would have been ironed out eventually, in one way or another, even in the absence of the Mediation Service. But when one considers that, in the great majority of cases, the opposing parties have not even begun to make concessions to each other up to the time of intervention, it is fairly evident that many more disputes would have resulted in open warfare, and that the average period of time required to bring about settlement would have been considerably longer if they had been left to their own devices.[11]

The mediation institution's usefulness is further attested by the high regard in which the organized workers and employers themselves hold it. This attitude is evidenced in the

[11] See the mediators' descriptive reports of their activities in the Social Board's annual publication (*Arbetsinställelser och Kollektivavtal samt Förlikningsmänens Verksamhet*). An instance of widely divergent demands being reconciled through mediation was described to the writer by Herr C. C. Schmidt, secretary of the Mediation Service. In the agreement negotiations between the Wood Pulp Association and the Paper Workers' National Union a few years ago, the workers demanded a 30 per cent increase in time rates, the shifting of several classes of workers into higher wage grades, and a number of important changes in the general provisions of the national agreement. The employers demanded a continuance of the status quo in time rates, a substantial increase in the rated "normal production" (on which piecework payments are based), and more freedom in moving workers from one job to another. The commission of three mediators chosen to handle this case decided, on the basis of past experience, that a "gradualistic" approach offered the best possibilities of settlement. They therefore tackled the nonwage questions first. A special committee of five (two employers, two union men, one mediator) was appointed to iron out the grading problem. Another such committee took up the question of "normal production." In this or some similar way, compromises were effected on all the nonwage issues. By the time this was done the opposing negotiators had become accustomed to dealing with each other on a give-and-take basis, and were thus in a better frame of mind to tackle the touchy subject of wage rates, where the gap between employer and union demands was widest of all. After some days of intensive effort on the part of the mediators the gap was finally bridged, the workers accepting a 12 per cent increase as against the 30 per cent originally demanded.

afore-mentioned practice, adopted by nearly all the contracting parties of national scope, of calling in a member of the Mediation Service staff in the early stages of their agreement making conferences to conduct the proceedings in the capacity of neutral chairman.[12] Moreover, prominent leaders on both sides have on frequent occasions paid tribute to the mediators' impartiality and have expressed the belief that their work has aided materially in reducing strikes and lockouts.[13] As one of the most experienced and successful of the official peacemakers has himself stated it, "the clearest proof of its (the Service's) importance lies in the confidence which both sides place in it, and in the fact that neither side would want to see it abolished." [14]

WHY GOVERNMENT INTERVENTION "WORKS" IN SWEDEN

All in all, one may fairly conclude that the Swedish Mediation Service has proved its worth as a governmental agency for furthering peaceful settlement of employer-employee disputes. And the reasons for its effectiveness, or at least the principal ones, are not difficult to discover. The fact that its function is primarily that of a catalyst, with the parties themselve the actual reagents in the process, is unquestionably of first-rank importance. From the very beginning of large-scale bargaining early in the century down to the present day both workers and management have been strongly averse

[12] Chapter IX, p. 148.

[13] Statements to this effect were made to the writer by August Lindberg, chairman of the S. F. T. U., Gustaf Söderlund, executive director of the S. E. F., and a number of other officials high in union and employer-association circles. Cf. S. Hansson, *Svenskt Fackföreningsliv under Fem Decennier*, p. 102.

[14] O. Ekblom, "Staatlichen Verordnungen zur Beilegung von Arbeitsstreitigkeiten in den Nordischen Ländern," *Schriften des Vereins für Sozialpolitik*, 1930, pp. 129–130. There are, moreover, definite indications that as their confidence has increased through the years, the disputants have availed themselves of the mediators' services more and more frequently. For example, if one compares the first columns in each of the foregoing tables, one notices that the proportion of all mediated disputes which have not resulted in a stoppage *prior* to intervention is 66 and 81 per cent for the periods 1930–1933 and 1934–1936, as against 55 per cent for each of the two earlier periods.

to having "outside" persons, whether public or private, *decide on* the terms of employment. It is true that arbitration was resorted to quite frequently in the nineties, but it should be remembered that both the interested parties were usually represented on the decision-making bodies, so that even these were more of the nature of conciliation boards than courts of arbitration.

Since then, even so mild a form of external control as self-initiated arbitration has lost favor. An arbitration service (*skiljedomareinstitution*) composed of seven arbitrators (one stationed in each of the seven mediation districts) was set up in 1920, to assist in settling those cases in which the parties should decide of their own accord to resort to arbitration. But little use has been made of this agency. During the first five years of it existence, there were less than one fifth as many cases of arbitration as of mediation.[15] And in more recent years the number has been even smaller — so small, in fact, that for most purposes the arbitration service may be considered defunct.

Since 1928, to be sure, obligatory last-resort referring of *interpretational* disputes to an arbitrational body — the Labor Court — has been prescribed by law.[16] But the parties to the labor bargain regard these disagreements as being in a wholly different class from interest disputes. It is in deciding what the terms of employment shall be that they demand complete self-determination. Once these terms have been settled, it is not considered absolutely essential to retain full freedom of action regarding differences of viewpoint as to the exact meaning of the various clauses.

Fully as important as the character of the Service (mediation rather than arbitration) is the fact that from its very inception it has been staffed by unusually well-qualified men. As the institution has developed through the years, the post of state mediator has come to be a career job in a very real sense of the term. The appointees have been chosen pri-

[15] *Statens Offentliga Utredningar, 1927:4* (*Utredningar Till Belysande av Arbetsfredsfrågan*), pp. 24–25.

[16] See Chapter XV.

marily on the basis of personal merits and training, and entirely apart from political considerations. Most of them have served for long periods, usually in the same district throughout.

In all, twenty-six men have held mediatorships during the three decades of the institution's existence, which makes the average term of tenure slightly more than nine years. However, this figure considerably understates the usual period of actual service. Five of the twenty-six resigned soon after taking office, because of illness or for other personal reasons. Three others — the most recent appointees — are as yet only at the beginning of their careers. Seven of the remaining eighteen, all of them highly successful mediators, have been promoted to provincial governorships or other high administrative or judicial offices after from ten to fifteen years of service on the staff, and most of these have continued to serve as special mediators in "emergency" situations for many years afterward.[17]

Two of the seven original appointees, S. H. Kvarnzelius and Allan Cederborg, did some of their most valuable work during the big conflicts of the middle twenties, nearly a decade after their promotion to higher posts. Even more persevering was Dr. Henning Elmquist, already referred to in connection with the machinery trades negotiations of 1903–1905, who continued to act as go-between in large-scale disputes for more than thirty years. His last job was the settlement of a wage quarrel in the building materials industry in 1933, shortly before his death.[18] These pioneer mediators, by winning and holding the confidence of the organizations on both sides and by building up a flexible and practicable

[17] The above data were obtained from the accounts of the mediators' activities in the Social Board's annual reports — *Statens Forlikningsmännens Verksamhet* (for years 1907–1922), and *Arbetsinställelser och Kollektivavtal samt Förlikningsmännens Verksamhet* (for 1923–1936).

[18] It was Elmquist who, with the aid of two associates, Gunnar Huss and Nils Bergsten, really "founded" and built up the Mediation Service. As director of the labor section of the Board of Trade and later of the Social Board, he carried the burden of organizing the work and selecting suitable men for more than a decade after the inception of the service.

method of procedure, set a standard which their successors could hardly have done better than follow.

It is difficult to say whether inherent personal suitability or long experience is the more important requisite to success as a mediator in labor disputes, but the reports of the Swedish mediators' activities indicate that the latter means a great deal. A man who serves continuously in the same district for ten or twelve years is bound to acquire a more intimate knowledge of the problems confronting the particular industries and occupations falling within his purview than an occasional mediator or one whose activities are spread out over a wider geographical or industrial area. Moreover, he has a better opportunity to study the personal traits and idiosyncrasies of the particular persons — employers and union leaders — who actually confront each other at the conference table, which gives him a definite advantage in deciding how to approach a given set of contestants.

Even under such relatively favorable circumstances, the mediator's job is often an extremely difficult one. The mere fact that a mediator is needed usually indicates a wide gap between the employers' and workers' demands, and a propensity on the part of each side to hold out for its own terms. Nor is it always merely a case of knowing what sort of compromise to propose — on some occasions it is more important to know whether to make any proposal at all. If, as not infrequently happens, there is a definite sentiment on one side or the other to precipitate an open conflict at all costs, the best thing the mediator can do is to call the conference off and let matters take their course for the time being. If he misjudges the situation and comes forward with a proposal, which is then thrown down, he may be making it far more difficult to effect a settlement at a later date. For then he must make a new proposal with altered terms, and the side whose terms have been worsened is sure to accuse him of bad faith.

In concluding, it should be emphasized that the principal effect of official mediation in Swedish labor relations has been a reduction in the number and duration of disputes.

Its effect on wages or working conditions has probably been quite small.[19] There must, of course, have been *some* reaction on the terms of employment, for the intervention of a mediator in a dispute, at a time when one side or the other has any advantage at all in bargaining, inevitably tends to bolster the weaker side.

Whatever influence the use of mediation has on the final outcome of agreement negotiations must be in the direction of making the *changes* in the contractual terms over time smaller. However, compared with the more objective factors — the swings of the business cycle, the degree of organization on both sides, and so forth — the effect of mediation on the final outcome of the bargaining process is probably of minor significance.

[19] Cf. O. Ekblom, *op. cit.*, p. 130.

PART FOUR

BARGAINING WITHIN THE AGREEMENT FRAMEWORK

CHAPTER XII

LOCAL BARGAINING: INTERPRETATION AND GRIEVANCE ADJUSTMENT

UP TO THIS POINT our discussion of the bargaining mechanism has been confined mainly to the making and revising of agreements and to disputes and conflicts which arise in connection with this process. Hence the major emphasis has of necessity fallen on the negotiations which take place between central worker and employer organizations in the various branches of Swedish industry, since the national agreements constitute by far the larger and more significant part of the bargaining institution's end-result.

But it must be obvious that the occasion for dealings between the parties does not vanish abruptly with the concluding of the contract. Questions as to the meaning or manner of carrying out certain provisions, differences as to the applicability of particular wage rates to particular jobs — these and various other kinds of disputes frequently arise during the period of the agreement's operation. To meet such contingencies, a body of rules and practices has been built up which is fairly distinct from and supplementary to the agreement making process. In the present chapter we shall describe the main features of this "auxiliary" adjustment machinery.

The rubric "local bargaining" is somewhat inaccurate. In certain few industries the collective contracts themselves cover only single plants or localities; hence the negotiations by which they are concluded are primarily a local function. Moreover, the type of bargaining we are considering here is not necessarily confined within this narrow sphere. However, it is practically always initiated at the individual workplace, for it is not until the local dealings have failed that the central organizations come into the picture.

The kinds of questions which arise during the life of an agreement may for convenience be divided into three groups, as follows:

(*a*) Interpretation and application of "general" (nonwage) provisions in the agreement — or more briefly, nonwage interpretational disputes.

(*b*) Determination of the workers' share in "running the business."

(*c*) Wage adjustment disputes.

NONWAGE INTERPRETATIONAL DISPUTES

Questions of the first type vary widely in nature. The contractual basis of the practice followed in most industries in handling such differences is the "disputes clause." [1] In order to bring out more clearly the connection between the written rule and actual practice, it will be well to set down this clause again:

> When differences arise as to the meaning or application of this agreement, negotiations shall be instituted first between the immediately affected parties, and thereafter (if no settlement can be reached) between the respective central organizations. Such differences may not be made the occasion for stoppages of work — whether by strike, blockade, lockout, or any other method — until an attempt at peaceful settlement has been made in the manner prescribed above.

Specific stipulations as to who shall do the negotiating and what procedure shall be followed are relatively rare. However, certain practices have been built up, and while these are by no means identical from industry to industry, they are sufficiently similar so that one may speak in terms of a generally accepted method.

In the initial parleys the conferring body is usually composed of two or three representatives of the particular employer (departmental or works managers, production engineers, etc.) and an equal number of officers of the union covering the same establishment. In minor disputes involv-

[1] *Supra*, pp. 82–84.

ing only one or a few work people, it is not uncommon to begin with even more localized negotiations — e.g., between the affected workers and their foreman. Or a representative of the particular group may be present when the management and the local officers confer. In any case, the negotiators are not ordinarily chosen beforehand, but rather from time to time as the occasion arises.[2]

When the parties at the individual workplace are unable to agree, the dispute is usually transferred directly to "central negotiations" — a conference held under the auspices of the national organizations to which the disputants belong. While both local and national leaders take part in these proceedings, it is the latter who "do the deciding" — on the union side, at any rate. The local representatives serve mainly in the capacity of witnesses.

In a few industries, an additional stage is interposed between the "workplace" and "central" negotiations. For example, in the pipe fitting trades a dispute which fails of settlement at the workplace is taken up next by the respective "locality organizations" of the Associated Pipe Fitting Firms and the Metal Workers' Union. From here it goes to the corresponding national bodies.

Even when the worker and employer delegates are able to reach an agreement, the dispute is not (except in rare cases) thereby definitively settled. The proposed solution must be submitted to the affected union members for their acceptance or rejection — and sometimes, when the question at issue involves several concerns, to the employers also. If either side turns in an adverse vote, the proposal approved by the delegates is invalidated.

Prior to 1928 a number of national agreements — approximately one third of the total — stipulated that interpretational disputes not settled at the central negotiations should be disposed of through arbitration. To this end, special

[2] An exception to this rule is found in the tobacco products industry where, at each workplace, local disputes are handled by management and union "shop committees," appointed for a stated period. *Statens Offentliga Utredningar, 1927:4*, pp. 118–119.

boards of arbitrators were established in each industry. But with the passage in that year of the Labor Court Law, making final adjudication of such disputes by the court compulsory for all industries, this step in the procedure became more or less superfluous. Accordingly, during the succeeding four or five years most of the above-mentioned boards were abolished. The only important branches of business in which "special" arbitration of interpretational disputes is still used are newspaper printing, railways (privately owned), the telegraph and telephone system, and the building trades.[3]

Nonwage interpretational disputes are not ordinarily concerned with the meaning and phraseology of agreement provisions, but rather with their application to particular instances or particular groups of workers. More specifically, they usually result from complaints of alleged violation, made by one side or the other, hence might be termed interpretational *grievances*.

As one might surmise, most grievances originate on the worker side. Among the more common types are those arising in connection with hours of work, overtime, vacations, and medical care. For example, a group of workers may challenge the employer's right to postpone their lunch period until one o'clock, when the agreement specifies that it shall begin at twelve. Another group may claim that the employer, in requiring them to do regular work after hours, is violating the clause which states that overtime must be confined to such work as is "necessary for the normal operation of the enterprise." An industrial worker who has been employed the required length of time with the exception of a month's involuntary layoff demands compensation for the vacation period. And so on.

Grievances brought by employers, while less numerous, are by no means unimportant. For instance, when a crew of workmen leave their jobs because of the heat, or as

[3] The building trades arbitration board, which is of more than ordinary interest because of the peculiar wage-making problems with which it has to deal, will be described in a subsequent chapter.

a protest against some action on the employer's part, the latter will very likely bring the matter before the union, on the ground that the men are violating the clause prohibiting stoppages of any kind during the agreement period. Employer-initiated disputes are, for the most part, confined to cases involving aggregations of workers. When the grievance concerns only one or a few men, the employer usually "complains" by discharging them.

Oftentimes grievances arise in connection with conditions and occurrences not covered in the agreement. Although relatively few contracts contain any provision as to how such cases shall be handled, in practice the procedure used is usually the same as for interpretational grievances proper. We may therefore dispense with a separate discussion of these extracontractual disputes. Moreover, many of the "secondary" terms of employment which are specifically stated in the more elaborate documents are omitted in those industries having simpler, less detailed agreements;[4] hence it is difficult to draw any definite dividing line between the two classes of complaints.

WORKER PARTICIPATION IN RUNNING THE BUSINESS

We come now to a class of questions which, while similar in nature to interpretational disputes, are usually considered in Sweden as constituting a distinct type of problem — i.e., those having to do with the employer's "right to run his own business" and with the degree of the workers' participation in or encroachment on that right.

Among these, the problems which arise in connection with the hiring, discharging, and laying off of workers are of predominant importance. The "Section 23 clause" in the national agreements, it will be remembered, accords the employer "full freedom to take on and discharge workers, to

[4] The agreement for the shoe industry requires workers to give notice before leaving the employer's service, forbids the changing of clothes during working hours, and stipulates fines for lateness. There are no corresponding provisions in, e.g., the sawmill, pulp, and iron and steel agreements. Cf. *Landsorganisationens Berättelse*, 1936, pp. 226–227.

lead and allot the work, and to employ workers regardless of whether they belong to organizations or not," subject to the limitation that he may not impair the workers' right to organize.[5] This clause reflects the sentiment, long prevalent among Swedish employers, that hiring and termination are matters for management alone to decide. The organized wage earners quite naturally do not concur in this view, believing that the question of whether he is employed or not is of such vital importance to the individual worker that his union should, of right, have some voice in deciding it. But the employer's insistence on retaining the clause has been so strong and so unified that all past attempts of the national unions to delete or modify it have met with failure.[6] Moreover, it has been quite generally adhered to in practice — outwardly, at any rate.

HIRING

So far as hiring is concerned, the fact of sole employer discretion is of relatively minor significance. With a large majority of the workers in most industries organized, the average employer has little choice but to hire union help. In a few of the less well-organized lines, to be sure, certain concerns have shown an inclination to discriminate, and here the national unions have attempted to obtain a measure of control over hiring. For example, the Wood Products Union, in concluding contracts with non-S. E. F. employers, insists that they agree to file the names of all newly hired workers with the local union headquarters. The Transport Workers' Union has adopted a more direct form of "exerting influence." Its agreement with the dockwork firms of Stockholm provides that when vacancies occur in the "regu-

[5] See *supra*, p. 31.

[6] This statement requires modification in the light of a very recent episode, the significance of which is not as yet wholly apparent. With the conclusion, in December, 1938, of a "master agreement" between the S. E. F. and the S. F. T. U., providing for bilateral negotiation of questions relating to dismissals and layoffs, a notable first step in replacing the Section 23 clause with an arrangement more palatable to the unions has been taken. This episode is described more fully in Chapter XVIII.

lar corps" of dockworkers, the union may present "recommendations" for filling them.[7]

But by and large the organized workers are not greatly disturbed over the hiring question, knowing as they do that the great majority of employers are neither capable nor desirous of using their "exclusive right of control" as a means of weakening the unions' position. A tripartite commission, appointed by the government in 1920 to investigate the extent of worker participation in management, aptly summarized the then-existing (and, to an even greater extent, the present-day) situation in these words: "Among the Swedish workers the question of hiring is not considered to be nearly so vital as, for instance, that of the right to organize. This is undoubtedly a consequence of the fact that the employers do not ordinarily exercise their power to hire for the purpose of fighting unionism but rather, in many cases, prefer that their workers belong to an organization." [8]

LAYOFFS, REHIRING AND DIVISION OF WORK

What has been said above about the initial placement of workers also applies, albeit with some modification, to *rehiring*. However, this subject is so closely allied to that of layoffs that we may well discuss the two as a single topic.

Provisions as to the order of termination and reinstatement of workers during and after periods of slack business, or as to dividing up the available work, are almost entirely absent in the Swedish agreements. These matters are considered, both legally and by tacit agreement between the parties, as falling within the scope of the employer's "right to take on and dismiss workers, and to lead and allot the work." In practice, moreover, it is the employer who — nominally, at least — most often makes the decisions and issues the orders.

[7] Agreement for 1937–1938, p. 6. To the best of the writer's knowledge, this is the only branch of economic activity in which "union hiring" is used to any appreciable extent.

[8] *Statens Offentliga Utredningar, 1923:29* (*Den Industriella Demokratins Problem*), pp. 108–109.

In view of the vehemence with which organized workers in the United States have fought for seniority clauses in collective agreements, it may seem strange that such a powerful group of organizations as the Swedish unions should not have sought and obtained some contractual regulation of layoffs and rehiring. Certain of the national unions have, it is true, made sporadic attempts along this line, and resolutions have been brought before two or three of the most recent S. F. T. U. congresses proposing that the unions should seek a direct share in deciding not only on layoffs, but on the entire complex of questions now included in the category of sole employer discretion. But despite the strongly favorable sentiment toward the *idea* of seniority among the rank and file, there has never been any united drive for agreement-regulated layoff and hiring schedules from the union side.

However, the reasons for this lukewarmness toward what American unionists regard as a very vital issue are not too difficult to discern. First in order of importance, no doubt, is the fact that most Swedish employers cannot utilize the layoff as a means of replacing union with nonunion men — and would not do so even if they could. Another reason is that many local union leaders are unwilling to assume the responsibility that would be theirs if slack-period employment were jointly determined. Both sides are agreed that "straight seniority" is undesirable, because of its failure to take account of newly hired individuals in needy circumstances, such as supporters of large families. Any scheme of layoffs that might be adopted, therefore, would almost certainly be a more or less flexible one, entailing a good deal of empirical selecting on each separate occasion. And the duty of singling out people for termination would fall, in part at least, to responsible union officials. It is at this duty that the local leaders balk. Quite naturally they do not relish the idea of losing favor with a sizable proportion of their own constituents.[9]

[9] Numerous instances of local officers declining to be parties to the making of layoff lists were related to the writer, both by employers and prominent unionists. This attitude is, however, by no means universal. Several of the

Finally, despite the relatively rare occurrence of any direct, explicit control, the unions do exert a very considerable *indirect* influence over layoffs. There is no doubt that, if they were entirely free to do so, many employers would follow the practice of retaining only the most capable and diligent workers without much regard for their period of service or need for the work. But the fact remains that the principle of seniority, tempered by consideration for the economic needs of individual workers, is very widely adhered to in Swedish industry. And the reason therefor is plain: the employers fully realize that if they failed to take cognizance of the widespread sentiment in favor of this method on the worker side, the unions would soon be up in arms to force its introduction. In other words, it is a case of concession by foresight rather than hindsight.

On the other hand, division of the available work with no reduction of the labor force is not often encountered nowadays. There is some support of the idea on the part of the unions, but the majority of the employers whom the writer interviewed are unfavorably disposed toward it, claiming that it militates against productive efficiency. And as with union sentiment regarding seniority, the prevailing employer opinion with respect to equal division of work appears to be sufficiently strong so that the other side does not deem it expedient to press the point.[10]

---

union leaders interviewed mentioned particular workplaces (e.g., in the match and paper industries) where conferences between representatives of the management and of the unions, for the purpose of ironing out layoff problems, are a matter of standard practice. Cf. *Statens Offentliga Utredningar, 1923:29*, p. 116.

[10] Apparently there has been a considerable shift in practice concerning division of work since the early twenties. The Commission on Industrial Democracy, referred to above, reported in 1923 that "the current industrial depression has furnished many examples of employers . . . taking measures to divide up the work among the undiminished worker staff, through reducing the number of working hours per day, or working days per week." *Statens Offentliga Utredningar, 1923:29*, p. 116.

DISPLACEMENT BY INNOVATIONS

Another kind of curtailment about which nothing specific is said in the agreements is that which occurs in connection with the introduction of labor-saving methods and machinery. Here again the employers have sole discretion, but as with layoffs, they do not ordinarily utilize their power *à outrance*. One fairly common practice is to find work for the displaced workers, or a portion of them, in other departments or occupations. Some of the employers who adhere to this policy profess to be actuated solely by humanitarian motives. Others, particularly those in wood pulp and steel production — predominantly mill village industries — assert that in the long run the extra cost involved in keeping the displaced men at work is not a major item, since if let go they would become dependent on local relief funds, of which "the company" supplies the major part. It seems probable also (although there is less willingness to admit this) that the prospect of drastic measures from the union side plays a not inconsiderable role in deterring the employers from wholesale dismissals. At all events, there has been relatively little out-and-out "technological firing" in recent years, except in sawmills and one or two other less important industries in which the rate of mechanization has been unusually rapid during and since the depression.

"DISMISSALS FOR CAUSE"

With respect to the dismissal of individuals on grounds of unsatisfactory work or comportment, union participation is considerably more direct and visible than in the case of layoffs and reductions resulting from improved methods of production. It may seem somewhat illogical that the employer's "exclusive right to run" should include layoffs and not individual dismissals. However, it will be remembered that most of the national agreements contain a modification of the "Section 23 clause," which provides that if a worker believes he has been discharged in violation of the right to organize he may, through his organization, "demand an investigation." It is in connection with discharges for alleged incompetence and unseemly behavior that this provision is usually invoked. That is to say, such cases are regarded as regular interpretational disputes rather than matters for management alone to decide.

The question most frequently raised in dismissal disputes is not that of merely belonging to a union (which, as we have shown, is largely a closed issue in Sweden) but rather that of union *activity*. The controversies usually center around local leaders or other prominent or outspoken unionists, and the charge customarily brought is that they have been discriminated against because of their zeal in upholding union interests.

It is not difficult to understand why such disputes should be both numerous and difficult to iron out. The union, for its part, may construe almost any dismissal as a case of discrimination by applying a suitable interpretation to the phrase "the right to organize." The employer, on the other hand, has ample opportunity to find "legitimate" reasons for discharging workers whom he considers undesirable.

Management policy in this regard appears to vary considerably. Some employers follow the practice of dismissing union leaders only in cases of extreme incompetence or insubordination, in order to avoid stirring up ill will in their plants. Others, particularly members of such militant organizations as the Machine Industry Association, do not hesitate to get rid of workers — prominent unionists as well as others — whom they regard as trouble makers. However, it is important to note that even such employers usually take pains not to make their "purges" too obvious. For example, the hiring-and-firing authority in one large machinery plant told the writer that his usual method is to transfer troublesome *bråkmakare* to some other department, and then wait for a convenient period of slack business to "lay them off."

The organized workers, too, have adopted certain defense measures in their fight to prevent the employers from discriminating. Most important among these, perhaps, is the practice, widely followed in recent years, of electing only workmen of unquestioned skill and diligence to union offices. Governor Ekblom, one of the keenest observers of trends and tendencies in the industrial relations field, avers that the degree of worker competence among union leaders is much higher nowadays than it was a decade ago.

The "investigation" stipulated in the discrimination clause customarily begins with a conference between representatives of the management and the local union, at which the discharged worker may testify in his own behalf. Because the views of the opposing parties are usually based on opinion rather than fact, such conferences frequently break down, and it becomes necessary to carry them to central negotiations. Nearly a hundred dismissal cases have been referred to the National Labor Court — the final authority in interpretational disputes — during the past nine years, and several of these have resulted in important precedent-setting decisions. The effect of these decisions on the status of the employer's right to discharge will be discussed subsequently, in connection with the functioning and significance of the court.[11]

All in all, it is apparent that while the managers of Swedish business enterprise, through the Section 23 clause, nominally have sole discretion in matters pertaining to the termination of the employment relationship, actually they pay a great deal of attention to the workers' collective sentiments and desires in making their decisions. And the impression one gets as one talks with the employers about this aspect of "running the business" is that their insistence on the retention of Section 23 in the contracts is largely due to psychological factors. They seem to derive considerable satisfaction from being the nominal rulers and issuing the orders, even though they are well aware that union sentiment has played an important part in determining the decisions on which the orders are based.

Nor is dismissal of workers the only aspect of management in which this idiosyncrasy of the employers manifests

[11] See Chapter XV, pp. 260–263.

itself. A similar situation often comes about when workers complain about the behavior of foremen. Only on rare occasions will employers accede directly to a request by a union that a foreman be removed. Instead, they usually eliminate the cause of the irritation in a more roundabout way, so as to avoid the appearance of sharing their autonomy. One method of doing this was described by the Molders' Union in 1923, in answer to a questionnaire regarding the subject of worker dissatisfaction with foremen issued by the National Commission on Industrial Democracy. The union stated that "because of the employers' insistence on the principle that they alone shall have the right to decide on such questions, without any interference from the workers' side, it is not ordinarily possible to secure the immediate dismissal of a foreman. What happens most frequently is that some time later the foreman is transferred to a different post, ostensibly for a different reason; but in reality the transfer is almost always a direct result of the workers' complaint."[12]

UNION-MANAGEMENT COÖPERATION IN SWEDEN

Union influence over hiring and firing is essentially negative in nature, since its chief purpose is to restrain employers from making decisions against the workers' best interests. To round out the picture, it seems apropos also to tell something about the status of *positive* participation in the decision-making function — the kind of participation, that is to say, in which the workers try to help the employer improve the efficiency of the enterprise.

Contrary to what one might expect, formal collaboration between unions and employers for the purpose of effecting economies and improvements in production is rarely encountered in Swedish industry. In a few of the more "progressive" concerns — such as the Sandviken steel works and the Nyman bicycle plant in Uppsala — union-management coöperation of a sort has been an established part of the internal bargaining setup for some years, but even here it can hardly be said to have progressed very far.

[12] *Statens Offentliga Utredningar, 1923:29*, p. 125.

The idea evokes very little response among the employers, and many of them are definitely opposed to it.[13] The reason most commonly given is that the possibilities of fruitful results are too small. Present-day processes and machines, it is claimed, are already so highly perfected that only experts are competent to find ways of making further improvements. As one factory executive put it, "I have a whole staff of trained engineers, whose sole job consists in discovering new and better ways of doing things. If a worker does get an idea, the chances are that some engineer has already thought of it long before." [14] On the worker side too, the preponderance of opinion is unfavorable to coöperation in effecting improvements. To be sure, the leaders of the S. F. T. U. and of a number of national unions are, and have been for years, strong advocates of it, their argument being that labor's only hope of achieving a continuously improving living standard lies in a continuous improvement in productive efficiency. However, the bulk of the rank and file have shown little inclination to help the employers save on labor and other costs. And most of the national union leaders admit that their crusading and preaching have so far failed to stir up any appreciable enthusiasm.[15]

Of the various reasons for the workers' apathy, two seem to be outstanding. They are still too preoccupied with obtaining *direct* gains, such as better wages and longer vacations; and they have no great confidence that the employers will share the fruits of improved efficiency with them.

On two occasions the government has attempted to stir up interest in "industrial democracy." The above-mentioned commission of 1920 — composed of union leaders, employers, and members of the Social-Democratic government —

[13] Practically all the employer-association executives interviewed asserted that the sentiment in their respective industries was generally adverse.

[14] Interview, Västerås, August 9, 1938.

[15] An official of the Wood Products Union tells of admonishing the joinery and furniture workers in the Gothenburg export factories that they would have to step in and help the employers "rationalize" the industry or lose their jobs to foreign competitors. The response, however, was practically nil — even after his prediction had begun to be fulfilled.

proposed the passage of legislation providing for the setting up of "shop committees" (*driftsnämnder*), as a means of encouraging worker-management coöperation. But the employer members submitted a sharply dissenting minority opinion.[16] Indeed, the proposal stirred up strong adverse feeling among employers all along the line, and it was this, probably more than anything else, which led to its being tabled. In 1928 the Social Minister called a number of worker and employer leaders to a conference in Stockholm, principally for the purpose of discussing this same question. The sentiments expressed by the respective sides at this "labor peace conference" (*arbetsfredskonferens*) were, in general, the same as those of the two factions in the 1920 commission. One prominent employer, Director Hugo Hammar of the *Götaverken* shipyards in Gothenburg, reported that a system of suggesting improvements under union auspices had been in existence in his plant for more than a decade and that it had resulted in a number of useful innovations and corrections.[17] However, when the writer talked with him ten years later (September, 1938), he averred that the workers' interest in the idea had been gradually decreasing for a number of years, and was now practically extinct.

WAGE ADJUSTMENT DISPUTES

We have seen in an earlier chapter [18] that of the disputes which result in stoppages, those having to do with wages outnumber by far all other kinds. However, it must be remembered that stoppages are confined almost exclusively to interest disputes — i.e., disputes incident to the agreement *making* procedure. Only on rare occasions do interpretational quarrels or other differences arising during an agreement's period of operations lead to strikes or lockouts nowadays.

[16] *Statens Offentliga Utredningar, 1923:29*, pp. 228–239.

[17] Socialdepartmentet, *Arbetsfredskonferensen i Stockholm* (Stockholm, 1929), pp. 25–37.

[18] Chapter X, p. 169.

True, wage questions are more frequently the subject of interpretational disputes than any other single class of question, but their predominance is by no means as great as in interest disputes. According to the records of the above-mentioned shipbuilding concern, approximately 50 per cent of the 153 cases handled by the "plant committees" during the period 1926–1932 had to do with one aspect or another of the wage problem.[19] This proportion is undoubtedly higher than the corresponding percentage for Swedish industry as a whole, but it is probably safe to say that wage adjustment disputes constitute, for most lines of business, from a third to a half of the total.

The relatively less frequent occurrence of the wage issue in interpretational disputes is due, in part at least, to the prevalence of national wage scales. Figures are unambiguous locally as well as nationally, whereas rules covering, for example, the dismissal of workers or the right to vacations may or may not be, depending on particular circumstances.

The three phases of the collective employment contract which give rise to the bulk of wage adjustment disputes are piece rate schedules, time rate provisions, and stipulations regarding "extra compensation." It will be convenient to discuss these in the reverse order.

The extra-compensation provisions concerning which local disputes most frequently arise are those relating to overtime and vacations. The point at issue in overtime disputes is usually some variant of either of two questions: whether the work done may properly be classified as overtime, or what base rate the compensatory "overpercentage" shall be applied to. The overpercentages themselves are rarely the subject of disputes, since they are customarily specified in the agreement and are in most cases the same for all classes of workers.[20]

Debatable claims for vacation compensation are, if anything, an even more common source of local disputes than

[19] Data obtained from Herr Hugo Hammar, executive Director of AB Götaverken, Gothenburg.

[20] Cf. Arbetsdomstolen, *Sakregister till Arbetsdomstolens Domar* (Stockholm, 1936), pp. 111–113.

the overtime problem. Such cases center around two categories of workers: those who have been employed irregularly during the year and those who have severed their connection with the affected concern a short time prior to the beginning of the vacation period.[21]

Provision is also made in many agreements for "waiting time compensation" (time rate pay for pieceworkers, while waiting for materials, repairs, etc.), traveling expenses, and various other kinds of "extra" emolument; but disputes concerning such stipulations are relatively few and far between.

In the time rate provisions, as in those relating to overtime, the essential numerical data are usually explicitly specified, hence there is seldom any occasion for differences of interpretation on this score. However, difficulties frequently do arise in allocating particular workers, or groups of workers, to the proper wage grade. Thus a gang of laborers who have been put to work painting a factory building may demand that while engaged at this task they be rated as semiskilled rather than unskilled workers. A plumber's helper who spends a considerable portion of his time doing regular journeyman's work may feel entitled to promotion to the highest time rate grade. And so on.[22]

No less troublesome is the problem of classifying border-

[21] The following excerpts from the topical index of the national Labor Court's decisions will serve to illustrate these two kinds of "vacation disputes":

1. According to the agreement, a worker is not entitled to vacation pay if he has been absent from work a certain length of time, except on grounds of sickness or other specified circumstances. Question concerns the application of this provision

(a) when the worker has been laid off because of slack business . . . 1933: Decision No. 78

(b) when the working day at the affected plant has been shortened . . . 1932:145

(c) when the worker has taken part in a strike. . . . 1934:164.

2. Since the agreement contains no provisions to the contrary, a worker who has given up his job before the beginning of the vacation period is not considered to be entitled to compensation. (*Sakregister till Arbetsdomstolens Domar*, pp. 73–75.)

[22] "The agreement stipulates different wage rates for, on the one hand, com-

line workers for time rate purposes, according to age and/or experience, to the satisfaction of both parties concerned. The following illustration is fairly typical:

> The wage clauses in an agreement in the merchandising industry make explicit provision only for workers who have reached the age of 18, and stipulate, besides the beginner's wage, higher wage classes to which the wage earner attains after he has had 1, 2, 3, and 4 years' experience in the occupation, respectively. The questions at issue are: (a) May experience obtained before the age of 18 be considered in determining promotion to a higher wage class? (b) Is "experience in the occupation" synonymous with period of employment? [23]

Of the various other time rate provisions which lead to disputes, mention should perhaps be made of the group which permits the employer to give particular employees lower rates than those specified in the agreement — for example, if they are not "competent" (*fullgoda*) workers, or if their capacity to work has been reduced through "age, illness, or disability." Occasionally, too, questions arise as to the proper cost-of-living group classification of certain concerns, especially new adherents to national agreements. But as compared to the grading and classification schemes, these provisions present only minor problems.

SETTLING PIECEWORK QUESTIONS

Considerably more numerous than either time rate or "compensation" disputes are those which occur incident to the operation of piece rate schedules. Indeed, taking Swedish industry as a whole, the administration of the piecework system probably gives rise to a greater volume of local bargaining than any other phase of industrial relations, whether wage or nonwage.

---

petent woodworking machinery operators and, on the other, helpers and general workers. Question: In which category should a worker be placed whose job consists in tending a splitting-saw?" (*Sakregister till Arbetsdomstolens Domar*, p. 47.)

[23] *Ibid.*, p. 62.

As between *adjustment* and *application* of rates, the former is the less prolific source of disagreement. Since the wage contracts are established for definite periods of time in most industries, the need of adjusting piece rates between agreement dates seldom arises, except when new machines or methods of production are introduced. To take care of such contingencies, it will be remembered, the national agreements usually contain a clause to the effect that the rates of payment may be changed, through negotiation, during the life of the (agreed-on) schedule.[24] In addition, it is often stipulated that during the period when the new rates are being worked out, wages shall be reckoned per hour — not infrequently on the basis of the affected workers' total earnings during the preceding twelve months.[25] But beyond this the agreements seldom go. There are rarely any specific provisions as to representation and procedure in the negotiations, or as to the method of determining the new rates.[26]

In practice, however, it is customary to begin by making a trial run on the new machine or method and to translate the results of this run into a tentative rate, on the basis either of average earnings under the old method or the workers' established time rates plus a certain "overpercentage." Final adjustments of the tentative rate are then made through negotiations between managerial and local union representatives. In one industry — wood pulp — the negotiations are instituted in the first instance by the *central* organizations.

[24] See *supra*, pp. 89–90.

[25] See, e.g., the national agreement between the Iron Masters' Association and the Metal Workers Union, 1938–1939, p. 3.

[26] The national agreement for the textile industry is one of the few that go into details. It stipulates among other things that "if the question concerns a rate which is to be incorporated in a fixed rate schedule, the (affected) worker has the right to negotiate through his union." It specifies further that "either side may require that an investigation be made into the productive method on which the rate is to be set. . . . The management and the workers, acting jointly, shall designate the particular workers on the basis of whose production the rates shall be determined, and the union may take part in the investigation." Agreement between the Textile Industry Association and the Textile Workers' Union, 1937–1938, pp. 7–9.

With bilateral handling of this touchy problem, it is obvious that some friction is bound to result. The most common subject of disagreement is, as one might expect, the magnitude of the new rate, but disputes over other aspects of the innovation are by no means unknown. For example, the union may hold that the change in question does not constitute an "introduction of a new method" at all. On the employer side, the usual complaint is that the workers withhold their best efforts during the trial run. According to several employers interviewed by the writer, "soldiering" on such occasions is a very widespread practice, and one that is practically impossible to prevent.

Taking the country's economic activity in the large, disputes over the application of piece rates are considerably more numerous than adjustment disputes. But when individual lines of business are considered, this statement requires qualification. In industries producing uniform "semiprocessed" goods, such as lumber and pulp, the problem of application is a fairly simple one. Specific rates are established for stated quantities of designated products and, barring the introduction of new methods or processes, there is seldom much room for debate as to what a given designation covers. Consequently, the number of piecework disputes in these industries is relatively small.

Conversely, in the production or handling of highly fabricated and heterogeneous commodities, it is often very difficult to specify a particular object or operation unequivocally — so as to leave no chance for argument — and here piece rates are a very fruitful source of disagreement and verbal strife. Such lines as wood products, garment making, and dockwork (loading and unloading of vessels) fall within this category.

However, there are two branches of Swedish industry in which the piecework problem overshadows all others to such an extent as to put them in a class by themselves. The first of these is building construction, where the wide variations in a given type of work from job to job make frequent applicational disputes a foregone conclusion. The second is the group of related lines of manufacturing which we have designated as the machinery trades. Besides being unusually numerous, the wage problems encountered in these industries are more or less special in nature. It has therefore seemed worth while to discuss them at some length in separate chapters.

CHAPTER XIII

WAGE BARGAINING IN THE BUILDING TRADES

THE TERM "building trades," as generally used, covers not only occupations concerned with the actual process of erecting buildings but also the "auxiliary" occupations, the most important of which are painting, pipe fitting, and electrical installation work. In the present chapter, however, we shall confine our attention mainly to the wage problems of the building workers proper — carpenters, masons, and building laborers [1] — since these are in large measure typical of the industry as a whole.

THE WAGE-MAKING STRUCTURE

According to the national agreement between the Master Builders' Association, on the one side, and the Wood Construction Workers', Masons', and Laborers' and Factory Workers' Unions, on the other, all work for which prices are published in the national piece rate schedules must be paid for according to results.[2] For work of "such a nature that the setting of fixed rates has not previously been possible," either side may demand that negotiations be instituted for the purpose of establishing piece rates during the period of the agreement's operation. For all work not covered by the fixed lists nor by rates established through interim negotiations, payment is reckoned by the hour, on the basis of the time rates specified in the agreement.[3]

The time rate arrangement is comparatively brief and

[1] "Building laborer" (*byggnadsgrovarbetare*) is the general appellation applied to hodcarriers, cement workers, pick-and-shovel men, and all other kinds of workers not included in the more highly skilled occupations.

[2] The schedules (for all three occupations) examined by the writer were negotiated in the Summer of 1937, and remained in force until April, 1940 — a period of nearly three years.

[3] Agreement of June 12, 1937, pp. 8–9.

simple. Masons and carpenters, in order to qualify for the specified hourly rates, must be able to show that they "have learned the trade, or have worked at it for at least three years, inclusive of the apprenticeship period." The only corresponding stipulation for laborers is that they must have reached the age of eighteen.

The rates for masons and carpenters are identical and range from 1.65 kronor per hour in the first cost-of-living area (Stockholm) down to 1.20 kronor in the eighth, while those for laborers run from 1.50 to 1.08 kronor — approximately 10 per cent lower throughout.[4] For workers not fulfilling the stated requirements, the rates may be set lower, but not by more than 15 per cent.

The piece rate schedules, on the other hand, are voluminous and highly technical. The building laborers have four separate schedules — applying to the Stockholm area, and to southern, western, and middle and northern Sweden, respectively — whereas the masons and carpenters have only two each: one for Stockholm and one for the rest of the country.[5] The carpenters' lists are especially lengthy and

[4] This difference between the hourly rates for skilled and for unskilled building workers is unusually small, as compared with the corresponding disparity in, e.g., the United States. It will be recalled, however, that the proportion of total working time paid for on a piecework basis is more than twice as large for masons and carpenters as for laborers (*supra*, p. 132). And when it is considered that the average building worker earns at least 50 per cent more per hour on piecework than on straight timework, it is evident that the difference in actual earnings is considerably greater than the gap between the time rates would indicate.

[5] For masons and carpenters, the living cost differential device is applied to the piecework schedules in the following manner: the "all-Sweden" schedule is called normal for the fifth cost-of-living area; that is, wages are computed directly from the established rates. In the fourth area, all prices in the schedule are multiplied by the ratio

$$\frac{\text{Time rate (fourth area)}}{\text{Time rate (fifth area)}};$$

similarly for the second and third areas. (The first area, Stockholm, has its own special piece rate schedule.) In the sixth, seventh, and eighth areas, however, piecework wages are not reduced, but follow the standard schedule "as is." The differential scheme for building laborers is essentially the same as that used for the two skilled trades.

detailed, each comprising approximately 140 pages of tables and specifications.

Of the two forms of wage reckoning used in the building trades, it is piecework which commands our principal attention — not only because of its predominance but also because it gives rise to an unusually large amount of debate and disputation, which in turn necessitates a great deal of "specialized bargaining" between the employers and the workers. What is perhaps more important, the long experience of the Swedish contractors and building workers with the productivity wage affords a basis for discussing the timely question of whether payment by results is a more efficient, or in any other sense a *better* method than timework as a means of determining wages in this industry. Before we attempt any such discussion, however, it will be necessary to tell something about the makeup and operation of the piecework system used in the building trades.

From the very nature of the work, it is obvious that the time and effort required to construct piece rate schedules which are to any degree generally applicable must be considerable, and the schedules themselves must of necessity be highly ramified, to take care of variations in the character of the work to be done. In this connection, it should be observed that the building trades piece rates have been built almost entirely on experience and trial-and-error, supplemented by higgling and bargaining between the parties. The possibility of using formal time studies has come in for a good deal of discussion, but up to now very little has been done along this line. It is generally conceded that the predominance of hand operations in building work makes it too difficult to determine a "normal" intensity of effort within any reasonable limits. This difficulty is, of course, much less serious in factory production, where the speed of the machinery affords a considerable degree of objective control.

Some idea of the volume and detail of the piece rates in the building industry may be gained from the following partial list of prices for floor laying, reproduced from the wood construction workers' (carpenters') "all-Sweden" schedule.

These represent merely a few of the 160 items in the floor laying price list. And the laying of floors, it must be remembered, is one of the relatively simple and straightfor-

PIECE RATES FOR THE LAYING OF FLOORS

Item No.			Thickness of flooring (in millimeters) up to and including			
			25	31	37	50
1.	Floor laying with planed and matched stock, including leveling up of joists, for finished board width of:					
	a 137 mm. & above	per sq. meter	.78 kr.	.85 kr.	.92 kr.	1.05 kr.
	b 125–137 mm.	" " "	.81	.87	.94	1.08
	c 112–125 mm.	" " "	.84	.91	.97	1.11
	d 100–112 mm.	" " "	.86	.93	1.00	1.13
	e 87–100 mm.	" " "	.90	.96	1.03	1.17
	f 75– 87 mm.	" " "	.92	.99	1.05	1.19
	g 62– 75 mm.	" " "	.95	1.02	1.09	1.22
2.	Laying of base floor for hardwood flooring shall be paid according to the above table, with prices reduced by 10 per cent.					
3.	For laying of border flooring:					
	a Single board	per linear meter				.33 kr.
	b Two boards in width	" " "				.48
4.	For laying of border flooring along curved partitions:					
	a Single board	per linear meter				.71
	b Two boards in width	" " "				.97
5.	For joints or corners on border flooring	each				.37
	. . . .					
11.	For right angle fitting to border flooring:					
	a With square or beveled edge	per linear meter				.40
	b With grooved edge	" " "				.72
12.	For fitting of flooring to another floor surface, laid at right angles to it	per linear meter				.40
13.	For oblique fitting, the prices in items 11 and 12 shall be increased by 20 per cent.					
	. . . .					
20.	For leveling up of joists, when average spacing from center to center is at least 60 cm.	per sq. meter				.38
	For closer spacing, the price shall be increased 10 per cent for each "commenced" (*påbörjad*) 10 cm. reduction in average distance between joists.					

Source: *Ackordsprislista för Byggnadsträarbete i Sverige År 1937* (Stockholm, 1937), pp. 76–77.

ward operations connected with the construction of buildings. All in all, the wood construction workers' schedule comprises more than 2500 prices, covering almost every conceivable kind of woodwork encountered in house building.

The building laborers' schedule, while less voluminous than that of the woodworkers, is still a fairly formidable document, containing in all somewhat less than a thousand prices. The following extract from the list for hodcarrying is illustrative of the methods employed in pricing this type of work.

PIECE RATES FOR THE CARRYING OF MORTAR FOR BRICKLAYING (BY HAND)

	kr.
(a) Base price, per 1000 brick	
for brick 12 by 6 by 3 inches	4.35
for brick 10 by 5 by 3 inches	3.92
for brick 10 by 5 by 2½ inches	3.92
(b) Additional for each meter of height of the building, per 1000 brick	
for brick 12 by 6 by 3 inches	0.196
for brick 10 by 5 by 3 inches	0.176
for brick 10 by 5 by 2½ inches	0.176

Source: Piece Rate Schedule for Building Laborers in the Stockholm District, 1934 (*Ackordsprislista för Byggnadsgrovarbete i Stockholm, 1934*) (Stockholm, 1934), p. 49.

Other phases of construction covered in this document include excavating, pile driving, blasting, foundation laying, insulating, and a dozen or more classes of operations connected with concrete construction work.

The price list for masonry work is considerably simpler than either of the other two, although comparable in length to the building laborers' schedule. Four kinds of building work — bricklaying, plastering, tile floor laying, and tile roofing — comprise most of its contents, and practically all prices are expressed in kronor per unit of areal or linear measure.

CONSTRUCTION PIECE RATES IN OPERATION

The operation of the building trades piecework system also presents a number of novel aspects, as compared with the more familiar method of reckoning wages by the hour. Work on new construction is usually carried out on a "piecework job" (*ackord*) basis — i.e., in instalments, each of which constitutes a more or less integral part of the whole construction project, and as a rule the grouping of the prices in the piece rate schedules follows this demarcation of the work. Thus in the building of a frame house, the preparing and raising of the frame constitutes one job, the boarding in of the walls and roof another, the fitting and hanging of window sash another, and so on. Piecework earnings are customarily computed at the completion of each job or group of closely related jobs. For jobs lasting four months or over, however, the building trades agreement specifies that a reckoning and payment of 75 per cent of the "current overage" (see below) shall be made at the end of each three-month interval. It also stipulates that if a job is held up for more than fourteen days, either side may require that a reckoning and 75 per cent payment be made.[6]

Payment for piecework is divided into two parts: the "weekly wage" and the "piecework overage" (*ackordsöverskott*). Each week the worker receives an amount equal to the product of his time rate and the number of hours he has worked. After the job is completed, the total of weekly payments made during the period is deducted from the piecework earnings and the "overage" is paid in a lump sum.

The masons and carpenters usually work in teams or gangs (*arbetslag*), running anywhere from three to fifteen or twenty members. That is to say, the piecework jobs are carried out *collectively*, rather than by individual workers. This arrangement is also used in the less skilled occupations (hodcarrying, cement pouring, grading, and so forth), although to a smaller extent.

In each gang, one man is designated as the "leading hand" or working foreman (*lagbas*).[7] In addition to his regular work of bricklaying, plastering, or woodworking (as the

[6] For delays or hindrances which require the workers to *wait*, it is specified that they shall be paid according to their time rates. This does not apply, however, to hindrances which are due to "circumstances beyond the employer's control."

[7] Usually, the employer hires all the workers, and the *lagbas* is elected by members of the gang. Not infrequently, however, the employer hires only the *lagbas*, who then procures his own gang.

case may be) this individual has certain duties of a supervisory nature. He is responsible for delegating the work and seeing that it is properly carried out. He also keeps track of the number of hours worked by each member of the gang, whether on piecework or by the hour. Finally, he acts as a sort of paymaster. At the completion of each job, the group's overage (in this case the difference between the piecework proceeds and the *sum of the several members'* weekly wages) is paid to the foreman, who distributes it among the members, in proportion to individual time rates and number of hours worked by each man.[8] However, he is not a boss or driver, or in any other sense an agent of the employer, nor does he ordinarily have any authority to discipline or discharge members of the gang.

The computing of piecework earnings is in itself a rather formidable undertaking. In the building trades proper, each of the three national unions employs a number of surveyors (*ackordsmätare*), allocated district-wise throughout the country, to carry out this work. The Master Builders' Association also has its corps of surveyors to uphold the employers' interests.

When a piecework job is finished, the gang foreman notifies his local union headquarters to that effect, and some time within the next day or two a surveyor arrives on the scene. With tape measure and tally sheet, he proceeds to "measure" the amount of each kind of work done. In the case of interior finish in a dwelling house or office building, for example, he determines the number of doors and windows fitted and equipped, the area of floor laid, the linear meters of baseboard and molding installed, and so forth. Each of these amounts is multiplied by its proper price as listed in the piece rate schedule and a total struck for the entire job or series of related jobs.

The employer's surveyor goes through a similar procedure,

[8] The intervals at which building workers receive their overage may vary from a week (e.g., several accumulated short jobs) to three months for a very long job. The average is probably somewhere between four and five weeks.

either independently or in conjunction with the union estimator's survey. The two then compare notes and attempt to iron out, through compromise, any differences in measurement or pricing. If and when this process is successfully completed, the results of the survey are turned over to the employer and the overage is paid out to the workers on the next regular payday. The surveyors (both workers' and employers') are usually paid on a commission basis. In the ordinary case, the cost of surveying amounts to between 1.5 and 2 per cent of the total piecework proceeds.[9]

ADJUSTING PIECEWORK DISPUTES

From the foregoing description, it is evident that the application of the piecework principle in the building industry must be a fruitful source of disagreement and dispute. This is further attested by the special arrangement which the parties to the building trades agreement have instituted for settling such disputes. All questions of agreement interpretation and application *other* than those pertaining to piecework are handled in the regular way — by the local parties first, then by the central organizations, finally by the Labor Court. But in disputes relating to the piece rate schedules, or to questions as to whether a given kind of work is or should be covered by them, only the first two steps of this procedure apply. Final disposition of such quarrels is effected through a national board of arbitration, set up exclusively to handle appeals of piecework cases in the building industry.

The board of arbitrators, which is permanent, consists of three representatives of the Master Builders' Association, a like number from each of the three workers' organizations (Carpenters', Masons', and Laborers' and Factory Workers' Unions), and a neutral chairman, chosen either by agreement between the parties or by the chief of the Royal Social Board. In any given case brought before the board, the worker representation comprises only those members whose union is immediately affected by the question at issue. Either side

[9] Cf. *Statens Offentliga Utredningar, 1938:10* (*Byggnadsindustrin i Sverige, Del. I*), p. 376.

may appeal piecework cases to the board, and its decision is absolutely "binding on both parties." [10]

PROS AND CONS OF PIECEWORK IN BUILDING

We may now turn our attention to some of the merits and deficiencies of piecework as a method of determining wages in the building industry. The frequency and seriousness of the disputes to which it gives rise is unquestionably one of the principal drawbacks of the Swedish building trades setup.[11] These disputes vary widely in nature, but most of them fall in one or another of four general categories. First of all, there is the difficult question of whether "extra work" shall be included in the piecework price. Unforeseen tasks — blasting or breaking out ledges, fitting around pipes or wires, repairing or adjusting imperfect material, etc. — are continually cropping up in building work, and the inevitable result is a retardation of the worker's rate of accomplishment. No less troublesome are the frequent discrepancies in measurement of the amount of work done.

The introduction of new kinds of material or new styles of fixtures provides still another source of disagreement. For example, if the new material requires a greater amount of effort per unit of accomplishment than the old, the work-

[10] Building trades agreement of June 12, 1937, pp. 20–23. One of the principal reasons for having a separate arbitration board for piecework disputes, according to leaders on both sides, is that the Labor Court is not competent to handle such specialized problems. The questions at issue are usually highly technical in nature, and special knowledge and training are required for their proper appraisal. It is this technical knowledge which the unions and the employers' association have attempted to supply in setting up the Board of Arbitration.

[11] According to Director Holmén of the Master Builders' Association, the Board of Arbitration (of which he is a member) handles approximately 300 disputes per year. This is nearly twice the number of cases heard annually by the National Labor Court, which represents the total of the "finally appealed" interpretational disputes for *all the rest* of Swedish industry. While this comparison undoubtedly gives an exaggerated picture, due to the fact that the parties in the building trades are less reluctant to appeal than those in other industries, it leaves no doubt as to the relatively high frequency of piecework disputes in the building industry.

ers usually demand that a new rate be negotiated, while the employer prefers to apply the old rate. In the opposite case (i.e., when the new material *decreases* the effort required) the incentives are, of course, reversed. The introduction of labor-saving machinery raises similar difficulties, except that here the demand for the new rates almost invariably comes from the employer side. This problem of mechanizing the building industry will be discussed more fully in a subsequent section.

Closely allied to the difficulties of applying piece rates are the inequalities in wages which result from them. The empirical methods pursued in setting rates make it practically impossible to insure any uniformity in income from job to job, even when the intensity of effort remains the same. Discrepancies in hourly piecework earnings ranging as high as 30 per cent above or below the average are a common occurrence.[12]

Another feature of the building trades piecework scheme which many people consider unfortunate is that it tends to drive out the older and slower workers. Since the earnings of each individual wage earner depend on the collective efforts of the entire gang, the faster workers are naturally averse to having as fellow members any who are less speedy and less physically rugged than themselves. Hence the older and slower men, even though they may be highly skilled and competent craftsmen, find it difficult to remain in the gangs, and must either be content with meager time work jobs or seek employment in some other industry.[13]

[12] It should also be remembered that the distribution of income *over time* is considerably out of balance. The "weekly wage" (time rate $\times$ hours) ordinarily comprises only one-half to two-thirds of the total piecework earnings. On the average job, therefore, the worker has to wait an unduly long time (usually a month or more) for a large fraction of the pay which he has already earned.

[13] If *individual* rather than gang piecework were utilized, the tendency would be reversed — i.e., the older and slower workers would remain in the industry longer than under straight timework. For under timework the *employer* is more averse to retaining men whose rate of output is low than he would be if each man were paid in proportion to the results of his own

Finally, the use of piecework undoubtedly lowers the quality of the workmanship to a certain extent. However, the importance of this factor should not be exaggerated. The intrinsic qualities (durability, heat-insulating properties, etc.) of most buildings depend fully as much on the quality of the materials used as on the degree of care exercised by the workers who handle them. The main result of slow and careful workmanship is to give a better *appearance* than can be obtained at higher intensities of effort. And the writer has been unable to detect any great differences, even in this respect, between Swedish buildings erected by pieceworkers and comparable American structures built on a "straight" time work basis.

All in all, the drawbacks enumerated constitute a serious indictment of the building trades piecework system. Yet it has a number of important advantages which go far toward offsetting the drawbacks and may indeed more than offset them. In the first place, there is no doubt that the speed and efficiency of the Swedish building workers are unusually high. Most competent observers of the national scene in building are in accord on this point.[14] And after one has watched a crew of bricklayers putting up a wall, or a gang of carpenters framing and raising a wooden dwelling house, one is inclined to agree with them.

However, the mere fact of piecework itself does not account entirely for this high intensity. The gang system, with its tendency to weed out the weak and slow workers and retain only those with the greatest stamina and natural dexterity, probably plays as large a part — if not, indeed, a larger one. This may be bad for the workers who lose their

efforts. The piecework system, it should be noted, also places obstacles in the way of supplying the industry with *new* workers, since the pieceworkers are reluctant to take "time out" to give them instruction.

[14] Among the people whom the writer quizzed on this matter were a number of leading union and employer association officials, two prominent members of the Mediation Service, the secretary of the Building Trades Board of Arbitration, and several functionaries of the Royal Social Board, all of whom expressed the belief that no comparable rate of output could be expected under a straight time work system.

jobs, but it is unquestionably good for the industry and for the purchasers of houses and other buildings.

But the group piecework scheme also has beneficial features from the standpoint of the workers — that is, those who remain in the industry. For one thing, it gives them a large measure of independence and freedom from irksome pressure from above, since the employers seldom find it necessary to hire bosses or "chasers" (*påfösare*) to egg them on. Even on the largest construction projects there are rarely more than one or two general overseers (*verkmästare*) in addition to the employer himself, and their duties usually consist of supervising the technical details rather than driving or disciplining the workers.

A second advantage for the wage earners lies in the fact that under the gang arrangement the work is carried out on a collective rather than an individual basis. In the American building industry, where timework is practically universal, contractors frequently employ the device of assigning a number of men to the same kind of work simultaneously. For example, five carpenters may be put to work installing doors, one on each floor of a five-story building. The usual result is (as the employer intends it to be) a race to see who can finish first. From the trade unionist viewpoint this is definitely bad, since it creates dissension and ill feeling among the workers and thus tends to undermine union solidarity. It is also disadvantageous to the individual worker, who is led to exert himself to the utmost but receives no reward for his extra effort.

In Swedish "gang piecework," however, there is little incentive to race, since no matter how much faster or harder than his fellows any one member of the gang works, he must divide the proceeds of his "differential exertion" equally with the rest of the members. Nevertheless, there is a real inducement for the group *as a whole* to work more efficiently, not only through increased intensity of effort but also through specialization and coördination of the various tasks and operations, since every improvement in this direction pays tangible and substantial dividends.

For the employer, too, the piecework system has certain undeniable advantages over time work. As has been said, piecework permits him to dispense almost entirely with subordinate executives. This not only cuts out a considerable item of overhead, but also prevents those disruptions in smooth industrial relations which occur when independent-minded workers rebel against bullying bosses. Another important point is that with piecework the employer gets his project completed in a shorter time than he would if wages were paid by the hour. Indeed, this factor counts more heavily in the building industry than in almost any other line of business, for construction contractors are practically always under pressure to reduce the time required for completion. Finally, in submitting bids to prospective clients, the building entrepreneur is able to estimate his costs more accurately when he has definite prices per quantity of output to go by. To be sure, there are many doubtful items in every such estimate, but in the ordinary case the uncertainty is confined mainly to special jobs and "extras," which constitute only a minor part of the entire project. For such major construction operations as excavating, foundation work, framing, and roofing the piece rates are well established and — except for buildings of quite unusual design — unambiguous; hence the prospective costs can be gauged with a degree of accuracy considerably greater than would be possible under time work.

THE BUILDING TRADES AND MECHANIZATION

The question of mechanical equipment versus hand methods in construction work has been the subject of so much discussion, both in Sweden and elsewhere, that it merits special attention. There is no doubt that the prevalence of collectively determined piece rates in the building trades tends to retard the introduction of labor-saving machinery. The workers on any particular job naturally do not welcome the advent of a new mechanical device, since some of them must inevitably be displaced by it. And the piecework system affords them a means of delaying its introduction. When, as usually happens, the employer asks for a reduction in the affected piece rates to compensate him for his investment, the workers may hold out for a smaller decrease or (if they have sufficient bargaining power) refuse to take any cut at all. In either event, unless the saving in time and expense engendered by the new machine is unusually large, the employer may deem it unprofitable to procure it. According to Director Holmén of the Master Builders' Association, the Wood Construction Workers' Union has used this method quite extensively in opposing the introduction of such devices as circular saws and mechanical planers.

But it is not always the workers who hold back innovations. A large proportion of the Swedish contractors are "small entrepreneurs" (*småföretagare*) who operate with very limited capital resources. For many such employers the purchase of expensive equipment entails such great difficulties that they do not attempt to mechanize, even when the workers are willing to accept a reduction in rates. And the fact that the rate of output is already relatively high acts as an additional damper on incentive in this respect.

Nor is it, in every case, practicable for the employer to introduce machinery, even though he may have the necessary capital to buy it. In the laying of floors in an office building, for instance, it may be considerably more time-consuming for the carpenters at work in the various rooms and stories to carry their material to and from a circular saw, located at some central place, than it would be to cut it by hand on the spot. Several instances of contractors who have had such experiences with mechanical saws, planing machinery, and other similar devices, and who have subsequently abandoned them, were related to the writer.

Despite these deterrents, the construction of buildings in Sweden is by no means a purely handwork occupation. A very considerable amount of rationalization has been effected in recent years, especially by the larger contracting firms. In a cursory survey of apartment house and other construction projects in Stockholm in the summer of 1938, the writer found the following types of equipment in widespread use: gasoline compressors (for drilling rock, concrete walls, etc.), cement and mortar mixers, electrically driven hoists and elevators, oxyacetylene cutting and welding torches, and various kinds of power-driven metal working devices. Mechanical excavators, sand-blasting equipment, and spray-painting apparatus were also being utilized in a number of places.[15]

This advance in mechanization is reflected in the piece rate schedules, which now contain many alternative prices, for work done by other-than-hand methods. Indeed, rates for mechnically aided operations have in some cases supplanted the old handwork prices. For example, in the most recent building laborers' schedule, the standard rate for the preparation of concrete (70 öre per cubic meter) applies to material mixed in motor-driven mixers. For "mixing by hand, or with hand-driven mixers," this base price is increased by 130 öre.[16]

In fact, it is quite apparent that the chief effect of the piecework system has been to postpone, rather than prevent the substitution of machinery for hand methods. Moreover, as both interested and neutral observers testify, the organized workers have not usually wanted to shut out the new devices entirely, but merely to insure themselves against arbitrary and wholesale losses of work and wages. For the average worker — especially if he has a strong organization behind him — the desire to be quit of the monotonous and back-breaking toil which most construction machinery is designed to eliminate far outweighs the fear of displacement and lowered earnings. Anyone who has ever shifted from pounding stonesteel with a sledge hammer to the relatively pleasant task of compressor drilling will appreciate how strong this motive may be.

[15] A brief account of the present-day use of labor-saving methods in the Swedish building industry is given in *Statens Offentliga Utredningar, 1938:10 (Byggnadsindustrin i Sverige, Del. I)*, pp. 592–593.

[16] Piece Rate Schedule for Building Laborers in Middle and Northern Sweden, 1937 (Stockholm, 1937), pp. 28–29.

PIECEWORK IN BUILDING CONSTRUCTION FURTHER CONSIDERED

Before we conclude our discussion of piecework in the building trades, mention should be made of a somewhat similar analysis contained in a report issued by the "Building Industry Experts of 1934," a three-man commission appointed by the government to investigate the industry and its problems. The commission's survey was mainly concerned with such matters as production costs, unemployment, and rationalization in the industry, and with property values and rents. Its investigation of the piecework system was more or less incidental to these larger problems.

In their report on piecework, the commissioners present the case for and against payment by results along approximately the same lines as outlined above, but with considerably greater emphasis on the disadvantages of piecework as compared with payment by the hour. In conclusion they recommend "a change-over, or perhaps more correctly, a reversion to the time rate system." [17]

However, they tacitly admit that this is a theoretically desirable rather than a practically attainable goal:

> Such a reform can only be effected through agreement between the employers' and workers' organizations.[18]

That an agreement of this sort would be exceedingly difficult to bring about is apparent from the commissioners' own account of a conference between themselves and representatives of the unions and employers, held in 1935. The opposing parties' views on the question of substituting time wages for piece rate payment are summarized in the commission's report as follows:

> The sentiment on the employer side was divided. The representative of the Master Builders' Association was, to a certain extent, sympathetic toward the idea *in principle*,[19] while those of the pipe

[17] *Statens Offentliga Utredningar, 1938:10*, p. 381. The entire report on piecework covers pp. 360–381.

[18] *Ibid.*

[19] Author's italics. The writer has subsequently been informed by the Asso-

fitting and electrical installation firms were definitely opposed to it. The master painters' representative felt that a greater continuity of operations would result if work on new buildings were paid for by results, and repair work — with the possible exception of Stockholm, Gothenburg, and Malmö — by the hour.

The strongest opposition to time work on the workers' side appears to come from the woodworkers, painters, pipe fitters and electricians. Opposition from the masons seems to be somewhat less widespread. The Laborers' and Factory Workers' Union was at one time opposed to payment by the piece, but nowadays the majority of its members prefer piecework.[20]

Thus it is evident that the contracting parties themselves were definitely unreceptive to the commission's recommendation. And, if one may judge from the opinions expressed by leading employer and worker representatives at a later date,[21] the prevailing sentiment is still against a return to time work.

Nor is it, in the writer's judgment, necessarily desirable that the piecework system be abandoned, even apart from the practical obstacle interposed by union and employer hostility toward such a move. On the contrary: in view of the inherent inefficiency of the building process itself, as compared with that of manufacturing, it would seem to be the more sensible policy to continue in force a scheme of wage determination which tends to select and retain in the industry only the strongest, fastest, and naturally most dexterous workers and make them utilize their attributes to the utmost. By so doing, it offsets — to some extent at least — the intrinsic disadvantage under which the building industry labors,[22] and aids in establishing a measure of com-

---

ciation's executive director that in practice the great majority of the employers still prefer piecework.

[20] Statens Offentliga Utredningar, 1938: 10, pp. 372–373.

[21] E.g., Nils Linde, chairman of the Wood Construction Workers' Union, V. Björkman, chairman of the Masons' Union, and F. Holmén, director of the Master Builders' Association — all of whom the writer interviewed during the summer of 1938.

[22] The widest possible use of labor-saving machinery in the construction of buildings could obviously not offset this disadvantage, except to a minor

petitive balance between houses and other commodities which are better adapted to being produced by machinery in factories.

The complexity of the price-making problem and the large volume of bargaining which it entails are, of course, serious drawbacks. But these difficulties can be substantially reduced by modifying the piecework system somewhat. The more special details and operations, involving wide possibilities of variation from job to job, can be placed on a time work basis, leaving only the more straightforward, readily measurable work to be paid for in proportion to results.

A comparison of the present and recent status of building construction in Sweden and in the United States strengthens the case for piecework. In America, where time work is practically the universal rule, privately sponsored building has been in the doldrums for nearly a decade. In Sweden, on the other hand, private construction has been in a decidedly healthy condition during most of that period, and during the past three years a veritable boom has prevailed. This despite the fact that the level of wages in the building trades is nearly twice as high as in manufacturing. While the prevalence of piecework is not the only reason why Sweden can afford to build, there are, as we have seen, good grounds for believing that it is one of the more important ones.

---

degree. In building, a major part of the whole productive process must be performed at the "point of consumption," which is a different site in each case; and this drawback would be present, no matter how many machines were introduced.

CHAPTER XIV

WAGE BARGAINING IN THE MACHINERY INDUSTRY

THE VERKSTADSINDUSTRI, or machinery industry, as we have termed it,[1] differs markedly from building construction, the branch of activity discussed in the preceding chapter. In fact, it is not a single industry, in the ordinary sense of the term, but an aggregation of firms producing a wide variety of technical metal products — including machine tools, hand tools, ball and roller bearings, electrical machinery and apparatus, armaments, bicycles, automobiles, railroad equipment, steamships, and many others.

Oddly enough, most of the machinery manufacturers are banded together in a single, closely knit organization — the Machine Industry Association — while the building trades employers are split up among five different groups, covering construction work proper and four auxiliary activities. Similarly on the worker side; approximately 95 per cent of the organized wage earners in the machinery industry belong to the Metal Workers' Union,[2] whereas in building each occupational group (with the exception of laborers and pipe fitters) has its own separate union.

But so far as employer-employee relations are concerned, the two industries have one important feature in common — decentralization in wage bargaining. Indeed, collective wage making is even more of a local function in the machinery trades than in building construction. This does not mean that the central workers' and employers' organizations play no part in determining what the wage rates shall be. On the contrary, the very foundation-stone of the machine

[1] The British term "engineering trades" is perhaps more accurate, but its use in the present study has seemed inadvisable, mainly because the word "engineering" has a different meaning in American industrial parlance.

[2] The remaining 5 per cent are foundry workers, organized in the Molders' Union.

industry's wage-making scheme — the national schedule of minimum time rates, graduated according to the worker's age, experience, and skill, and the cost of living — is laid at the central negotiations. Moreover, when the national agreement expires and a new one is drawn up, some change in the *level* of wages — for all plants and all classes of workers in the industry — is usually negotiated at the central parleys.

FIXED AND TEMPORARY PIECE RATES

However, actual wages are in most cases determined by the amount of output rather than the time spent. And since very few plants in the "industry" are engaged in making the same specific commodity, it is obvious that the piece rate schedules cannot be established on a national basis, but must be designed to conform to the product and technique of each particular workplace. This fact accounts for a considerable proportion of the wage making which takes place in individual plants in the machinery trades. But the bulk of the local bargaining is due to another factor — the variation in wage scales *over time*.

Two kinds of piece rates — fixed and "temporary" (*tillfälliga*) — are provided for in the national agreement. The pertinent clauses read as follows:

> In any plant where "factory production" (*fabriksmässig tillverkning*) is carried on, price lists shall be established which shall remain in force for a certain fixed period, ordinarily a year. . . .
>
> On all piecework, prices for which cannot be established in such fixed schedules, the rates shall, in each particular instance, be determined through free negotiation between the employer or his representative and the individual worker or workers to whom the work is proffered; and agreement shall be reached before the work is begun.

One important distinction between these two kinds of piece rates is that the duration of fixed rates is contractually established for a definite period of time, whereas temporary rates may be terminated whenever a particular task or lot of work is completed. The other is that in making temporary rates the employer deals with the "individual worker or workers," while in fixed rate making the contracting entity on the worker side is the local union.

The apparent intent of these provisions is that fixed schedules are to be used wherever the article produced or operation performed remains the same over extended periods of time, and temporary rates only where the product changes. In practice, however, the bulk of piece rates in machinery plants are temporary.

In the making of "order goods" — e.g., machine tools and electric generators — flexibility of this sort is indispensable, since the style and construction of the machinery may change radically from one order to the next. But in such lines as bicycle, typewriter, and hand tool manufacturing, where production is largely "for stock," many of the major parts and operations remain substantially unchanged year after year, and here the use of temporary rates is less a matter of technical necessity than of deliberate employer policy. This policy, and the sharp controversy between the Machine Industry Association and the Metal Workers' Union which has resulted from it, will be described in a subsequent section of the present chapter.

In most plants where the shifting nature of production necessitates the frequent setting of new rates, the procedure followed is not a literal application of the "free negotiation" clause but rather a modification of it. The rate setter or "time study engineer" determines, in the first instance, what the price is to be, and the worker practically always accepts it — tentatively at least — and goes ahead with the work. If he is dissatisfied with the rate given him, he brings his complaint to the rate setter or his foreman, but not until the job is completed. In case they fail to reach an agreement, the dispute is referred to successively higher authorities for settlement — first to the head of the shop union (*verkstadsklubb*) and the management, then to the central workers' and employers' organizations, finally to the National Labor Court in Stockholm. If the decision favors the worker and the rate is raised, it applies retroactively to the work already completed.

AN ILLUSTRATIVE CASE

In order to convey a clearer idea of how temporary piece rates are set in practice, it will be well to take a specific example. The method chosen for illustration is that used in the rotating machinery division of a well-known electrical equipment concern.[3]

As in most other piecework establishments, the basic determinants in the rate making process are a series of time rates. The schedule used in this plant for adult male workers on individual (non-group) piecework is reproduced below.

HOURLY RATINGS ON MOTOR AND GENERATOR PRODUCTION
(IN KRONOR)

Preponderantly Handwork			Machine Work		
Moving Materials	Spooling Winding Stamping Grinding	Mounting Filing Welding Drilling	Lathe Work Drilling Planing: Requiring Less Than Average Skill	Lathe Work Drilling Planing: Requiring More Than Average Skill	Special Work
1.16	1.22	1.29	1.32	1.36	1.42

These rates apply chiefly to the production of motors and generators, of which the company manufactures a wide variety of sizes and styles, principally "on order."

It should be observed that the determination of these "actual hourly ratings" (*timlöner*) is left in large measure to the parties on the ground. The *minimum* time rates for adult male workers as specified in the machinery trades national agreement for the cost-of-living group in which this plant falls, are as follows:

For skilled workers who have attained the age of 24, and who have worked at the trade at least 7 years .... 88 öre
For skilled workers who have attained the age of 21, and who have worked at the trade at least 3 years .... 81 öre
For workers (unskilled) who have attained the age of 20 75 öre

[3] Interview with managerial officials and tour of plant, August 1938.

The plant classification, it will be noted, is based on the degree of skill alone, whereas the national agreement scheme also takes account of age and experience. There is, never-the less, a certain correlation between the two, since the "preponderantly handwork" operations are performed mainly by younger workers, while machine work jobs are usually held by older and more experienced men. Moreover, although there are six rates in the plant as against three in the national schedule, the percentage spread between the rates for unskilled and highly skilled workers is roughly the same in both cases. The reason for this similarity is, as one might expect, that the national agreement was taken as the basic model in setting up the local arrangement.

It is in establishing the margin between the regular ratings and the minimum rates that local bargaining plays the principal role. Its magnitude depends primarily on the individual concern's ability to pay and the relative bargaining strength of the opposing parties. Because of the national union's policy of demanding "what the traffic will bear," this differential varies markedly from plant to plant, the figure in the present case — approximately 55 per cent — being considerably above the average.

As noted, the chief purpose of the hourly ratings is to serve as a basis for the setting of "temporary" piece rates. The other criteria needed are obtained from time study data. In setting up the piece rate schedule for a particular operation, the rate setter does not make a separate time study analysis for each size of motor or generator part that may conceivably be wanted, but merely for a few selected sizes. In the case of machining out stator frames for induction motors, for example, he takes a "time run" on each of three or four sizes of frames — those, let us say, whose diameters are 20, 35, 50, and 65 centimeters. He then computes the price per piece in each case by taking the product of the time consumed and the hourly rating for this class of work (1.36 kronor). Finally, he "spots" these results on a chart, with surface area machined as the horizontal coördinate, and draws a smooth curve through the points thus determined, as shown in the accompanying diagram. This curve enables him to estimate with reasonable accuracy the rate for machining any size of frame within the range covered by the series of time studies.

This scheme, or some variant of it, is in force not only in

ILLUSTRATIVE PIECE RATE CURVE FOR MACHINING OF CAST MOTOR AND GENERATOR PARTS

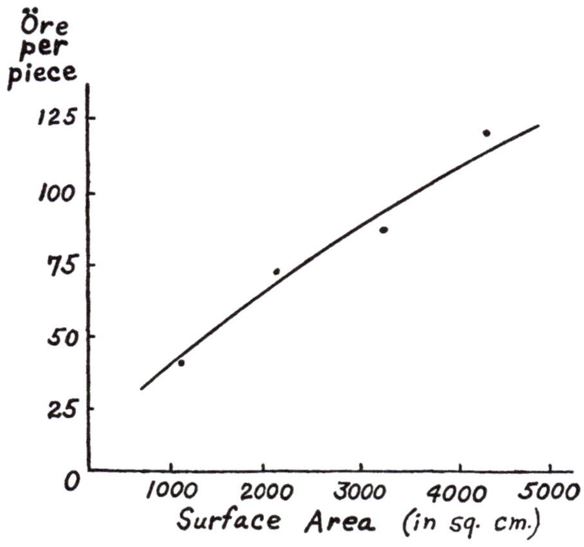

the motor and generator departments but largely throughout the entire enterprise, for most of this company's products are made in a variety of sizes. Nor is its use confined to individual models or styles of a particular product. Even when the apparatus to be made involves a substantial departure from the standard technical design, there is usually sufficient similarity in the nature of the operations required so that the established "piece rate curves" may be used as a basis for determining the prices.

So far as its outward functioning is concerned, the rate-setting method outlined above obviously resembles wage making by decree more than it does collective bargaining, since the process of arriving at piece rates and the decisions as to what rates shall be assigned to each job are left almost entirely to the discretion of the rate setter — a representative of the employer. Nevertheless, the majority of the workers are quite favorably disposed toward it. This may seem strange, at first sight, for collective wage determination is a basic tenet of Swedish unionism. However, the reasons underlying the acquiescent attitude toward unilateral rate setting at this particular plant are fairly apparent.

In the first place the workers, and more especially the local leaders, appreciate that with production constantly shifting from one size of machine to another, and from old to new designs, the volume of bargaining would be almost prohibitively great if all rates had to be decided on through the usual process of union-management negotiation. Moreover, they know that the method used is based on well-tried engineering principles and that it has produced equitable results in the past. Finally, pieceworkers are always kept informed as to the price and "normal time" of every job they undertake, hence are enabled to keep a close check on their earnings from hour to hour.

The absence of hostility toward temporary piece rates in the present instance is, of course, not due entirely to the management's astuteness in establishing a "scientific" rate making scheme. As already noted, if a worker feels dissatisfied with the rate given him for a particular job, he has the right to protest it and to call on his organization to protect his interests. As the rule is applied in the plants operated by this concern, the worker first contacts his rate setter. The latter usually has considerable leeway in making adjustments, and consequently most complaints are settled at this first stage. Should they fail to reach a settlement, the case is next taken up at a conference between the "chief engineer in charge of operations" and an authorized representative (ordinarily an official) of the shop union.[4] One of

[4] These "official bargainers" (one in each major department) are usually assigned to non-production jobs, which they can leave at any time without

the common boasts of the company officials is that it is almost never necessary to carry piece rate complaints to the next stage — negotiations between the central organizations — or to the Labor Court.

In addition to its active function — giving the worker a means of redress against rates which have been set too low — this right of appeal also has a passive effect, in that it tends to restrain the rate setters from paring the rates down to a level where complaints will result. Nor is this factor wholly a function of the individual rate setter's discretion, for the top management's primary aim is prevention, rather than mere early settlement, of piece work disputes.[5]

An interesting feature of the wage making setup at this factory is the procedure followed in adjusting piece rates when new machines or methods of production are introduced. On such occasions it is frequently necessary to make new time studies, even though no change in the technical design of the product is involved. The usual practice is to let the affected workers continue at the old rate for a few weeks or months, depending on the degree of difficulty involved in learning how to operate the new machine. When they have "gotten their hand in" on it, a series of time runs is taken by the rate setter. This is, of course, a management-initiated device, for the employers do not want too wide a disparity between the "time study speed" and the rate of output on subsequent production after the piece rate has been set. But there is also a limit on the "high side" here, for it is a matter

---

interfering with smooth operations. They are paid on a straight time rate basis.

[5] The plant officials claim to have something like a record in this respect. According to Herr H——, the chief engineer, there are seldom more than one or two complaints per week, whereas the number of rates "set" normally runs to several hundred per day. This claim appears to be substantiated by the records of the Metal Workers' Union. According to the union's annual reports, the plant in question had no "recorded" piecework disputes (i.e., disputes which are referred to the local unions for settlement) during the period 1936–1937, whereas most other concerns of comparable size had at least three or four. See *Svenska Metallindustriarbetareförbundets Verksamhetsberättelser*, 1936, pp. 116–135, and 1937, pp. 212–230.

of management policy (induced, no doubt, by union pressure) that in making time studies on new production methods the rate setter shall not require the trial run to be made at the highest possible speed of the machine, but at some speed well below it. This insures the workers of a fair margin of possible increase in output after the rate has been established. The fact that the average hourly earnings of machine workers in this plant are approximately 1.50 kronor,[6] as against an average hourly time rating of only 1.36, indicates that the workers do manage to increase their speed and efficiency with time.

All in all, there can be no doubt that the method of payment by results works unusually well in this establishment, despite the wide variety of types, designs, and sizes of products manufactured. According to the chief engineer it is, indeed, the only workable method, his contention being that if time work were adopted, unit costs would be so much higher as to make it impossible to compete with foreign producers. He did not deny that it might be possible to keep the rate of output at the same level if incentive wages were abandoned, but declared that this would necessitate hiring a large number of additional foremen and overseers without permitting any reduction in the hourly wages paid. He stated further that this added expense would not be offset by a reduction in inspection costs. In fact, he maintained that the difference between the amount of quality supervision necessary on piecework and on time work is so small as to be practically negligible. Substantially the same opinion was held by a number of other representatives of the machinery industry — both employers and unionists — whom the writer interviewed, and there is little reason to doubt its accuracy. The detection of bad workmanship is a relatively easy matter on most manufactured technical apparatus, and the fear of having their work rejected keeps the workers from neglecting accuracy in their desire to turn out more work.

The problem of avoiding "holdups" on piecework production appears to be very competently handled in this plant.

[6] Chief engineer's estimate.

The company employs a "toolmaster" (*verktygsmästare*), whose sole responsibility is to provide workers with the proper cutting tools and other implements, and a "stock router," who is charged with the duty of keeping them supplied with materials. Repairing of machinery is done after hours, so far as possible. On the rare occasions when delays do occur, the workers are paid according to their regular hourly rating.[7]

One of the bargaining practices followed aptly illustrates the superiority of the temporary rate device over fixed price schedules in plants where the nature of the work changes from day to day. Sometimes — and despite the widespread use of time studies — piece rates are inadvertently set too high, and when this occurs, the rate setter has to try to scale it down to a more equitable figure. The workers to whom the rate has been assigned will naturally object to having their incomes reduced, so the rate setter usually resorts to the expedient of "making a trade" — he offers them small increases in several other rates, which have previously been on the low side, in return for a substantial reduction in the high rate. Such an adjustment would be extremely difficult, not to say impossible, if the rates were incorporated in fixed schedules.

BAD BLOOD OVER TEMPORARY RATES

Although the setup described above has been used to illustrate the wage making process in the machinery industry, the status of collective bargaining in this concern is not be regarded as typical of the industry as a whole.[8] Indeed, the relations between the employers and workers in a majority of the other machine-making establishments, and between the two central organizations, are decidedly less amicable than they are in our illustrative equipment plant. The chief

[7] This situation is fairly representative of the Swedish machinery industry as a whole. According to Gustav Vahlberg, vice-president of the Metal Workers' Union, the number of instances of workers complaining of delays and holdups is almost negligible.

[8] In view of the many different lines of production comprising the machinery trades it would of course be quite impossible to find such a "typical" plant.

reason therefor is their inability to agree as to the most desirable method of determining piece wages.

As has been pointed out, there are many concerns in the industry whose product is not diversified and shifting in nature, as in the case of electrical apparatus, but relatively uniform and steady. Yet these concerns, aided and abetted by their national employers' alliance, the Machine Industry Association, have insisted that the temporary rate device be used on all piecework and have, moreover, been able to attain their end in most instances.

The metal workers have no quarrel with temporary rates in places where the conditions of work make frequent changes necessary, as the situation described above amply attests. But they feel that when the productive operations are uniform and continuous, the rates could and should be established in written contracts and for definite periods, with the local union rather than the individual wage earner as the contracting party on the workers' side.

According to Herr Styrman, the executive director of the Machine Industry Association, the employers' chief objection to the fixed-rate system is that it is too cumbersome and costly. In drawing up fixed schedules, delegations of the management and the union must meet and negotiate, and this, they contend, is always a long and troublesome procedure. When the rate contract is concluded, formal lists must be compiled, printed, and distributed. Further difficulties are encountered when contractually fixed rates are found to be too high or too low, or when new methods of production are introduced, since the rates can be changed only through the unwieldy and time-consuming process of formal union-management negotiations. These nuisance factors, they hold, are either greatly reduced or entirely absent when "temporary" rates, established through direct dealings between the rate setter and the individual worker, are used.

However, the leaders of the Metal Workers' Union do not admit the validity of these objections. They contend that in factories where the output is confined to one or a few products, the design of which does not change radically from year to year, fixed schedules are no more difficult to make or administer than temporary rates. They point out that in iron and steel — the other major industry with which the union bargains on a nation-wide scale — fixed rates are used almost exclusively, and that the iron masters are well satisfied with the arrangement. The desirability of the fixed rate system from the worker's viewpoint is beyond all dispute, since it gives him positive insurance against arbitrary reductions in his rate of income for a definite period of time.

Indeed, it is quite apparent that the employers have other, and perhaps even more important, reasons for insisting on the retention of temporary rates than those which they openly declare. For one thing, it permits them to deal, in the first instance, not with the union but with the individual workman, hence gives them a certain bargaining advantage. To be sure, it is not ordinarily the employer himself but one of his representatives who computes the price and proffers it to the man at the machine. But the rate setter is usually an engineering graduate or other technically trained person, with an intimate knowledge of the employer's affairs and a plentiful store of bargaining experience. He is, therefore, to a considerable extent able to impose his will on the relatively unschooled worker, who knows little about the art of bargaining and even less about the wages which the company can afford to pay. True, the worker may subsequently protest the rate agreed upon, if he finds that the income it yields is too low, but this is always a bothersome and embarrassing procedure, and many workers will continue working at a low rate rather than go to the trouble of protesting it.

Another *sub rosa* reason for the employers' partiality toward temporary rates is the ease with which they can be terminated. The national agreement specifies that (new) rates shall be determined "in each particular instance"; and it is the employer who determines what the duration of each "instance" shall be. He is, therefore, in a position to take advantage of any opportunities which may arise for lowering his wage costs without consulting union sentiment in the matter.

An apt illustration of how the employers sometimes avail themselves of this feature of temporary piece rates is afforded by a recent episode which took place in one of Sweden's largest armament works. In accordance with an understanding between the management and the local union at this plant, piece rates which had been applied to the same type of work a number of times without change were recorded in a card file and were thereafter regarded as fixed rates — i.e., they could not be changed during the remainder of the (national) agreement period.

In the instance under consideration a mature worker, whose rate had been recorded in this manner, was replaced by a youth of eighteen, and at the same time the rate was reduced, approximately in proportion to the difference between the minimum rates for adult and under-age workers in the national agreement. According to the writer's informant, Herr Vahlberg of the Metal Workers' Union, the department head had just discovered that the work could be done by a less experienced worker and was anxious to take advantage of his discovery before the expiration of the agreement.

The Metal Workers' Union brought the case before the Labor Court, claiming that the rate in question was *de facto* fixed and that consequently the company was violating the contract in reducing it. However, the court decreed that since the original agreement had been made with an individual worker and not with the local union, the rate must be considered as temporary, hence amenable to being changed at any time.[9]

Whatever the reasons for the employers' insistence on the "flexible" rate making scheme, the fact remains that they have been able to keep it in force over most of the industry in the face of repeated attempts by the organized workers to obtain fixed schedules.[10] And their success on this score must be attributed, in large measure at least, to superior

[9] *Arbetsdomstolens Domar, 1934,* Decision No. 189, pp. 922–924.

[10] According to Herr Vahlberg, approximately 85 per cent of the piecework in the machinery industry is still priced on a "temporary" basis.

bargaining strength. The Metal Workers' Union, for all that it is the largest of the Swedish worker organizations, has never been quite a match for the Machine Industry Association, with its closely knit organizational structure, ample financial resources, and hard-boiled leaders.

During the last two or three years, however, the indications have pointed toward a change in the piecework situation in the machinery trades. The union has succeeded (whether through a stiffening of its own front or a softening of the employers', it is difficult to judge) in obtaining several concessions which should make it considerably easier for the unions in mass production plants to replace temporary piece rates with fixed schedules. For example, in 1936 the following clause was added to the "temporary rate" clause in the national agreement:

> Such piece rates, provided they are based on time studies or are otherwise controlled, and are kept at the same level on successive occasions, shall, if the employer and the affected workers so agree, be incorporated in the plant's fixed piece rate system. . . .

It will be noted that this clause still puts the major emphasis on the individual worker rather than his organization. In 1938, however, a paragraph was introduced which definitely makes the local union the responsible entity on the workers' side in effecting such change-overs.[11]

It is still too early to determine the practical effect of these new provisions. The union leaders claim that they have already begun to tell, while the few employers whom the writer questioned were inclined to belittle their significance. At all events, it is evident that the union has at last managed to insert an entering wedge. The course of the next few years may very well show a distinct trend in the direction of contractually established piece rates in the machinery industry.

[11] See machinery trades national agreement for 1938, p. 28.

CHAPTER XV

THE COLLECTIVE AGREEMENT LAW AND THE LABOR COURT

It is noteworthy that in the development of the Swedish collective bargaining institution, law and governmental authority have played only a minor part. The procedure followed in making agreements, the bulk of their contents, and the machinery for settling disputes concerning their proper applications were worked out, during the first quarter of the present century, between the contracting parties themselves and quite independently of legislative influence. Not until 1928, when this evolutionary process was practically completed, were collective contracts defined and regulated by law. And even then the rules laid down were, for the most part, merely a codification of practices previously established through unregulated parleying and compromise.

EARLY SENTIMENT FOR STATE-REGULATED BARGAINING

The "labor legislation" passed prior to 1928 did, it is true, impose some restrictions on the parties to the employment bargain. The Forty-eight Hour Law, for example, set a definite upper limit to hours of work. And the Mediation Law of 1906 provided for intervention by an impartial third party in all "serious" disputes. But these statutes still left the principle of independent decision intact — the former because it applied only to a particular condition of work, the latter because it did not put either side under any compulsion to accept a mediation proposal.

However, a sentiment in favor of state interference of a more drastic sort was in evidence during most of the period, and from time to time this sentiment manifested itself in attempts to place legislative checks on the activities of the organized workers and employers. The earliest of these attempts, sponsored by conservative legislators in 1899 and aimed at the unions alone, actually succeeded in becoming a law. This *Åkarpslag*, as it was called, made it a criminal offense for any person "to force (another) to take part in a strike, or to prevent anyone from returning to work or from accepting profferred work." Despite repeated efforts by the Social Democrats in the Riksdag to get it repealed, this act remains a part of the Swedish penal code to this day, and workers are still occasionally fined or imprisoned for violating it. However, it has had little effect in preventing the use of the strike-and-blockade weapon by organized labor. Indeed, the number of attempts by employers to "carry on" with strikebreakers has grown smaller each year, and today this form of counterpressure is practically unknown.

The second legislative campaign, launched in 1905, was also directed against the organized workers. This time the act of striking itself, if it resulted in "serious damage to property" or "danger to life and health," was to be made a punishable offense. All strikes "against the public interest" (*samhällsfarliga strejker*) — by railroad workers, power plant employees, etc. — were to be strictly prohibited. The proposal was thrown down in the Second Chamber of the Riksdag, albeit by a very narrow margin.

The first real attempt to place restrictions on organized workers and employers as parties to collective agreements was made in 1910. In this instance, the conservative government sought to make the agreements legally enforceable and to prohibit stoppages in interpretational disputes. A special labor court was to be set up to handle such disputes. Sympathetic strikes and lockouts were to be permitted, provided the primary conflict was legal.

Despite the fact that this proposal put limitations on both sides, the unionists and their political allies, the Social-Democrats, regarded it as a proemployer measure, especially the part allowing sympathetic stoppages. Accordingly, they took a definite stand against it and, with the aid of a group of Liberals in the lower house, finally succeeded in killing it. The bill was revived the following year, but again went down before the Labor-Liberal coalition.

In 1916 the government — still conservative — delegated to the Social Board the task of framing a law "to promote industrial peace." In its recommendation, the board, taking the same approach as the legislators six years earlier, proposed to regulate "legal" (interpretational) disputes only, leaving disputes incident to the making of new agreements to be handled by the Mediation Service. The collective aggreement was defined and delimited, and was to be legalized, in the sense that either party might sue the other for breach of contract. Stoppages in interpretational disputes were explicitly specified as one type of breach. Damage suits were to be brought to a court of seven judges, set up expressly for this purpose.[1]

This proposal was never presented to the Riksdag, the government leaders deeming it inexpedient to risk stirring up unrest among the workers at a time when proletarian revolutions were in the wind. Thereafter no serious attempts were made to revive the issue for nearly a decade.

Meanwhile, in 1915, the collective contract had been legalized in another way. In that year the Supreme Court handed down a decision, in connection with a lawsuit arising out of the general strike of 1909, to the effect that trade unions and employers' organizations were responsible at law for breaches of agreement obligations. However, this precedent was rarely used as the basis of litigation in the years that followed. The regular law courts were notoriously slow in handling civil cases, and neither the unions nor the employers were anxious to start suits which might drag out over a year or more.

THE LEGISLATION OF 1928

Early in 1928 a bill, embodying in two separate laws the main features of the proposals of 1910 and 1916, was laid before the Riksdag by the Independent-Liberal coalition government.[2] Its initiator, Social Minister Jakob Petterson,

[1] Kungliga Socialstyrelsen, *Underdånigt Utlåtande med Förslag till Lag om Vissa Åtgärder till Främjande av Arbetsfred* (Stockholm, 1916), pp. 40–55.

[2] *Utkast till Lag om Kollektivavtal jämte Kortfattad Motivering* (Stock-

although a Liberal in politics, was a jurist by profession and a strong advocate of legal regulation of worker-employer relations. The support for this proposition came partly from his fellow Liberals in Parliament, and partly from the organized employers, who dominated the Conservative Party.[3] The employers, while opposed to coercive interference in interest disputes, favored mandatory adjudication of interpretational disputes. They argued that under the existing arrangement it was too difficult for them to get redress when the unions failed to live up to agreement obligations, and that the only way to insure observance was through explicit legislation, properly implemented.

The unionists and Social-Democrats fought the bill vigorously at every step. A law creating the right to sue for breach of a collective contract would, they maintained, inure to the workers' disadvantage, since damages awarded in their favor would never amount to more than the wages lost, whereas verdicts against them might include all conceivable losses incurred by the employer. They also objected to the establishment of a judiciary tribunal with precedent-setting powers, on the ground that this would tend to "freeze" existing provisions and practices, and thus prevent the workers from winning further improvements in the conditions of work.

The laborites' opposition reached its climax on May 22, when the Federation of Trade Unions called a one-day protest strike, in which some 370,000 workers took part. Despite all their efforts the bill was passed, and on January 1, 1929 the two new statutes — the Collective Agreement Law and the Law Providing for a Labor Court — went into effect.[4]

---

holm, 1927), p. 15. The new legislation was prepared by a commission of experts, consisting of Henning Elmquist and Gunnar Huss of the Social Board, who had worked out the 1916 proposal, and Arthur Lindhagen, a jurist with wide experience in the field of labor law.

[3] Cf. V. Spångberg, *Från Arvid Posse till Per Albin Hansson* (Stockholm, 1936), p. 210.

[4] These laws are reproduced in A. Molin, *Svensk Arbetslagstiftning*, second edition, pp. 243–263.

LAW NO. 1: CODIFICATION OF ACCEPTED PRACTICE

The Collective Agreement Law lays down certain rules regarding the making, scope, enforcement, and termination of contracts between unions of workers and employers or employers' associations. Among other things, it stipulates that every such contract must be made and terminated in writing; that it is binding on all members of the contracting organizations, whether they have come in before or after the date on which it was concluded; that if a member leaves an organization, he is not on that account freed from his agreement obligations; that if workers and employers who are bound by the same contract make other agreements which conflict with it, such agreements are invalid.

The meat of the act is contained in Sections 4 and 8. The substance of the former is that no dispute regarding the interpretation or application of an agreement may be made the occasion for lockouts, strikes, blockades, or boycotts, and that sympathetic stoppages are forbidden "if (the organization being supported) does not itself possess the right to take coercive measures." Section 8 provides that if either of the parties to an agreement evades any of the responsibilities undertaken therein, it may be held liable for any loss or damage sustained by the other party. However, in addition to this "general" provision, there is a supplementary clause which reads as follows:

> If the degree of the defendant's guilt, the injured party's connection with the origin of the dispute, the magnitude of the injury inflicted or other circumstances warrant it, the amount of the damages awarded may be reduced, even to the extent of full exoneration from liability. In no case may an individual worker be required to pay damages in excess of 200 kronor.

This clause as originally drafted said nothing about reducing the damages, nor about a maximum levy on individual workers. These features were added in the later stages of the act's legislative career, in an attempt to appease the workers' hostility toward it.

For the majority of organized workers and employers the introduction of this law, taken by itself, was obviously not an epochal event, since most of the national agreements already prohibited strikes and lockouts in interpretational disputes. True, such stoppages still occurred, despite the contractual ban, but they were, for the most part, small and unimportant, and comprised only a very minor proportion of the total annual number of workers affected by stoppages of all kinds.[5]

It should be noted, too, that the qualifying appendage in the provision forbidding sympathetic stoppages — which excepts cases where the primary conflict is legal — has practically the same import as the "sympathy clause" found in all the larger collective contracts.[6] Thus in another important respect the advent of the Collective Agreement Law did not seriously affect the contractual status of the parties to the national agreements. Incidentally, the inclusion of this provision was a victory for the employers. For the sympathetic stoppage weapon has been used more frequently and more effectively by the employers' organizations than by the unions. The chief significance of the clause is that it permits a member association of the S. E. F. to declare a lockout in sympathy with another constituent body which is involved in an agreement *making* dispute, even though the "sympathizing" association's contract is still in force.

LAW NO. 2: THE LABOR COURT

Section 8, which makes the collective agreement a legally enforceable document, is still another "codification of earlier practice," since it repeats the essential substance of the Supreme Court decision of 1915. Nevertheless, this provision is of great practical importance, in that it provides the definitive basis for the second of the twin laws — the Labor Court Act. By this act a tribunal was set up especially for the purpose of dealing with interpretational and other similar disputes and for awarding damages to injured agreement

[5] See Chapter X, p. 169.

[6] See Chapter V, pp. 86–88.

signatories. The main purpose of the lawmakers in establishing this body was to secure a more competent and speedy adjudication of such cases than was possible in the regular law courts.

The law specifies that the Labor Court shall consist of a chairman and six members. The chairman and two of the members, appointed by the government for a "specified term," must be chosen from among persons who "cannot be considered as upholding employer or worker interests." The chairman and one of these neutral members (who is designated as vice-chairman) must be "well versed in the law and experienced in the practice of judgeship." The second neutral member must be a person of "special insight and experience in labor relations and allied questions." Of the remaining four members, two are to be selected from among nominees submitted by the Swedish Employers' Advisory Board,[7] and two from a similar slate presented by the Federation of Trade Unions. Their appointments run for two years at a time.

The present chairman of the court is Arthur Lindhagen, the jurist who participated in drawing up the two laws. The other neutral members are Johan Hagander, an official in the Department of Justice, and Nils Bergsten, chief of the Bureau of Labor Statistics in the Social Board. Erik Paues, chairman of the Textile Industry Association, and Ivar Larson, vice-director of the S. E. F., comprise the employer delegation. The two labor members are Oscar Karlén and Oscar Westerlund, the heads of the Wood Products Union and the Metal Workers' Union, respectively.

THE COURT AT WORK

The Labor Court has unquestionably fulfilled the expectations of its originators to a high degree, both as to competence and dispatch in handling agreement suits. In the scant dozen years since its establishment it has disposed of more than 1800 disputes, in every case within a few weeks

[7] A body representing the Swedish Employers' Federation and a number of the larger non–S. E. F. associations.

of the initiation of proceedings. And most of its decisions have been acceptable, if not always entirely satisfactory, to both sides.[8]

One of the reasons for the court's favorable showing is to be found in its organizational makeup, and more especially in the particular men who serve on it. The chairman and vice-chairman are eminent jurists, both entirely competent to keep the proceedings and the judgments within the framework of the law and to furnish the knowledge necessary to understand the questions at issue from the legal standpoint. Herr Bergsten, the third neutral member, is one of the country's leading authorities on collective agreements, and has at his command a wealth of factual information on the subject which his bureau has gathered in the course of the past thirty years.

The chief value of the union and employer members lies in their close connection with and knowledge of the technical details which local interpretational quarrels frequently involve. Sometimes, to be sure, the subject of the dispute is an entirely unique feature of the particular workplace, and in such cases the knowledge of these "experts" is of no great help.[9] But by and large, their close acquaintance with actual worker-employer relationships and actual productive processes enables them to contribute materially to a proper comprehension of the pros and cons of alleged breaches of contract.

The efficiency of the court's functioning is also due, in no small measure, to the straightforward and standardized procedure by which each case is handled, both before and during the trial. The plaintiffs and defendants are required to submit statements of their respective versions of the issues

[8] It is interesting to note, in this connection, that more than two thirds of the decisions have been unanimous. Lode Wistrand, *Kollektivavtalslagen och Arbetsdomstolen* (Stockholm, 1936), p. 20.

[9] When the question at issue concerns some tangible object or condition — such as machinery, safety devices, sanitary facilities, etc. — the entire membership sometimes pays a visit to the particular workplace, in order to study the problem at first hand. *Ibid.*, pp. 86–87.

to the court, in writing, at least a week before the date of the trial. The chairman studies these statements carefully, after which he confers with the parties by telephone and informs them that they must be prepared to substantiate certain of their statements with further evidence. The other judges also acquaint themselves with the facts of the case ahead of time. Finally, all the principally interested people on both sides are required to present themselves as witnesses. When the trial begins, therefore, the ground is cleared for a quick review of all the relevant facts, and prompt answers to most of the questions that arise are assured.

The court convenes one day each week, usually on Friday. Between ten in the forenoon and four in the afternoon it tries four cases, one hour being allowed for each. The proceedings themselves are conducted on an informal basis, yet with surprising smoothness and dispatch. Legal language is almost totally absent. The chairman guides the course of the trial, acting both as cross-examiner and presiding judge.[10]

All representatives and witnesses for the complainant party are heard from before any of the defense's testimony is given. Later, rebuttals are made by both sides. In most local disputes involving national agreements, officers of the affected national union and employers' association act as principal spokesmen for their respective suborganizations or members.[11] In addition, a number of representatives of

[10] The part played by the present chairman, Herr Lindhagen, in making the court an effectively functioning institution can hardly be overemphasized. The skill and tact with which he elicits information from the reluctant witnesses is little short of remarkable. To quote one prominent unionist, "It is practically impossible to keep anything a secret from the chairman. With an unerring technique he pries out of the witness all he knows, and oftentimes induces him to express himself on matters that he had no intention of saying anything about." (Frithiof Ekman, in *Nutida Svenskt Arbetsliv*, p. 145.) He is no less skillful in sifting out the significant facts from a mass of testimony and in piecing them together in such a way as to bring out the relative merits of the opposing parties' cases. The impression one gets, after attending a session of the court, is that its success in "producing results" is very largely Chairman Lindhagen's doing.

[11] It should be remembered that, in accordance with the "disputes clause" in the national agreements, such cases will ordinarily have been through two

the directly interested local parties — plant executives, union leaders, and individual workers — are usually present. The litigants sometimes hire lawyers to represent them, but this occurs chiefly when the employer in the case is unorganized.

The main object of these hearings is to enable the judges to appraise each case on its merits and arrive at an impartial conclusion.[12] However, no verdict is given out at the open session. All four cases are heard in sequence, after which the court is adjourned. At the end of the day, the judges meet behind closed doors and a vote is taken on each case. The only task remaining after this is the writing of the "judgments" (*domar*), which is usually finished within two weeks after the trial.[13] The parties are then notified of the verdict and presented with copies of the judgment. This ends the matter; there is no appeal from the Labor Court's decisions.

COURT ACTION BY THE UNIONS

The Labor Court has now completed its twelfth year of existence. It seems apropos, therefore, to examine briefly what it has done, and to try to obtain some idea as to how its advent has affected the status of employer-employee relations in Sweden.

Of the 1,450 cases tried during the period 1929–1936, nearly 1,200 were initiated on the worker side.[14] In view of the strong union hostility toward the Collective Agreement and Labor Court laws prior to their passage, this seems

---

stages of unarbitrated negotiation (local and central) before coming to the court. In fact, the Labor Court Law specifically states (Section 14) that if the agreement contains a disputes adjustment clause, such negotiations must have taken place before a case may be brought before the court.

[12] If the case involves the "home organization" of one of the union or employer members, he usually refrains from participating and his place is filled by an alternate.

[13] Each judgment comprises three main parts, as follows: a statement of the issue, together with the agreement provisions involved, and other pertinent data; a summary of the opposing parties' contentions; and the court's opinion. In cases where the vote is not unanimous, the opinions of the dissenters are also included.

[14] S. Hansson, *Den Svenska Fackföreningsrörelsen*, sixth edition, p. 245.

somewhat paradoxical at first sight. However, the workers' attitude has undergone considerable modification since the court's establishment, and this undoubtedly accounts in some measure for their willingness to put it to use. But the real reason for the high proportion of worker-initiated suits is to be found in the nature of the agreement relationship itself. For it is usually the employer who determines, in the first instance, how a given provision shall be interpreted and applied. For example, he may decide that a clause stipulating extra compensation for overtime applies only to hours worked in excess of the total number specified per week, rather than to those falling outside the particular interval constituting the regular working day. Or he may choose to reckon payment for a certain operation on a time work basis, on the ground that it is not one which "can be adapted to piecework without inconvenience." [15] Consequently, in most cases, it falls to the individual worker or his organization to take the offensive in cases involving alleged breach of agreement obligations.

There are, to be sure, many provisions which explicitly require the workers themselves to do, or refrain from doing, a particular thing (e.g., to exercise due care in using the employer's property or to abstain from proselytizing during working hours). But when an employer believes that such rules are being transgressed, he will ordinarily avail himself of his "full freedom to hire and fire" and dismiss the offenders. Hence in this type of case, too, it devolves upon the discharged workers or their union to institute the breach of contract proceedings — if the matter is to be litigated at all.

No attempt will be made here to catalog all the different kinds of disputes brought before the court by the unions. As one might expect, the range of questions covered is approximately the same as that for local disputes in general, as outlined in Chapter XII. Among the categories listed in the index of the Labor Court's decisions, the following may be mentioned as containing the largest number of cases:

[15] Cf. Agreement between Wood Products Association and Wood Products Union, 1937, p. 7.

Hiring, Dismissal, Hours of Work, Time Rate Classification, Piecework, Overtime, Vacations, and Sickness Compensation. The dismissal group — comprising mainly union allegations of unjustifiable discharge — is especially noteworthy, in that the great majority of these cases have gone against the workers. Even when the complaints have alleged discrimination because of union activity, the court has decided on a number of occasions that no breach of the "right to organize" clause had occurred.[16] On the other hand most of the decisions in sickness compensation cases have been favorable to the workers.[17] In the other categories mentioned, the outcome has been more or less evenly divided between union and employer victories.

EMPLOYER-INITIATED DAMAGE SUITS

Most of the employer-initiated suits are concerned with incidents involving fairly sizable numbers of workers — ordinarily at least five, frequently more.[18] By far the most common complaint is that of "unlawful coercive action" (*avtalsstridig stridsåtgärd*) — i.e., striking and/or blockading during the agreement period. Although they constitute only a small proportion of all stoppages in point of total workers involved, local strikes and blockades of this sort still occur now and then, especially in the more recently organized and less well-disciplined occupations, and among the building workers — the "bad boys" of the Swedish trade union family. When such measures are carried out in the open, the complainant concern usually has a clearcut case, since the Collective Agreement Law expressly prohibits stoppages during a contract's operable life. Consequently in most

[16] See, e.g., Labor Court judgments listed in *Sakregister till Arbetsdomstolens Domar*, 1929–1934, pp. 25–36, 39–40.

[17] *Ibid.*, pp. 77–81.

[18] This obviously follows from what has been said above. Only when the number of workpeople breaking an agreement provision is sufficiently large so that it becomes inexpedient to dispense with their services will the employer refrain from exercising his "right to fire" and institute legal proceedings to enforce compliance instead.

instances of this kind, the plaintiff wins an easy victory and collects heavy damages.

Occasionally, however, a group of workers will resort to "undercover" methods of applying pressure, and then it becomes a much more difficult matter to show that a breach of agreement obligation has been committed. Suppose, for example, that the owner of a printing establishment dismisses a certain worker who is a prominent member of the local union, in the face of protests from the rest of the workpeople in his plant. A day or two later one of them "hands in his notice" and leaves. The next day another one quits. Others follow suit, at intervals of two or three days until at last the shop is practically depopulated and the owner either has to curtail production or shut down entirely. An action of this sort, if undertaken collectively and with coercive intent against the employer, constitutes a "secret strike."

The employer now advertises for new help but very few people apply, and those who do, and are accepted, leave after a week or so. If this situation comes about because the "self-dismissed" workers, either directly or through their local union, have persuaded other printers in the locality not to work for the "struck" employer, it is considered to be a "secret blockade."

It may, obviously, be next to impossible to prove conclusively that such occurrences are based on concerted action, especially if the workers involved are well organized and highly solidaristic — as they are in most of the older Swedish unions. For this reason an employer usually thinks twice before instituting legal proceedings, even when he is convinced that the union is carrying on an undercover campaign against him. Nevertheless, at least a dozen cases of alleged secret coercive action have been brought before the Labor Court, and in almost every instance the worker side has been found guilty of breach of contract and has had to pay damages.[19]

[19] See, e.g., the following decisions of the court (published in *Arbetsdomstolens Domar* for the respective years): 1931, No. 52; 1932, Nos. 44, 85; 1934, Nos. 61, 62, 64; 1937, Nos. 93, 124.

Another way in which local groups of workers sometimes attempt to apply pressure is by deliberate reduction of their working speed. This may occur when an employer decides to place on a time rate basis a job which the workers feel should be paid for by results. Such cases are seldom litigated, mainly because of the extreme difficulty of establishing objective evidence that conscious withholding of effort has taken place. However, in one famous suit, the court found that a gang of bricklayers on an apartment house project in Stockholm "had carried on the work at a slower rate than that which (the employer), with full consideration of the difficulties involved, had a right to expect . . . manifestly for the purpose of exerting influence in the matter of piece rate setting." The eleven workers were therefore ordered to pay damages of 200 kronor each, and the employer was freed from any liability for having discharged them.[20]

PRECEDENT-MAKING DECISIONS AND UNION SENTIMENT

The Labor Court is now an established part of the country's bargaining institution and is generally recognized as such, both in union and in employer circles. Its acceptance by the unions is particularly noteworthy, in view of their earlier hostility toward any judicial intervention by the state. The discovery that the power to sue could be used effectively against as well as by the employers, coupled with the legal limitation on the amount of damages which individual workers could be required to pay, was undoubtedly a major factor in bringing about this change of attitude. In all probability, the large number of unanimous decisions has also had a good deal to do with it. Not infrequently, in such cases, the verdict goes against the union; when this happens, the workers' dissatisfaction with the outcome is bound to be tempered somewhat by the knowledge that their own representatives have concurred in it.

Nevertheless, there is a feeling prevalent on the worker side that the unions have not fared as well at the Labor

[20] See *Arbetsdomstolens Domar*, 1934, Decision No. 132.

Court's hands as the employers have. The chief source of grievance is the fact that the court's decisions frequently assume the character of legal precedents, applicable to all subsequent cases in which the issue and attendant circumstances are similar in nature. This, it is claimed, tends to freeze the conditions of employment in their present status, and thus militates against the attainment of a "fair balance of advantage" between workers and employers — a state of affairs which, according to union philosophy, is still far from being established.

This argument seems invalid at first sight, for the court's function is to *interpret* collective contracts, which implies neither improvement nor worsening of the terms during life of the agreement. However, it should be remembered that every agreement contains certain provisions which are capable of precise interpretation only when applied to specific occurrences. (Clauses dealing with discriminatory treatment and dismissals "for cause" are illustrative.) When a judgment involving such a provision is rendered, it will usually reflect not only the social and economic philosophy of the court's membership but also, in some measure, current public opinion in the matter.

The implications of the precedent-setting rule in such instances are fairly clear. Thus a decision handed down in 1940, if based on a precedent established ten years previously, would tend to perpetuate the pro-status quo sentiment of the semi-conservative government then in power, which had appointed the neutral members of the court; whereas if the case were decided on its own merits, the fact of a labor government and a strongly pro-labor public opinion in 1940 would very likely influence the opinion of the judges in the direction favorable to an extension of "workers' rights."

A cursory survey of the more important precedent-setting decisions indicates that the misgivings of the unionists are not entirely unfounded, for most of them have been unfavorable to the union cause. Several of the decisions already mentioned are of this kind — e.g., the one upholding "temporary" piece rates [21] and those condemning secret strikes and blockades.

The most significant of all these "anti-union" precedents, however, is that contained in Judgment No. 1932: 100. In this case a chauffeurs' union in Gothenburg was suing a local transportation company, the allegation being that it had discharged a certain bus driver without proper cause. The court declared that the matter was concerned exclusively with the (verbal) "work contract" between the individual worker and the employer, and that, consequently, the company was under no legal obligation to give any reasons at all for dismissing the bus driver.

In effect, this ruling put the stamp of legal sanction on the "Section 23 clause" in the S. E. F. agreements, which gives the employer the right "to engage and dismiss workers at his own discretion." [22] What is more, the principle now applied to *non*-S. E. F. employers as well, provided nothing to the contrary was specified in their contracts.

The organized workers, who had been striving for more than a decade to secure a modification of this provision, regarded the decision as a serious blow to their aspirations. And such, indeed, it proved to be. In the immediately ensuing years, the employers — both organized and independent — became increasingly militant in wielding the discharge weapon, and with the Labor Court rigorously applying the precedent of 1932, the unions found it difficult to offer any effective resistance to their aggression.

The balance of legal approval was partially restored in 1936, when Parliament passed an act which established by law, for the first time, the right of associations of workers to exist and to bargain with employers. This law was not designed primarily to fortify the position of the wage earners, since their organizing and bargaining rights were already well established *de facto*, but rather to extend these rights to the "white collar" workers — office clerks, bank personnel, foremen, etc. — whose attempts to organize had

[21] See Chapter XIV, p. 244.

[22] Cf. Chapter V, p. 88.

always been vigorously opposed by the managers in most lines of business.[23] But it did have the effect of making the employers, especially those outside the S. E. F., more circumspect in exercising the dismissal prerogative. For the new law placed a definitive limitation on the 1932 precedent, saying, in effect, that the employer's "full freedom" to terminate the individual employment contract only applied in so far as it did not infringe on the employee's right to organize and bargain.

Now and again a precedent-making decision has gone in favor of the worker side. The best known of these, perhaps, is the so-called "burden of proof ruling," handed down in 1931.[24] The gist of this decision is that in cases of alleged discrimination against workers for union activity, the employer must furnish satisfactory evidence of the existence of other valid and sufficient grounds for the punitive action. However, the fruits of this victory have been rather meager. In at least half the discrimination suits subsequently brought before the court, the judges have deemed the evidence produced by the defendants to be "sufficient," and have forthwith disallowed the unions' contentions.

The present attitude of organized Swedish labor toward the Collective Agreement Law and the Labor Court is summarized fairly accurately in the following resolution, adopted by the 1936 S. F. T. U. congress:

> The resolutions committee supports the view . . . that the solution of true interpretational disputes (*verkliga rättstvister*) through coercive measures is not to be recommended.
>
> The presupposition for all legislation has always been that of equality of advantage between opposing parties, in the eyes of the law. Such equality does not exist at the present time in the sphere of the collective agreement and, as a consequence, the application of the law has worked to the detriment of the workers in certain respects. The committee discerns in the rise of the working class as a force in the community a possibility of revising

[23] The significance of this law to the white collar workers is discussed in Chapter XVIII.

[24] Decision No. 107.

> the currently effective statutes in the field of labor law . . . and proposes that the congress declare itself in favor of undertaking such measures in connection with these statutes as will guarantee to the workers that position of equality which constitutes the foundation of all law making.[25]

In a word, the unions are in favor of changing, rather than repealing, the laws. And with organized labor's own party at the helm of government, it is not at all unlikely that they might succeed in doing so. Just what changes they propose to make has, however, not yet been revealed.

[25] *Protokoll Förda Vid Landsorganisationens Elfte Ordinarie Kongress* (Stockholm, 1936), p. 560.

PART FIVE

CONCLUSION

CHAPTER XVI

THE SIGNIFICANCE OF THE SWEDISH SYSTEM OF BARGAINING

As STATED at the outset, the primary purpose of this book has been to present an expository picture of the Swedish collective bargaining system. The foregoing account of how agreements are regulated by law brings to a close the writer's attempt to fulfill this task. However, a study of collective bargaining could hardly be called complete without some appraisal of its *results* — that is, of the effects of this institution on the operation of the entire economic and social unit of which it is a part.

CHARACTERISTICS OF THE SYSTEM IN SUMMARY

Before essaying such an appraisal, it will be well to review briefly the main features of the bargaining system, particularly those which are generally approved of on both sides and which, consequently, constitute the permanent basis of the country's industrial-relations setup at the present time.

In the first place, the bulk of both workers and employers are banded together by industries, in associations of nation-wide scope. On the management side, this form of organization was a foregone conclusion almost from the start. Industrial unionism is of more recent origin, but it has unquestionably come to stay. No other structural makeup would be acceptable to the employers; and the wage earner groups which still cling to craftism comprise only a small proportion of organized workerdom.

The framework of the bargaining institution is also both national and industrial in character, since each of the major agreements covers an entire industry, and all wage earner occupations within that industry. These agreements are, therefore, essentially sets of standards, making the conditions of work uniform throughout the respective branches of economic activity to which they apply. And while it is recognized that large-scale bargaining does not preclude inequities in particular instances, both sides maintain that it produces the most satisfactory *overall* results.

With respect to general working conditions (as distinguished from the terms of payment for work) the degree of standardization is even greater than the existence of an agreement for each industry would indicate. Many of the provisions relating to this phase of the labor bargain are either identical or closely similar in *all* agreements, thus constituting, in effect, standards or norms for the country's working force as a whole. These "common rules" reflect the influence of the central employers' organization, on the one hand, and of the federation of national unions, on the other.

Minimum hourly rates, graduated according to age, experience, skill requirements, and geographical variations in the cost of living, constitute the fundamental wage determinants of the agreement system. In addition to defining the least permissible amount of hourly earnings, these rates are taken as the starting point in negotiating all other terms of payment for labor.

Actual compensation for work is based on the amount of work done, rather than on the time spent, in all industries and occupations which are adapted to this method of determining wages. Piece rates are usually, though not always, established through large-scale bargaining, and incorporated in collective wage contracts which run concurrently with the main agreements.

The bargaining process falls into two distinct phases: agreement making and adjustment. The making of new agreements, while based on accepted practices rather than written rules, follows an established procedure which is substantially the same in all industries. Most of this type of bargaining takes place at negotiation conferences between representative delegations of the national unions and the corresponding employers' associations.

Impartial mediators, appointed by the government, play an important part in expediting this process, and their intervention is approved of, and even solicited, by both workers and managers. But aside from the obligation to heed the mediators' call to negotiate, there are no legal restraints on freedom of action in contract making disputes. Nor would any such restraints be welcomed. Both sides jealously guard the right to resort to coercive measures, if satisfactory terms cannot be obtained through peaceful parleying. As a result, the concluding of new agreements is sometimes considerably delayed by the occurrence of strikes and lockouts. However, serious stoppages of work have been markedly less numerous in recent years than formerly.

The adjustment of disputes which arise while agreements are in force is primarily a local function. Even in this sphere of employer-employee relations established and uniform practices are adhered to over the larger part of the industrial field. Local differences which cannot be ironed out on the ground are commonly referred to the central worker and employer organizations for settlement. Strikes and lockouts occasioned by intra-agreement-period disputes are prohibited by the law of the land, which also prescribes the submission of such disputes to a special labor court for final adjudication. These legal checks, like state-sponsored mediation, have been accepted by both sides as justifiable encroachments on the traditional domain of free bilateral dealings.

COLLECTIVE BARGAINING AND THE NATIONAL INCOME

Owing to the difficulties of accounting for the many other variable factors acting on the productive and consumptive mechanism at any given time, no thoroughgoing analysis of the economic consequences of the Swedish method of trading in labor can be undertaken here. It is possible, however, to make a few general and more or less self-evident observations which may throw some light on the problem. In so doing, we shall consider first the incidence of collective bargaining on the Swedish economy as a whole, and thereafter its significance to the two economic groups most directly associated with it, namely labor and management.

If one were to put the question to a representative group of economists, a substantial proportion of them would undoubtedly hold that economic progress cannot be as rapid when collective bargaining prevails as when the terms of employment are determined by management alone. And it must be admitted that the arguments supporting this contention carry a great deal of weight. Strong unions are prone to demand ever higher and higher wages, which tends to reduce profits and hence to discourage businessmen from expanding their productive enterprises. They press for expensive improvements in working conditions, which further decreases the margin of profit. They impose restrictive rules regarding hours of work, hiring and dismissal, and the introduction of labor-saving machinery, which tie the entrepreneur's hands and prevent him from operating his establishment efficiently. Finally, bilateral determination of the terms of labor inevitably brings disagreements, and consequently stoppages of work, with resultant loss of production.

By most of these criteria, collective bargaining should have been acting as a definite drag on Sweden's economic advance. It cannot be said that the Swedish unions have been over-modest in their demands for better wages and conditions. True, they have not made restrictive working rules a major issue, nor have they been unduly aggressive with respect to hours of work. On the other hand, they have striven determinedly (and successfully) for longer paid vacations. Stoppages of work — lockouts as well as strikes — have been numerous and frequently long drawn out. Until recently, in fact, the proportion of workers involved in stoppages has, on the average, been rather higher in Sweden than in most other countries.[1]

But the presumption of relatively slow progress to which these facts point is not borne out by the record of the country's economic evolution. During the past forty years — approximately the period in which collective bargaining has been carried on on a national scale — Sweden has devel-

[1] See *supra*, p. 166.

oped from a poor farming country into a well-to-do and progressive nation. From 1900 to 1930, per capita real income increased by somewhat more than 60 per cent.[2] The volume of industrial production — i.e., the products of all factories — approximately trebled during this same interval, while the population grew by only 20 per cent. Agricultural production increased in about the same proportion as the population, so that the country continued to supply most of its own needs in the matter of food. The volume of foreign trade was more than twice as great at the end of the period as at the beginning.[3]

These indicators of economic advance compare very favorably with corresponding data for the United States, where unionism has been, on the whole, weak and ineffective, and where collective bargaining has affected the terms of employment only to a minor extent. The rise in real income per head in this country during the first three decades of the present century was, if anything, smaller than in Sweden, although the absolute level was undoubtedly higher throughout.[4] Industrial production increased in about the same proportion here as in Sweden,[5] but the population expanded by some 60 per cent, so that in per capita terms the rise in production was considerably smaller. In other branches of

[2] E. Lindahl and others, *National Income of Sweden, 1861–1930* (Stockholm, 1937), Part One, p. 248.

[3] Data from *Statistisk Årsbok för Sverige, 1937*. It may also be pointed out that Sweden competes successfully in the world markets with a number of relatively weakly unionized countries — with, e.g., Finland in lumber and pulp, and with the United States in various types of metal products.

[4] According to one fairly dependable estimate, national income per capita in the United States, in terms of "1926 dollars," rose by approximately 50 per cent from 1900 to 1930, the figure for the latter year being $661. (R. T. Bye and W. W. Hewett, *Applied Economics*, third edition, revised, New York, 1938, pp. 21–22.) The corresponding figure for Sweden for 1930, according to the University of Sockholm study, was 1370 kronor. (Lindahl, *op. cit.*, p. 237.) If one takes the real value of the krona as being somewhere between 35 and 40 cents (admittedly a very rough estimate) this figure becomes approximately $500.

[5] See S. H. Patterson and K. W. H. Scholz, *Economic Problems of Modern Life* (New York, 1937), p. 563.

economic activity, also, the record of the United States is certainly no more impressive than that of Sweden, and in some respects it is decidedly less so.

It cannot, of course, be claimed that the prevalence of collective bargaining is in any important degree the *cause* of the notable headway which Sweden has made in the economic sphere. The richness of the country's natural resources, the homogeneity, industry, and practical-mindedness of its people, its location, and other inherent factors have undoubtedly had more to do with it than any single institutional feature of the Swedish economy. On the other hand, unionism and bargaining cannot, on balance, have been retarding Sweden's progress. It is hardly possible that the country could have advanced as rapidly as it has if this were the case. In other words, there is reason to presume that large-scale collective bargaining as practised in Sweden has certain beneficial aspects which tend to offset the undesirable features enumerated above. In a subsequent section we shall attempt to show how the Swedish employers — and through them the nation as a whole — have derived positive advantages from deciding the terms of work collectively on a country-wide basis.

COLLECTIVE BARGAINING AND THE TREND IN TERMS OF WORK

Turning now to the second phase of our inquiry, we find that it is equally difficult to say with any definiteness whether the economic status of the Swedish wage earners has improved as a result of collective bargaining. According to the familiar argument of the union apologists, strong organizations, capable of forcing employer recognition and of holding their own both in conference and conflict, are the workers' only means of avoiding exploitation by the managers of enterprise — i.e., of receiving a reward equal to the full net value of their efforts, and not something less. If there is any validity in this contention, the workers of Sweden should be in a better position with respect to income than those of most other nations, for the Swedish union movement is one of the strongest, in proportion to the country's size, to be found anywhere.

The average real income of Swedish wage earners at the present time is, in point of fact, one of the highest in Europe.[6] But it would be invalid to say that the power of worker organization is the only or even the major force responsible for raising it to this high level. As in the case of average *national* income, it seems probable that other — mainly noninstitutional — factors have played at least as prominent a part.

This thesis is strengthened if one compares the available statistics on wages in Sweden and the United States. From 1900 to 1930 (to take the same interval as before) real annual wages in Sweden rose by approximately 55 per cent,[7] as against somewhat less than 50 per cent in the United States.[8] Considering the rather wide limits of error involved in the estimates on which these figures are based, it seems admissible to conclude that the increase in wages was substantially the same in both countries. The absolute level of wages, on the other hand, was at least 25 per cent higher in the United States throughout the entire period.[9] Thus, whatever role the power of unionism may have had in raising the standard of living of the Swedish wage earners, the data for the United States show beyond peradventure that a high wage scale can also be attained, in a country richly endowed with natural resources, even when organization among workers is comparatively weak and ineffective.

A comparison of the trend and present status of nonwage terms of work in the two countries shows a substantially similar picture. So far as hours of work are concerned, the

[6] See, e.g., the comparative wage figures in Styrman, *op. cit.*, p. 231, and G. R. Mitchison, "Wages and the Cost of Living," in *Democratic Sweden*, M. Cole and C. Smith, editors.

[7] G. Bagge and others, *Wages in Sweden, 1860–1930* (Stockholm, 1935), Part Two, p. 241; and Lindahl, *op. cit.*, Part One, p. 247.

[8] H. A. Millis and R. E. Montgomery, *Labor's Progress and Some Basic Labor Problems* (New York, 1938), pp. 98, 113, 120.

[9] Millis and Montgomery, *op. cit.*, p. 104; and *Lönestatistisk Årsbok*, 1936, p. 49.

available data indicate that Swedish and American workers have fared about equally well during most of the period, with a distinct advantage for the latter in very recent years. The average work week in Sweden, it will be remembered, was reduced from 55 to 48 hours in 1919, as a result of legislation passed in that year. In the United States, the average was still approximately 50 hours at this time, and it remained substantially unchanged until 1930.[10] Since then, however, hours in American industry have been shortened by more than 20 per cent,[11] whereas in Sweden they have decreased little, if at all, since the advent of the Forty-eight Hour Law.[12]

In the sphere of "job control" the honors are also about equally divided. The power of decision in matters pertaining to dismissals, layoffs, rehiring, etc., is still defined in the Swedish agreements as an exclusive function of management, although in practice the employer takes considerable account of union sentiment in deciding such questions. In many *union* plants in the United States, on the other hand, bilateral job control is expressly stipulated in the contract.[13]

In certain other respects the Swedish workers have done considerably better. For example, paid vacations have been the rule in Sweden for at least twenty years, whereas in this country they have become fairly common only within the past half-decade, and are still by no means universal. Similarly, sick-leave compensation and free medical care are far

[10] Millis and Montgomery, *op. cit.*, pp. 470, 474.

[11] *Ibid.*, p. 485.

[12] See Mitchison, *op. cit.*, p. 189.

[13] The validity of any comparisons in this phase of industrial relations on a country-wide basis must of necessity be very doubtful, owing to the highly dynamic status of unionism and collective bargaining in the United States at the present time. As to the handling of grievances, there is no doubt that, prior to the recent rapid advance of American unionism, the degree of protection against arbitrary treatment on the job was on the whole much higher in Sweden than in the United States. However, this statement requires modification in the light of more recent occurrences, for many of the new unions in this country have succeeded in introducing grievance-adjustment clauses in their contracts, and most of the schemes thus provided for seem to be "working" reasonably well.

more prevalent in the former country. But on the whole, the improvement in working conditions during the past quarter century has not been appreciably greater in Sweden than in the United States.

The indefiniteness which shrouds the problem of unionism's effectiveness in bettering the worker's economic status should not, however, be permitted to obscure the fact that Swedish wages and working conditions have improved very substantially during the period in which collective negotiation has been the accepted method of settling the terms of employment, and that Sweden is today well up in the forefront among nations in respect of wage earner living standards. It is fairly safe to conclude from this that the workers of Sweden are at least no worse off, pecuniarily speaking, than they would have been if they had never attempted to organize.

The importance of this conclusion becomes apparent if, instead of considering only the economic effects of collective bargaining, one takes a somewhat broader point of view. Unionism in Sweden represents, more truly perhaps than in any other country, a spontaneous movement of the mass of wage earners. The history of the Swedish labor movement establishes this as an indubitable fact. Unionization has proceeded steadily and surely, permeating ever more and more "unorganizable" industries and occupations, until today virtually every branch of economic activity is organized. And while union proselytizing in nonunion industries has played a not inconsiderable part in expediting the process, in the last analysis the great bulk of workers have "joined up" because they wanted to.

By the same token, collective settlement of the terms of work represents, in the first instance, the response to a demand emanating from the mass of Swedish workpeople. It is the logical concomitant, and indeed the principal *raison d'être*, of the union movement. And although the main motive behind this demand is, no doubt, the desire for more of the material perquisites of living, it is by no means the only motive. The workers of Sweden also regard collective bargaining as being, to an important degree, an end in itself. In other words, even if they did not believe that it would result in higher wages and a more satisfying existence in general, they would still want to have a voice in determining the circumstances of their workaday life.

When this *psychological* aspect is included in its purview, therefore, the answer to the question of whether the Swedish workers are better off under collective bargaining than they would otherwise have been becomes a simple and unequivocal affirmative. They can experience the fact of a higher level of living today than in the past. They know, also, that their confrères in most other countries are considerably less well off. Finally, they have what is perhaps the most valued imponderable possession of free men — a share in deciding the conditions in which they must move and have their being.[14]

UNIONISM, EMPLOYER ORGANIZATION AND PROFITS

Of the adverse aspects of collective bargaining, from the viewpoint of the owners and managers of enterprise, some mention has already been made. Restated briefly, the allegation is that the existence of strong unions, and the con-

[14] No less important is the part which union organization has played in enabling the Swedish workers to achieve unity and effective action in the political sphere. The Social-Democratic Party, which during the past four years has had a clear majority in both houses of Parliament and hence a safe control of the government, is in a very real sense the "political arm" of the Swedish labor movement. No detailed discussion of the various ways in which organization on the economic front has contributed to the attainment of solidarity on the political front will be attempted here. It is safe to say, however, that a political body with the numerical strength and militancy of the Swedish Social-Democratic Party of today could never have been built up if there had not been developed simultaneously, or rather slightly in advance of it, an equally powerful and militant wage earner organization. Most Swedish workers set a great deal of store in a high pecuniary level of living; and their strong faith in the possibility of obtaining more of the good things of life through trade union action has undoubtedly been an important factor in enabling them to hold together in the sphere of political activity, where the desired objectives are considerably more remote and less easily definable in terms of material benefits to the individual worker.

sequent necessity of consulting with them in setting the conditions of labor, increases production costs and prevents the businessman from operating his establishment at its optimum efficiency. The reward of ownership and management is thereby reduced and, as a secondary result, savers become reluctant to invest their capital, and managers their efforts, in business ventures.

However, as has been shown, it is unlikely that the *net* effect of unionism and bargaining on entrepreneurial incentive in Sweden has been an adverse one. It seems reasonable to suppose that the country's industrial apparatus could not have expanded threefold in thirty years if those responsible for its functioning were constantly facing losses, or even a serious curtailment in profits.

In order to verify the validity of this supposition, it would be desirable to have direct statistical evidence of the trend of industrial profits during the period under discussion. Unfortunately, such evidence is not available. Some indication of the movement of the return on capital and managerial ability may, however, be obtained from data already given. As noted, the average income of industrial wage earners rose by about 55 per cent during the first three decades of the century. In the same span of time the increase in the average income of *all* classes was somewhat more than 60 per cent. Making allowances for the rather wide margins of error involved in estimates of this type one would say, therefore, that wage earner and nonwage earner income increased at about the same rate.

Now "nonwage earner income" is not synonymous with "return to owners and managers of business enterprise," but, rather, considerably more inclusive. But it is possible to arrive at a somewhat closer approximation to the latter by a process of elimination. Thus we find that in the group of occupations including the independent professions and public administration, income rose somewhat more than in the economy as a whole, while in agriculture and forestry the rise was considerably less.[15] It follows that in the *remainder*

[15] Lindahl, *op. cit.*, p. 237.

of the economic structure, income must have increased in at least as great a proportion as total national income. And although this residue still includes other groups besides owners and managers of industry proper, it is close enough for practical purposes. One may conclude, then, that the reward for entrepreneurship showed an improvement at least equal to, and possibly somewhat better than, the return for wage work.

Nor is this result especially difficult to explain. It is probably due to some extent to a certain moderation on the part of the organized workers themselves. On the whole, the Swedish unions have not pressed unduly hard for limitations on the introduction of innovations and other restrictive rules, but have rather left these matters in large measure to managerial discretion. With respect to hours of work, also, the employers have no great cause to complain that the unions have obstructed efficiency. There has even been a tendency, especially in recent years, to keep demands for wage increases down to "reasonable" proportions — that is to say, within the limits dictated by marginal productivity considerations.[16] But the importance of this latter point must not be overemphasized; for if one takes the entire industrial-relations history of the country into account, the upward pressure exerted on wages by organized labor in Sweden has been quite in keeping with traditional union policy the world over.

From the evidence adduced in this study, however, it must be apparent that the principal reason why labor has not "taken out" a disproportionately large share of the fruits of enterprise is that there has been a constant and powerful counterpressure from the employer side. By forming strong combinations of their own, the business managers of Sweden have prevented the unions from gaining any permanent advantage over them; and have, moreover, been able to influence the development of collective bargaining very materially

[16] Such leaders of the S. F. T. U. as August Lindberg, Gunnar Andersson and Albin Lind have repeatedly advocated this policy in their talks and writings during the past few years. Among some of the older *constituent unions*, however, the idea finds considerably less favor.

in accordance with their own ideas and interests.[17] This "employers' united front" occupies such an important place in the Swedish industrial-relations setup that it seems worth while to recount some of its salient features, even at the risk of repetition.

It was started more than thirty years ago as a defense measure against union aggression, and its subsequent growth has followed closely that of the labor movement. At the present time the bulk of employers in each major branch of productive activity are organized in industry associations, most of which in turn are members of a comprehensive federation. While these associations are less inclusive, from the standpoint of worker coverage, than the trade unions, this disadvantage is largely offset by the more concentrated financial and administrative control which the organized managers have built up. This superior centralization manifests itself at the conference table, where the Employers' Federation can constitute itself the deciding entity in any important contingency, whereas the individual national unions have the final word on the worker side. It is also manifested in the large-scale lockout, in which coercive action can be instituted over a wide front, and backed by the financial strength of the entire Federation.

It is through this powerful coöperative apparatus that the managers of Sweden's industries have succeeded in keeping an effective checkrein on union demands. And the conclusion would seem warranted that it is this, more than any other single factor, which has enabled them to preserve a satisfactory margin between receipts and production costs.

That they might have fared even better if there had been no bargaining system at all, and all terms of work had been decided by management alone cannot, of course, be denied.

[17] For example, it may be recalled that pressure from the industrially organized employers played a prominent part in bringing about the "successive transition" from craft to industrial unionism. By contrast, American employers have taken little interest in the structural form of workers' organizations — a wholly understandable apathy, in view of the prevalent belief among them that there is no place in industry for unions of any kind.

But the posing of this possibility is hardly apposite to our discussion. For unionism was already a potent force in Sweden long before any definitive and representative employer policy had evolved, and hence managers in the unionized portion of industry had, in reality, no choice in the matter. When the first employer groups were finally formed in the early years of the present century they might, indeed, have made it their purpose to destroy the workers' organizations, just as certain employer alliances in the United States were doing. Instead they decided that the only feasible course was to recognize and bargain with the unions on an equal footing, and to depend on counterorganization for upholding their own interests. The adoption of this policy was based primarily on the fact that the existing unions were already too strong to be easily crushed. But it was also predicated in part on a belief that unionism would continue to gain headway, despite any efforts on their part to put it down.

In view of the spontaneous character of the Swedish labor movement, and of its almost phenomenal growth in the three ensuing decades, it is difficult to avoid the conclusion that the employers made a wise choice. At any rate, a policy designed to defeat or prevent worker organization would certainly have been far more costly and troublesome, and would probably have had to be abandoned eventually anyway.

It is worth reëmphasizing, at this point, that the process of unionization is today substantially completed. When one considers that business enterprise in Sweden is showing as good or better profits today than ever before, the significance of this fact for owners and managers becomes apparent. In the past, organized employerdom has constantly had to reckon with the prospective increase in the size and power of the opposition, the extent of which could never be accurately known.[18] But the numerical strength of the union movement

[18] That management's task is more difficult when unionism is expanding continually than when it remains quiescent or nearly so is fairly obvious. The United States furnishes an example of the latter situation. During the

has now reached a level not far from the upper limit of possibility, and any future growth can hardly add much to aggregate worker bargaining power. At the same time the employers have increased their own collective strength to a point where they are well able to hold their own against the unions. Thus one important source of uncertainty in the management of business has been largely, if not entirely, eliminated. To put it somewhat more generally, industrial relations in Sweden have attained a state of virtual equilibrium, at the stage of working class evolution where such equilibrium is most likely to be permanent.

HOW BARGAINING BENEFITS MANAGEMENT

In the foregoing discussion, we have dealt with advantages which the employers have gained primarily through their own capacity for effective organization. These are largely negative in nature, in that they simply enable management

period we are considering, the degree of unionization in this country has been comparatively small. In a number of important industries, worker organization has been practically non-existent up until very recently. Most other industries have been only partly organized, with the union plants usually in the minority. Whatever their ideas as to the proper or desirable wage level, the workers in the unionized plants, taken as a group, have had to keep their demands sufficiently modest to permit the employers to meet the competition of the nonunion establishments; or, failing to do so, have suffered a reduction in employment — either through a shift of consumers and investors to un-unionized concerns, or as a result of union plants migrating to nonunion territory.

At the same time, the prospect of future unionization has been no more than a minor source of concern to nonunion employers, for the progress of the American labor movement has been, on the average, very slow. On the whole, therefore, union pressure on the terms of work has not been a serious problem for management in the United States.

On the other hand, consideration of union demands has been an ever-present necessity in business planning in Sweden. In all the important fabrication industries, a majority of the establishments have been organized for at least two decades. Moreover, the un-unionized plants have been unable to ignore the factor of prospective organization, for the movement has been pushing forward almost continuously into new territory. This factor has also been a serious deterrent to savers seeking to shift their investments from union to nonunion concerns, and to employers who might entertain thoughts of migrating as a means of escaping the scourge.

to avoid the burdensome costs which unions, if left unchecked, are prone to impose on it. But the present status of Sweden's industrial relations also brings to the employers certain positive benefits — and certain disadvantages — which would scarcely be present in the absence of the bargaining system. In the main, the benefits are traceable to the fact that bargaining in Sweden has attained a mature stage of development, in makeup and functioning as well as extent of coverage — in other words, that it is a *system*, of truly national proportions.

To begin with, the bargaining process is in a real sense nationally standardized. The making of new agreements follows an established procedure which is substantially the same in all industries, and is carried on, for the most part, between corresponding national organizations. Even in "interim disputes," the adjustment of which is primarily a local function, established and uniform practices are adhered to practically throughout.

The terms of work arrived at through this process are also, in the main, industry-wide in scope. Indeed, as has been shown, the standardization with respect to nonwage terms is not confined within the limits of particular lines of business, but is substantially universal over all industry. What is more, this phase of the labor bargain is unlikely to undergo any drastic changes in the future, since in most instances the unions have already carried their drive for improved conditions well up toward the limit of bargaining possibilities. Wage terms, while necessarily more varied, are centrally determined in the majority of industries, and usually for a year or more in advance. In a few important lines, however, where the diversity of products or other circumstances render centralized wage making impracticable, the local bargaining parties are given considerable discretion. Nevertheless, schedules of minimum hourly rates, graduated according to the several criteria already enumerated, are taken as the fundamental wage determinants even in these industries.

Even the bargaining tactics employed by the parties to

the collective contract are fairly well standardized over the several branches of industry, and hence are essentially a part of the common stock of knowledge, rather than the individual property of the particular party. Moreover, as a result of having participated in the same agreement conferences for an extended period of years, the worker and employer representatives in each industry are well acquainted with each other's personal traits and idiosyncrasies — a highly important factor in the smooth operation of negotiation procedure. In short, each side is able to make a good estimate, in any given situation, of the stand which the other side is likely to take and the concessions it will be prepared to offer.

With the handling of labor relations thus codified and stabilized on a national basis, it must be apparent that the problem of managing business enterprise is considerably simplified. The individual employer, by delegating the bargaining and decision making power to his association, is spared the task of negotiating agreements with his own particular group of employees. At the same time, his chances of securing favorable terms are improved, for the "official negotiators" of the association are highly skilled and experienced specialists in the art of bargaining, and hence a better match for the union leaders than the employer himself would be.

Again, by being affiliated with the "system," he avoids much of the uncertainty ordinarily involved in business planning. Once the agreement is concluded, he is practically insured against stoppages or disruptions for the period of its operable life. Moreover, with wage rates fixed for a similar period in advance, the conjectural element in his production budget is materially reduced. And since he also knows what other firms and industries must pay for labor, he is able to make a more accurate estimate of the strength of potential competition than would otherwise be possible. In a word, the predictability factor in business management in Sweden has been markedly improved as a result of systematized collective bargaining.

BARGAINING AND PRODUCTIVE EFFICIENCY

The question may legitimately be raised, at this point, whether bargaining on an industry-wide basis does not also bring serious disadvantages to many employers. This question is particularly pertinent in connection with the high degree of uniformity which the national agreements prescribe with respect to the terms of employment. For example, how is it possible for the relatively inefficient concerns in a given industry association to continue paying the same wages, granting the same vacations, affording the same sick leave allowances, etc. as their more fortunately situated competitors?

In discussing this aspect of centralized collective bargaining, it should be recalled that the firms in a particular organization are not governed by identically the same *wage scale.* On the contrary, there are considerable differentials from group to group, as provided by the cost-of-living adjustment device — the higher scales being applied mainly in the cities, the lower ones in the smaller towns and rural villages.[19]

Now productive efficiency depends, of course, to a considerable extent on the size of the establishment — and more so in Sweden, perhaps, than in the United States. The larger firms are able to "rationalize" to a high degree — i.e., to utilize large-scale equipment and methods, and practise minute division of labor — whereas for most small concerns this is possible only to a minor extent. At the same time, there are few enterprises in Sweden sufficiently large to be "top-heavy." In many if not most industries, moreover, the larger establishments are located predominantly in the cities, and the smaller ones in the outlying districts. This is especially the case in such lines as lumber products, the building trades, printing, and garment making. But it is also true in large measure of certain of the mass production industries, particularly textiles and pulp manufacture.

Thus we see that under the Swedish bargaining scheme

[19] See *supra,* Chapter VII.

the *inherently* inefficient concerns (if one may term them such) are in reality afforded a considerable measure of assistance in the form of lower wage costs.[20] Nor is this by any means entirely a coincidence. When the geographical wage differentials were first established, this correlation between size of plant and efficiency was, in point of fact, a consideration only second in importance to the differences in the cost of living.

But there are also concerns which are inefficient for other reasons than those traceable to size of plant. In the main, such inefficiency is probably attributable to incompetent management. It may be said at once, however, that at the present time differences in efficiency arising from this cause do not constitute a serious obstacle to the smooth functioning of the centrally determined wage scheme. During the earlier stages of the bargaining system's development uniformity in wages and working conditions was, undoubtedly, oppressive to the firms with the least capable management. But with the continuance of uniformity through the ensuing decades these firms have of necessity had to reduce their other-than-labor expenses, in order to remain solvent. One would therefore expect that today, after thirty-five years of national collective bargaining, the total spread in efficiency among managers would be materially smaller, and consequently the burden of uniform labor costs for those in the lower half of the scale considerably less serious than formerly.[21]

[20] It should be remembered, too, that the prevalence of piecework is also an aid to backward concerns. Thus if, of two plants in the same cost-of-living group, one is equipped with slower, less up-to-date machinery than the other, its "production" wage costs will also be lower, approximately in proportion to the deficiency in its rate of output.

[21] In the above general discussion, no attempt has been made to explore all the factors underlying the widespread acceptance of industry-wide bargaining by Swedish business managers. In order to provide a really adequate explanation it would be necessary to take separate account of all the major industries, since the relevant circumstances are to a large extent different in each. This would require considerably closer and more detailed investigation than has been possible in the present survey.

The unions, for their part, are on the whole unsympathetic toward the idea of making special concessions to "high cost" employers. Instances of workers in particular establishments accepting lower wages in order to keep them from going under are not, it is true, entirely a rarity. An industry in which such instances are fairly common is iron and steel. In this industry, which is confined mainly to rural communities built around a single *järnbruk*, a rather wide divergence in interplant efficiency still persists. In setting the piece rates in many iron and steel plants, considerable weight is given to the individual employer's ability to pay. This practice has been followed for many years, and the Metal Workers' Union has not made any definitive attempt to do away with it. The principal reason for the union's acquiescence on this score is the low mobility of the *bruk* workers. Owing partly to their isolated location, and partly to the fact that the occupation is largely "hereditary," it would be very difficult to get them to move to other plants or industries if their own workplace should go to the wall.

But taking them by and large, the Swedish unions are opposed to making drastic exceptions to the national agreement rates for the sake of keeping backward concerns above water. Nor is there any widespread demand for such exceptions from the rank and file. Apart from the iron and steel workers and those in one or two other "mill village" occupations, the mobility of wage earners in Sweden is high in comparison with most other countries. For one thing, they have exceptionally small families. For another, they are more than ordinarily versatile in mechanical work, hence are able to shift from one type of work to another with comparative ease. Finally, the work opportunities are relatively plentiful, since most of Sweden's industries are composed of a large number of comparatively small firms. For the average Swedish worker, therefore, changing jobs is not an unduly serious matter, and consequently he has no great incentive to accept wage cuts in order to keep his present one.[22]

[22] Sweden also has an effectively functioning system of free public em-

It should be remembered, moreover, that the national unions, rather than the locals, are the significant units of worker organization in Sweden, and that a high degree of loyalty to the *förbund* exists among the individual members. Thus, even though the workers in a particular plant may be impelled, by the exigencies of their situation, to accept less than the "going rate," the desire to conform to the consensus of the national group acts as a powerful deterrent.

In the final analysis, however, the national agreement terms of work remain in force in the high cost plants because they are acceptable to the managers of these plants. And the ultimate reason therefor is, one may presume, that the advantages accruing from organization more than offset the hardships which these terms impose. It is, of course, impossible to compare these advantages and disadvantages quantitatively. But it must be evident that the need of a united front, sufficiently strong to meet the massed forces of the organized workers, is a factor of compelling importance to practically all productive enterprises in Sweden, whether below or above the average in technical efficiency. The fact remains, moreover, that a large number of comparatively inefficient firms have been adherents of the employers' movement for an extended period and — so far as one can judge — intend to remain within its fold. It would seem reasonable to suppose, therefore, that these concerns find it *profitable* to be a part of the centralized organizational scheme, despite the relatively high cost of labor which this entails.

---

ployment offices, which undoubtedly aids still further in keeping workers from feeling tied to a particular workplace. This system covers all fields of wage earner employment and is, moreover, nationally coördinated, so that an unemployed worker can be put in contact with a job opportunity anywhere in the country within a few days of its becoming available. During 1937 the employment service afforded placement for more than 350,000 applicants, approximately half of them in industry and trade. Kungliga Socialstyrelsen, *Social Work and Legislation in Sweden* (Stockholm, 1938), pp. 78–85. See also S. Skogh, "The Labor Market and Its Regulation," in *Social Problems and Policies in Sweden* (*Annals of the American Academy of Political and Social Science*, for May 1938).

By the same token, management's own evaluation of the bargaining system which national organization on both sides has made possible must carry a good deal of weight in any discussion of its results. The great majority of Swedish employers no longer regard unions and written collective contracts as necessary evils, but actually prefer them to verbal agreement with individual workers. On this point the writer has the assurance of the leaders of the Employers' Federation and its constituent associations, and of many other persons in a position to judge the consensus of employer opinion. By no means all the reasons underlying this change of attitude have been accounted for in our discussion. But one may safely say that it is due in large part to the substantial saving in time and trouble, the improvement in predictability, and above all the added stability which industry-wide collective bargaining has brought to the conduct of business enterprise.

CHAPTER XVII

WILL THE SWEDISH SCHEME OF BARGAINING WORK IN AMERICA?

TO THE AMERICAN READER, for whom this study is primarily intended, the discussion just concluded must inevitably suggest the question: Is the Swedish system of collective bargaining applicable in the United States? Employers in this country, in particular, have been much exercised over this question in the recent past.[1] We shall therefore consider it — albeit very briefly — from the employer's point of view.

[1] See, e.g., the papers and discussion presented at the American Management Association's Personnel Conference held at Chicago, February 15, 16, 17, 1939, and subsequently published by the association. Of especial interest are the two papers contained in the A.M.A.'s *Personnel Series No. 37*: "Objectives and Operations of the San Francisco Employers' Council," by Almon E. Roth; and "Are the British and Swedish Systems of Collective Bargaining Applicable in the United States?" by Ivan L. Willis. The first paper describes the makeup and functioning of a local "union of employers associations" in San Francisco, which is similar in many respects to the Swedish Employers Federation, albeit much narrower in scope. The aim of the San Francisco Council, according to Mr. Roth, is to enable the business managers in the area to meet the powerful and well-established unions on their own ground and deal with them effectively. Strong counterorganization for coercive purposes, coöperative financial assistance to besieged member firms, and centralized informational and negotiating services are the principal implementing means used to achieve this aim. Mr. Roth presents evidence to show that the Council is in fact helping the member firms to "hold up their end" against the unions, and that it has already had a considerable stabilizing effect on industrial relations in San Francisco.

The other paper is in essence a repetition of the time-worn employer assertion that trade unionism is inherently incompatible with the "American way of life." Mr. Willis climaxes his argument with the familiar but by now thoroughly discredited contention that collective bargaining is "a system that . . . even the American working man does not want." Most of what is said about Sweden is patently at variance with the factual essentials of that country's industrial-relations scheme, and no useful purpose would be served by reproducing it here. It is typified by the statement that "a Scandinavian industrialist aptly described the situation when he said 'I would not hesitate

SWEDISH AND AMERICAN EMPLOYER POLICIES COMPARED

In the first place, it should be noted that there has always been, and still is, a wide difference in management's attitude toward worker combinations in the two countries. The typical stand of American employers, especially in the manufacturing industries, has been that only in the absence of labor unions could satisfactory relations with employees be maintained, and to this end they have striven unceasingly to keep unions from being formed in their plants or, once started, to stamp them out. Again, there has never been anything resembling a general organization movement among employers in this country. In certain industries, it is true, managerial groups specifically concerned with labor relations have existed for more or less extended periods, and some of these have concluded written contracts with workers' organizations. But by and large the leaders of American industry have been opposed to collective bargaining in all its aspects.

However, it would be a mistake to accuse them of lack of business acumen in taking this position — despite the evidence adduced of benefits accruing to Swedish employers from a virtually opposite policy. For one thing, there has been no urgent need for them to do otherwise. The American labor movement has never represented more than a minor fraction of the country's aggregate wage earner force. This is attributable not only to employer hostility but also to various "internal" obstacles, such as racial heterogeneity and, most of all perhaps, to the absence of strong incentives to organization. Whatever the cause, the fact is that employers in this country, unlike those of Sweden, have not

---

to say that the workman in this country is a trade union slave.'" There is no reason to doubt that a particular employer might have made this statement, despite the fact that none of the nearly fifty Swedish employers and directors of employers' associations whom the writer interviewed expressed even a remotely similar sentiment. However, it is fairly clear from the evidence presented in this study that the Swedish workers who are in fact and by any criterion "trade union slaves" are decidedly in a minority.

been confronted with a widespread and insistent demand for collective bargaining from the worker side.

Moreover, employer-employee relations in this country have, on the whole, been reasonably satisfactory. Without the compulsion of union pressure, the employers have made substantial concessions to labor in the form of shorter hours and extra payment for overtime, through pension plans and profit-sharing devices, and in various other ways. And, as already pointed out, the improvement in wages in the United States has been quite comparable with that achieved by the Swedish workers.

In the past, therefore, anti-unionism has proved to be "sound business" for American managers, and there has been little occasion to abandon or modify it. That it will continue to work as well in the future is, however, extremely doubtful. Indeed, there are strong indications that its course as a practicable business policy is already run. During the last half decade, the union movement in the United States has been waging the most vigorous offensive campaign in its history. As a result, the major manufacturing industries, most of which had been entirely nonunion, are today at least partially and in many cases predominantly organized.

This increase in unionization, unlike earlier ones of comparable magnitude, is not due primarily to a heavy demand for labor. On the contrary, it has occurred during a period of severe unemployment. The principal stimuli behind the current upswing are to be found rather in the Wagner Act and other recent pro-labor measures, reflecting a consensus of popular sentiment strongly favorable to trade unionism. It is unlikely, therefore, that the recent gain in union strength will be followed by an early and drastic reversal, as has been the case with the "sellers' market" upsurges of the past. And a return of prosperity levels in economic activity and employment might very well bring a substantial further increase.

Apart from this essentially short-run movement, which may or may not be of lasting significance, there is good ground for believing that in the course of the next decade or two we shall witness the rise of a large and powerful labor movement in the United States. For the secular trend of sentiment among American wage earners is unmistakably in the direction favorable to organization. Immigration into this country has now been practically at a standstill for a full quarter century. As a result, the segment of the worker population which has been most difficult to organize is now rapidly being replaced by a generation fostered entirely on native soil. The members of this generation are essentially American rather than foreign in culture, and hence attach much less importance to differences of nationality than their parents. As the melting-pot process continues, therefore, this factor will gradually lose its potency as a barrier to worker solidarity, and will in time disappear altogether.

Moreover, the younger workers, both of immigrant and native stock, have had the advantage of a better education than those who preceded them at the machines and work-benches. And one need hardly cite Swedish experience to show that the more enlightened workers become, the greater is their desire for a voice in deciding matters pertaining to their own welfare. What is equally important, they become more and more conscious of their potential power in the community, both as workers and as voters. In other words, the desire for self-determination eventually materializes into an effective demand for it.

Finally, the average intelligent wage earner is bound to realize, sooner or later, that in an economy which is no longer expanding rapidly, his opportunities of raising himself above the level of his fellows are extremely limited. As this realization becomes prevalent, more and more workers will turn to organization as a means of bettering their *collective* lot.

The obvious inference from all this is that American employers would be well advised to follow the example of their Swedish confrères and accept unionism and collective bargaining in earnest — not merely for the duration of the New Deal administration, or until the advent of the next major depression, but as a positive long-range policy. However elementary and truistic this conclusion may be, it is nonetheless prerequisite to any valid discussion of the possibilities of applying Swedish bargaining experience and practice in American industry. Continued adherence to traditional anti-unionism could only lead to widespread and prolonged strife, with serious consequences for the efficient conduct of productive enterprise. And, as we have seen, it is likely that it would eventually have to be abandoned anyway.

It is equally clear that adoption of this policy will make it necessary for employers to build strong counterorganizations, specifically designed to uphold their common interests in dealing with the unions over the terms of employment. Only through this means can they be certain of keeping the costs incident to employing labor within limits consistent with continued profitable operations.

IS NATIONAL COLLECTIVE BARGAINING FEASIBLE IN THE UNITED STATES?

However, assuming *bona fide* acceptance of trade unions by management and the establishment of effective employers' associations, it does not necessarily follow that *national* collective bargaining, on the Swedish model, would work satisfactorily in the United States. Indeed, it would be extremely difficult even to discuss the question with reference to our productive economy as a whole. Owing to the wide differences — in size, geographic coverage, character of intraindustrial competition, etc. — existing among industries in this country, it is easily conceivable that a bargaining setup on this basis might function very well in some, and yet be entirely unworkable in others. Moreover, the corresponding industries in the two countries are in many cases so dissimilar in these and other respects that any blanket inferences from Swedish practice to American problems and difficulties would be of highly doubtful validity.

In this connection, it is important to note that collective labor relations on something approaching a national scale do, in fact, already obtain in a few major American industries, notably coal mining and railroad transportation. In the past, national collective bargaining in this country —

especially in coal mining — has had a rather checkered career, and its success or otherwise is largely a matter of debate. But it is worth noting that there has been a marked increase in the geographic coverage of worker and employer organization in recent years, both in the coal and railroad industries, and that, despite the resultant greater range and diversity of interests among the membership on both sides, the scheme of centralized negotiation and contract making has been preserved intact and appears to be working reasonably well.

In the great majority of American industries, however, national collective bargaining is still unknown, and any effort to introduce it in the near future would be bound to encounter serious obstacles. One such difficulty lies in the wide differences in conditions and costs of production which frequently exist between major units or sectors of the same industry. To take a rather extreme example: lumber in the Pacific Northwest is produced from giant virgin timber, in large-scale establishments employing the most modern mechanical equipment; whereas in the southern states the timber is mainly second growth, and is processed for the most part in small unmodernized mills. Wage rates of lumber workers in the South average scarcely more than half the rates paid by West Coast mills; yet the majority of southern lumber concerns make very small profits. Under these circumstances, it is highly doubtful whether the employers — or, for that matter, the workers — in the South and the Northwest could find sufficient common ground to unite in negotiating a collective employment contract covering both sectors of the industry. The limit of possibilities — for the near future, at any rate — would seem to be district-wide or regional bargaining; and so far as the South is concerned, even this is precluded, owing to the almost complete absence of any effective worker organization.

The idea that the individual firm is the "natural" unit in matters pertaining to labor relations, so common among employers of industrial wage earners in this country, constitutes another serious obstacle to the establishment of national collective bargaining. The typical large and medium-sized American manufacturing concern operates under its own personnel-management program, usually based on the principle of "individual bargaining" and covering all aspects of the employer-employee relationship — from wage making to the provision of after-hours recreation. In most cases these programs have been in force for an extended period of years, and have come to be regarded — by the managers and their underlings, if not always by the rank and file of the work-people — as an integral and essential part of the enterprise. The introduction of collective bargaining between a union and the management of the individual concern in such a situation requires a good deal of *procedural* adjustment, owing to the necessity of providing for worker participation in the making of decisions. Ordinarily, however, the transition can be effected without any important change in the structural framework of the scheme.

But with the extension of the scope of bargaining to the entire industry, major revisions in structure would almost certainly be necessary. Piece rate schedules would have to be altered, wage making methods revamped, layoff and dismissal stipulations changed to conform to a standardized pattern. Moreover the individual managing executive, long accustomed to making his own decisions in dealing with his employees — whether as individuals or collectively — would now be obliged to share this function with other managers in the industry, or delegate it to hired representatives. A large majority of industrial executives in this country, it is safe to say, would be opposed to such a drastic departure from the traditional "one big happy family" plan of conducting employer-employee affairs, and hence would regard with disfavor any proposal to introduce industry-wide collective bargaining.

Finally, it should be noted that many of our larger manufacturing industries are dominated by one or a few so-called giant corporations. In addition to being long-standing adherents of the happy family principle, most of these concerns are so large, and have command over such ample financial resources, that they have not yet felt the need of combining with other firms in order to hold their own against the unions.

These observations obviously do not warrant any definite conclusions or predictions with respect to our productive economy as a whole, for there are many industries — especially among those producing small articles for direct consumption — to which they do not apply, or apply only to a minor degree. Nevertheless, they are sufficient to indicate that no important extension of national collective bargaining is likely to occur in the United States in the near future. Those advantages of union-management dealings in Sweden which are mainly attributable to the fact that the contracting entities are centralized and coterminous can therefore probably not be realized in this country, at least for some years to come.

SWEDISH PRACTICE AND AMERICAN LABOR RELATIONS

This should not be interpreted to mean, however, that the institution we have been studying has nothing of value to contribute to the progress of American industrial relations. There are many constructive features of the Swedish setup which are unrelated, or related only incidentally, to the scheme of industry-wide negotiating and contract making, and which, in the present writer's opinion, could profitably be adopted in this country, even though the scope of collective dealings continued to be confined to individual concerns and localities.

In some instances, the initiative in introducing the Swedish practices would lie with management itself. For example, it would unquestionably promote the cause of peaceful labor relations if American employers generally copied the Swedish practice of closing down their plants during strikes. And it would probably conduce to more *efficient* relations if they took a strong stand in favor of the industrial form of worker organization, as against the out-moded and anomalous craft union. The Swedish employers adopted such a policy more than three decades ago, and have had little cause to regret it.

In others cases, the first move would have to come from the worker side. To take a single illustration: many unions in this country refuse to negotiate wage contracts on any other basis than "straight time work." It would be to the interests of all concerned, including the organized workers themselves, if this narrow policy were discarded and the principle of determining, through negotiation with the employers, the "most productive" method of reckoning wages adopted in its place. This would frequently mean acceptance of piecework, since for many types of work this method demonstrably results in a higher average product per unit of time worked, without discernible harm to the individual worker. But, as our survey of Swedish wage making procedure has shown, it is just as feasible for a union to bargain collectively over piece rates, and to protect its membership against unfair treatment or arbitrary reductions, as it is in the case of payment by the hour or day.

Much of the procedure followed in settling employer-employee differences in Sweden could be studied to good advantage by the labor market bargaining parties in this country, with a view to adapting it to their own needs. In most cases, the successful introduction of such procedural innovations would require the simultaneous consent of both parties. The initiative might be taken by either side, or by a disinterested third party. In the sphere of contract making procedure, for example, the practice of calling in the official mediators at the very start, as a means of preventing the negotiations from breaking down, has much to recommend it. This device is seldom used in the United States, but there seems no good reason to believe it would not work as satisfactorily here as it does in Sweden. The same may be said of the unwritten rule, always invoked when a breakdown occurs, whereby the aggressor party refrains from calling a stoppage until the mediators have made a further attempt to bring about a settlement by peaceful means.[2] In this con-

[2] As we have noted, this rule has recently been supplemented by a statutory stipulation to the effect that the stoppage may not be put into effect until seven days after the aggressor's intention has been announced.

nection it is pertinent to mention that the Swedish Mediation Service is much more adequately manned, in proportion to the industrial population which it serves, than are our own federal and state mediation agencies.

Of the many procedural devices for adjusting interim disputes, the Labor Court is perhaps the major focusing point of American interest. The great bulk of day-to-day differences, it is true, concern the application of agreement subject matter to particular situations and incidents in the individual workplace, and for these it is probably not necessary to have resort to governmental adjudication. Bargaining experience in a number of American industries — including coal mining, clothing and hosiery — shows that most such disputes can be satisfactorily settled "within the family," through the medium of shop committees, district or industry arbitration boards, "impartial chairmen," and other similar devices.

But for the more serious type of case which arises when one contracting party — whether local or national — accuses the other of overt breach of the agreement, there is plainly a need in this country for a federal judiciary agency, designed and staffed specifically to handle worker-employer disputes and vested with the power to pass final judgment on all cases brought before it. Our regular law courts, and particularly the State courts, have been notoriously inept in handling litigation in this sphere. As a result, both the unions and the employers who deal with them have become increasingly reluctant to submit breach-of-contract grievances to the ordinary judicial process. In fact, one of the chief objections raised against collective bargaining by American industrial managers is that they have no adequate means of obtaining redress when the entity on the worker side violates its agreement obligations.

In setting up a special labor market judiciary in the United States, it would not be feasible or even possible to transplant *in toto* the Swedish scheme which we have described. For one thing, owing to the great size and complexity of the American industrial economy, it would probably be necessary to have a number of courts, allocated region-wise throughout the country, rather than a single, centrally located body as in Sweden.

There are, however, a number of features of Sweden's practice in this field, at least a modified emulation of which would seem to be definitely called for. One may mention, for example, the Swedish court's composition, with its four partisan and three nonpartisan members — all of them experts in particular aspects of labor market problems; the requirement that litigants must have made an attempt to resolve the dispute through their intraindustrial adjustment machinery before it can be brought to the court; the simplified and expeditious procedure; and, not least, the rule limiting the amount of damages assessable to individual workers. In the writer's opinion, the establishment of a system of federal labor courts, with these features included, would go a long way toward overcoming the difficulties which have attended the litigation of breach-of-agreement suits in this country in the past.

These illustrative examples are not intended to suggest that there is any large-scale short cut to equilibrium in employer-employee relations. It is quite obvious, even to the casual observer, that the attainment of a stable and smoothly functioning collective bargaining scheme in this country will require many years of trial and error, and of peaceful adjustment to new ideas and ways of doing things. However, it seems reasonable to believe that with intelligent adaptation of these and other similar Swedish practices to American needs and situations, the evolutionary process can in some measure be expedited.

CHAPTER XVIII

BARGAINING IN SWEDEN COMES OF AGE

DESPITE its having attained a state of relative maturity, bargaining in Sweden has not stagnated into a mere routine of settling and resettling old issues and readjusting old disputes according to a set of fixed rules. On the contrary, the coming of age of "ordinary" bargaining — which may be said to have taken place about 1930 or soon after — marks the beginning of a new and, from one viewpoint, even more significant stage in the evolution of collective employer-employee dealings. In fact, it is the completion of the earlier phase of development which, more than anything else, has made the inauguration of the new phase possible. With the methods of handling the more immediate and pressing questions of wage making and disputes adjustment established on a stable basis and functioning with reasonable smoothness, the leaders on both sides have been able to turn their attention to other and broader aspects of industrial relations. And the events of the past few years indicate that this new approach has already borne fruit.[1]

THE DEPRESSION-RECOVERY COMPROMISE

One of the most interesting of these occurrences centered around the problem of adapting wage rates to the swings of the business cycle. The initiative in this instance was taken by the organized employers, and their action constituted a rather radical modification of accepted business practice.

In past periods of economic depression, business managers, in Sweden as in other countries, have customarily sought and obtained major reductions in wages, this being the most practicable and often the only effective means of bringing

[1] The proposed (and partly fulfilled) reform of the "balloting practice" and the "pretermination negotiations," referred to in Chapter IX, are cases in point.

costs into line with the fall in the prices of their products and thus making profitable production possible. The result of the widespread pursuance of this policy has been that, over the course of a particular downswing, wage rates have usually been reduced at least in proportion to the decline in commodity prices.

In formulating their new wage policy the Swedish employers, while fully cognizant of the importance of preserving a balance between costs and receipts, took the stand that their own current cycle problem called for a departure from the traditional procedure. In the depression of 1921–1922, they had gone the whole way in forcing wages down.[2] But the aftermath of this episode, and particularly the wave of retaliatory strikes during the subsequent years of prosperity, proved both troublesome and costly to the employers, and in the interim preceding the next major slump many of them began to revise their views on the subject. They came to believe that there was more to be gained by *not* making drastic wage reductions in times of depression. They felt that such a policy would make it easier to keep the workers' demands for increases during the ensuing recovery phase within reason, and that the resultant improvement in overall stability would more than offset the loss sustained through inadequate adjustment of wages to prices.

The full tide of the depression first struck Sweden in 1931. In the fall of that year the Employers' Federation drew up and adopted a plan of wage strategy, the main feature of which was that the five major industries whose products competed with foreign-made goods [3] should all seek reductions in wages, but that the amount of the decrease should be kept down to an irreducible minimum. The leaders of the Federation of Trade Unions tacitly accepted this program, and in the agreement conferences which followed — between the national unions and the individual employers' associations — they persuaded the affected constituent organizations to make peaceable settlements. The average cut in wage rates

[2] *Supra*, p. 163.

[3] Sawmills, wood pulp, paper, iron and steel, and machinery.

over all the industries was approximately 5 per cent — only a fraction of the percentage fall in prices.

The organized manufacturers have had no cause to regret their departure from traditional wage policies. In 1933 and 1934 they succeeded in keeping the level of wages unchanged, despite a substantial recovery in prices and in the demand for their products. In 1935 they managed to settle a mild wage movement, without stoppages or disruptions, by restoring to the workers the 5 per cent they had lost three years previously. Largely because of this favorable wage cost situation, the employers were able to exploit the unusual trade opportunities to the fullest extent. In consequence, the post-depression period has been one of the most prosperous in the history of Swedish industry.[4]

In the summer of 1937 the workers decided that the time had arrived to ask for a definitive increase. They felt that they had carried out their part of the depression-recovery bargain, that prosperity was now an established fact, and that they were entitled to a share of its fruits. The parleys which took place during the ensuing fall and winter testify to the progress the Swedes have made in the art of sensible bargaining. Between October and March new contracts were concluded for approximately half the country's industrial wage earners. In each case wages were raised, the average increase amounting to approximately 8 per cent; and if one excepts the much publicized but relatively insignificant hotel and restaurant conflict, all these adjustments were effected entirely through peaceable negotiating and compromise. This despite the uncertainty of the international situation and the rapidly deepening American recession, which might have provided the employers with good grounds for opposing any increase at all.

The success of this first experiment in "business cycle

[4] Some of the details of this episode are contained in *Svenska Arbetsgivareföreningens Styrelse- och Revisionsberättelser* (S. E. F. Yearbooks) and *Landsorganisationens Verksamhetsberättelser* (S. F. T. U. Yearbooks) for the years mentioned. The additional information needed to correlate these facts was obtained from the leaders of the S. E. F. and the S. F. T. U.

bargaining" has had a powerful influence on both the trade unions' and the employers' approach to the question of wage making. Both sides are now definitely committed to the policy of long-range wage bargaining as a means of softening the jars of boom and slump,[5] and it is almost a foregone conclusion that when the next downswing occurs, a definite agreement as to permissible wage cuts and subsequent increases will be concluded between the two top organizations.

THE "SOLIDARISTIC WAGE POLICY"

Another manifestation of the increasing emphasis on broader and longer-range objectives in bargaining is the so-called "solidaristic wage policy," which has come to the fore within the trade unions in recent years. Stated in general terms, the purport of this policy is that the union movement, taken as a whole, is pledged to support the workers in the lowest-paid industries, with a view to decreasing the disparity between their wages and those in the higher-paid branches of economic activity. The unions have, indeed, subscribed to this objective "in principle" for many years, the first formal utterance to that effect being a resolution passed at the S. F. T. U. congress of 1922. But little in the way of concrete action has ever been taken in the matter, up to within the past few years.

In the fall of 1937, however, the heads of the S. F. T. U. came forward with a proposal, specifically designed to effect a more equitable distribution of wages in the forest products industries. The essence of this proposal was that the sawmill and wood pulp workers, in terminating their agreements, should demand only a small increase in their wage level — i.e., less than the current prosperous status of these industries would justify — while the logging workers, whose low wages and miserable standard of living had long been a by-word in Sweden, should ask for a correspondingly larger increase.

[5] On this point the writer has the assurance of Gustaf Söderlund, administrative director of the S. E. F., August Lindberg, chairman of the S. F. T. U., and a number of other prominent men on both sides.

The rationale of the scheme was that neither the logging firms, on the one hand, nor the sawmill and pulp concerns, on the other, would be put at any serious disadvantage — for the former could recoup the "extra increase" in wages by raising the price of logs, while the lumber and pulp producers would be able to pay the higher price because of the relatively small increase in their wage bill.

The representatives of the pulp and sawmill workers were finally prevailed upon to accept this plan and, accordingly, scaled down their demands for higher wages from 15–20 per cent to 10 per cent. The logging workers' proposals specified a 25 per cent increase.

Whether the employers' response to these proposals constituted a tacit acceptance of the new policy or was merely the result of the pressure exerted by the Federation of Trade Unions, the writer has been unable to determine. In any event, the wage increases finally obtained by the loggers averaged well above 20 per cent, as against approximately 8 per cent for the pulp and sawmill workers. This first definitive attempt to apply the solidaristic wage policy may, therefore, be said to have worked out reasonably well.[6] At the present writing, plans are being formulated to extend the idea to other groups of allied industries.

It should be noted that in the effectuation of the "broad-view philosophy" in bargaining, as exemplified by the two episodes just described, the leadership on the worker side has been taken by the central organization rather than by the individual national unions. In fact, the new approach is largely the work of a small group of key men at the head of the Federation of Trade Unions. It is these men who have formulated the new union policies and who, through the exercise of personal influence, have "sold" them to the officials and the rank and file of the constituent bodies.[7]

[6] The facts concerning this episode were obtained from Chairman Lindberg of the S. F. T. U., and from Albin Lind, editor of *Fackföreningsrörelsen* (official journal of the S. F. T. U.). Cf. A. Lind, *Solidarisk Lönepolitik* (Stockholm, 1938), pp. 17–26, and *Fackföreningsrörelsen* for April 1, 1938, p. 298.

[7] It should be pointed out in this connection that most of the S. F. T. U.

Whether this *de facto* assumption of responsibility by the S. F. T. U. leaders marks the beginning of a definite trend toward greater centralization of the policy making and decision making power, it is still too early to ascertain. But if, as seems likely, collective bargaining in the future is to be concerned more and more with problems involving the whole of the country's industry, or large segments thereof, some shift in this direction is probably inevitable.

BARGAINING FOR WHITE COLLAR WORKERS

Still another recent innovation in the sphere of industrial relations is the advent of a definitive "bargaining movement" among nonwage earner employees. This does not represent any essential broadening of the scope of bargaining, so far as subject matter is concerned. It does, however, extend its potential coverage over a considerably larger segment of the population; hence some account of it must be included in our survey.

Organizations of particular groups of salaried workers — such as the Ships Officers' Association and the Bank Workers' Union — have existed for many years in Sweden. But it is only within the past decade, and particularly since the passage in 1936 of a "Law Concerning the Right to Organize and Bargain" (see below) that such organization has become in any sense general, and has attained a numerical strength at all comparable to that of the trade unions proper.

There are a number of reasons why the salaried workers should begin to combine so much later than the wage earners. In the average workplace in Sweden — as elsewhere — the divergences in position and occupation among foremen, technicians, and office workers (who comprise the bulk of the "white collar" movement) are comparatively wide. Consequently they have less of a "natural group" basis to build

leaders are either present or former national union officials. For example, Chairman Lindberg, and Vice-Chairman Andersson, who have done most of the effective work in promoting the broad-view approach, are ex-presidents, respectively, of the Sawmill Workers and the Metal Workers — two of the most progressive of the national unions.

on, and fewer interests in common, than the rank and file of manual workers. Moreover, they have considerably better opportunities for personal contact with management, and hence are likely to set a higher value on their chances of getting ahead as individuals. Finally, the Swedish employers, despite their ungrudging willingness to bargain collectively with wage earner groups, have never looked with favor on a similar arrangement with salaried employees.[8]

Whatever the reasons for the white collar workers' lack of organization, it has unquestionably cost them dearly. From 1913 to 1935, real annual income among "lower-rank" salaried persons increased by only 12 per cent, whereas that of wage earners rose by 45 per cent.[9] And while the difference in organizational strength is probably not the only factor accounting for this wide divergence, it is safe to say that the employers have "taken out of" the former group a good proportion of what they have had to yield to the latter. Nor have they fared much better in the matter of hours. To be sure, the *nominal* work week for salaried employees is somewhat shorter than that of piece and day

[8] See *Statens Offentliga Utredningar, 1935:59* (*Betänkande med Förslag till Lag om Förenings- och Förhandlingsrätt*), pp. 85–102. An investigation conducted by the government commission which issued this report showed that while the right of white collar workers to form organizations was generally recognized, the majority of employers refused to bargain with such organizations. The specific objection — of the Employers' Federation, at any rate — has been, not to "entering into discussion" with unions of salaried employees, but rather to concluding agreements with them concerning the terms of employment. (See, e.g., the statement of Administrative Director Söderlund of the S. E. F., *ibid.*, p. 150.) In view of their positive preference for such agreements with the wage earner organizations, this stand on the part of the employers seems somewhat inconsistent. Several employer association officials told the writer that the collective contract was considered by the employers to be ill adapted to regulating the *anställningsvillkor* of salaried workers; and the reason usually given was that their duties are, in most cases, largely supervisory or directive in nature, and that consequently their relationship to management is essentially individual and personal rather than collective.

[9] P. G. Stensland, *Tjänstemännens Ekonomiska och Sociala Problem* (Stockholm, 1938), p. 28.

workers. But in most workplaces overtime work is required of them as a "natural duty," and extra compensation is seldom made for such work.[10]

Gradually the white collar workers have come to realize the disadvantageousness of their position, and have begun to band together in organizations similar in scope and structure to the wage earners' unions. A number of organizations of this type were formed during the twenties, notably the Office Workers' Union (*Kontoristförbundet*), the Foremen's Union (*Arbetsledareförbundet*), and the Association of Industrial Salaried Personnel (*Industritjänstemannaförbundet*)—composed of white collar factory workers other than foremen. Since then several others have been founded. In 1931 a central organization, the Federation of Salaried Employees' Unions (*De Anställdas Centralorganisation*, or *DACO*) was formed, somewhat along the lines of the S. F. T. U. The aggregate membership of its constituent associations at the present time is approximately 50,000.[11]

The energetic political and publicity activities of this "top organization" of salaried workers, aided by the influence of the trade unions and of the Social-Democratic government itself, were largely responsible for the passage of the above-mentioned Law Concerning the Right to Organize and Bargain. With the enactment of this law, the right of aggregations of employed persons to exist and to bargain with employers concerning the terms of work became for the first time a part of explicit public policy in Sweden. So far as the organized wage earners were concerned, the statutory establishment of this right was, obviously, largely superfluous. To the white collar workers, however, it meant a great deal, since the bulk of employers were still unwilling to deal with them on a collective basis.[12]

[10] *Ibid.*, p. 38.

[11] De Anställdas Centralorganisation, *Vad är DACO?* (Stockholm, 1939), p. 12.

[12] The law was, in fact, written expressly for the benefit of the salaried workers. The stated task of the "commission of experts" which formulated it was "to investigate and work out proposals concerning the problem of legal

Moreover, it has already had a noticeable effect on the status of industrial relations for these workers. Within the past few years, the employers have retreated considerably from their former unyielding position. Most of the associations within the Employers' Federation are now willing to conclude "working condition agreements" with white collar organizations, although relatively few have as yet fully accepted the idea of contractual regulation of salaries. And there is little doubt that the advent of the new legislation has had a good deal to do with this moderation of earlier policy. The Swedish employers — like Swedes in general — are very conscientious about obeying the law, even when it does not wholly coincide with their own interests.

As a result of this change in the employers' attitude, the volume of bargaining between them and the organizations of *anställda* has shown a marked increase. Prior to 1936, only a few "special group" unions, such as the ships officers and the pharmacists, had collective contracts. But during the past two or three years, the Merchandising Employees' Union,[13] the Association of Industrial Salaried Personnel, and other broad-scope organizations have concluded agreements with several hundred individual employers, and even a few covering entire industries.[14] The effects of the legal establishment of the right to bargain are also reflected in a marked improvement in the numerical strength of the white collar unions. Since the law went into effect, the membership of DACO has increased by more than 25 per cent,[15] and from all indications it is still *en haussé*.

---

regulation of the privately employed salaried workers' employment contract and allied questions." It was as a solution to what it considered the most urgent of these "allied questions" that the commission drew up its proposal for a law establishing the right to organize and bargain collectively. See *Statens Offentliga Utredningar, 1935:59*, pp. 3–4.

[13] Not to be confused with the Merchandising *Workers'* Union, a wage earner organization consisting of the lower-paid types of wholesale and retail workers. There has been a considerable amount of controversy between DACO and the S. F. T. U. as to the dividing line between these two classes of workers.

[14] *Vad är DACO?*, pp. 42–57.

[15] *Ibid.*, pp. 12–13.

It is still too early to discern what the final status of bargaining in this sphere will be. The salaried workers' organizations are definitely committed to a program calling for bilateral regulation of both working conditions and terms of payment.[16] But the employers have not yet gone the whole way in acceding to this demand, especially in the matter of collectively determined salary scales. Whether the white collar workers can succeed in making their relations with management as all-encompassing as the wage earners have must be left for the future to reveal.

SECTION 23 AND THE "MASTER AGREEMENT"

One of the principal remaining sore spots in Swedish industrial relations is the lack of agreement over the question of the employer's "right to run his own business," particularly with regard to the discharging, laying off, and rehiring of workers. As has been noted, the organized employers have always insisted on the retention of the Section 23 clause in the national agreements. In fact, so strong is this insistence that any serious and unified attempt by the unions to have it struck out would, in all probability, be answered by a major lockout involving most if not all of the industry associations belonging to the Employers' Federation.

The workers, on their side, are equally strongly opposed to its being interpreted literally, insisting that their organizations share in the exercise of the decision making function; and there are many who advocate a drive to delete the clause entirely, regardless of cost. At all events, a large-scale move in any industry to apply it to the letter — for example, by laying off workers wholesale, without regard

[16] According to DACO's latest official brochure, the objectives of these organizations in the field of bargaining are as follows: "Reasonable salaries for all *anställda* — salaries sufficient for a decent living and the rearing of a family; increased security of tenure and guarantees against unjustified dismissals; a fair termination notice period; adequate sick leave compensation and old age pensions; vacation periods sufficient for proper relaxation and rehabilitation; reasonable working hours, an end to the inordinate amount of overtime work, and fair compensation for such overtime as is unavoidable." *Vad är DACO?*, pp. 39–40.

for seniority of tenure — would almost certainly result in a fight-to-the-finish strike of major, if not indeed "general" proportions.

In short, the situation with respect to "joint job control" may be described as a state of armed truce. It is, nevertheless, a stable situation, in that neither side would dare to provoke the other to the point of declaring a nation-wide stoppage. Each party to the labor bargain is fully aware of the other's solidarity and economic strength, and both appreciate that any such stoppage would of necessity be a long-drawn-out and attenuating affair, with dire consequences not only for the participants but also for the country at large.

To bring our study of Swedish bargaining fully up to date, however, this picture of a "swords' points" state of affairs on the dismissal-layoff question must be redrawn in the light of a very recent episode, the results of which have only been made manifest within the past year or two. In May, 1936, a joint committee — composed of the top officials of the Employers' Federation and the Federation of Trade Unions — was set up, with the object of working out a mutually acceptable formula for bilateral decision making in this still-unsettled sphere of industrial relations.[17] During the ensuing two and a half years, this committee held some ten or eleven lengthy sessions, but made no public disclosure of the purport of its discussions.

Finally, in December, 1938, the committee's work was declared finished. The principal product of its efforts was a written agreement, designated as the *Huvudavtal*, or "Master Agreement" — the first document of this type ever to be concluded between the two top organizations. In form, this

[17] The scope of the committee's work, as announced in the S. F. T. U.'s original proposal for its formation, included "all those problems of the labor market which may eventually be adjusted (through negotiation) between the two central organizations." It is common knowledge, however, that the conferences were concerned chiefly with the questions centering around "Section 23." Cf. S. Hansson, *Den Svenska Fackföreningsrörelsen*, sixth edition, pp. 291–292.

compact is similar to the "adjustment procedure" sections of the machinery trades and other national industrial agreements. Chapter I provides for the setting up of an adjustment board of six members — three from each side, chosen for a period of three years. This board is called the *Arbetsmarknadskommitté* or "Labor Market Committee."

Chapter II deals with the procedure to be gone through in settling disputes for which the board is to act as the "tribunal of last resort." Negotiations must be initiated by the local parties (individual employers and local unions). If no settlement can be reached on the ground, the dispute is next referred to the corresponding national entities (industry association and national union) and thence — if the dispute still remains unsettled — to the board. Time limits are prescribed, both with respect to the "age" of a question which may be brought up for adjustment, and the period which may be consumed by each of the several instances in handling it.

The subject matter to be handled according to this procedure — defined in Chapter III — is limited to questions concerning dismissals and layoffs. Dismissals of temporary workers and those "occasioned by comportment which gives the employer the right to terminate the individual work contract immediately" are excepted, as are layoffs of less than three weeks' (stipulated) duration and those occurring in "inherently seasonal" occupations. But of this section, more hereafter.

Chapter IV stipulates that each party to the agreement shall endeavor to prevent its constituent organizations and individual members from undertaking certain types of coercive measures, principally such as "are intended to inflict religious or political persecution" or are directed against "neutral third parties." It is worth noting that this chapter contains a provision specifically permitting sympathetic stoppages. Chapter V deals with conflicts involving services "essential to society." In effect it commits the two head organizations, acting through the Labor Market Committee, to use their influence in preventing or bringing an end to such conflicts.

The two last-named chapters, while by no means unimportant, are primarily "declarations of principle" rather than definitive innovations in the sphere of collective bargaining. It is to Chapter III, therefore, that our attention must be chiefly directed. The sections of this chapter which contain the essential "meat" of the Master Agreement are reproduced below.

Section 2

Upon occasion of dismissal or layoff of any worker with tenure of one year or more past, the employer shall, at least one week before notification (to the worker) of such dismissal or layoff, apprise the union's representative in the workplace of the contemplated action. . . . If either the employer or the union representative so desire, negotiations regarding such contemplated action shall be begun without delay. . . .

Section 3

If such dismissal or layoff has already been put into effect, and if the worker side wishes to negotiate concerning the effectuated action . . . the national union's executive board shall be apprised of the situation, and the latter may, if it sees fit, refer the matter to the Labor Market Committee for investigation. This stipulation shall apply even in cases where the employer has the right to terminate the individual work contract immediately.

Section 4

The committee shall . . . endeavor to obtain a true conception of all the circumstances under which the aforesaid action has been taken. In adjudging the situation account shall be taken of the importance to productive efficiency of an appropriate and capable labor force, and also of the workers' interest in security of employment. In conformance with this principle, consideration shall be given to the fact that the enterprise must, of necessity, be manned by suitable and competent workers and also — in cases where the employer has deemed it advisable, owing to slackness in his business, to dismiss or lay off workers *of equal suitability and competence* [18] — to length of service and family

[18] Author's italics.

responsibilities. . . . A decision concurred in by a majority of the committee shall be communicated to the affected national union and industry association, respectively . . . and it falls to these organizations to agree upon and effectuate the measures necessary for its proper execution.

The first of these three provisions is, obviously, a supersession of the Section 23 clause in the national industrial agreements, in so far as dismissals and layoffs are concerned. True, the unions have always participated indirectly — and even, in many cases, through actual negotiation — in deciding termination questions. But never before has such participation been explicitly provided for in a written collective contract. In agreeing to the inclusion of this clause, therefore, the Employers' Federation has plainly modified its stand-pat policy very materially.

But when we turn to Section 4, it becomes apparent that the signing of the Master Agreement by no means represents an out-and-out retreat on the employers' part. For it is clear from this clause that, in the settling of slack-period employment problems by the central adjustment board, individual ability and skill are to have precedence over seniority of service and family obligations. And it is safe to predict that this will also become the pattern for local and "industry" negotiations involving such questions.

The Swedish unions, as already explained, do not — and need not — attach as much importance to observance of the seniority principle as worker organizations in the United States. But they have always held that length of service and family responsibility should be given at least as much consideration as individual capability in performing the job. Consequently it may be said that Chapter III, Section 4 of the Master Agreement represents a distinct counterconcession from the worker side.

It is impossible, at this stage, to tell whether or not the Master Agreement constitutes an important permanent addition to collective bargaining in Sweden. For one thing, before it can become effective for any particular national organization, it must be "re-negotiated" by each of the unions and employers' associations which conclude national agreements with each other, and some of the less tractable of the former have already indicated that they do not intend to "go along."[19] Moreover, at least two or three years of experience will be required to determine whether the local unions will avail themselves of the new "right" to any considerable extent and, if so, whether the outcome of dismissal and layoff actions will be materially different from what it has been in the past.

At the same time, the significance of this new wrinkle in Swedish negotiation machinery and procedure should not be minimized. For it is plain that the ice which has for so many years surrounded the issue of Section 23 has at long last been broken. What is no less noteworthy, the means adopted for resolving this issue shows that it is possible to include within the framework of a single, voluntarily worked-out bargaining arrangement not merely one branch of economic activity but practically the whole of a country's industry.

CENTRALIZED WAGE ADJUSTMENT IN TIME OF CRISIS

A still more recent occurrence illustrates in striking fashion the important potentialities of "inter-federation bargaining." In December, 1939 a joint committee of S. F. T. U. and S. E. F. leaders met in Stockholm and drew up a "directive central wage agreement." The purpose of this agreement is to provide a method and implementing rules for adjusting wage rates to compensate for fluctuations in the cost of living during the crisis occasioned by the outbreak of the present war. Briefly stated, it stipulates that at the end of each quarterly period subsequent to the date of its formal adoption (January 1, 1940) all wage rates specified in currently effective contracts between the several constituent unions and employers' associations shall be adjusted in approximate proportion to the change in the Social Board's cost-of-living index during the period. In order to ease the burden of large

[19] Cf. *Fackföreningsrörelsen*, May 12, 1939, p. 426. The Master Agreement has already been approved by the S. F. T. U. Council.

potential increases in living costs on workpeople in the lower wage brackets, it provides further that the wages of all adult male workers in a given plant or industry (depending on the coverage of the wage contract) shall be changed by the same *integral* amount — and similarly for adult female and under-age workers.

This agreement was unanimously accepted by the S. F. T. U. representative council (which, indeed, took the initiative in proposing the idea) and has since been incorporated in practically all the individual plant and industry contracts. As a result of its acceptance and the subsequent rise in the Social Board's index, some 500,000 Swedish workers received a wage increase of approximately 3.5 per cent in the spring of 1940.[20]

The importance of this arrangement for the preservation of peaceful and orderly labor relations in Sweden during the present critical period can hardly be overemphasized. With the country's economy so highly dependent on foreign trade for its effective functioning, and with that trade largely disrupted by the blockades and counterblockades of the warring great powers, prices in Sweden are almost certain to undergo severe and rapid fluctuations as long as hostilities last, and probably for a considerable period thereafter. Under such circumstances, it is obvious that some provision for fairly frequent revisions in wage rates is necessary, if serious discontent — and, concomitantly, overt protest — on the worker or the employer side is to be avoided.[21]

The fact that the central worker and employer federations

[20] The details of this episode are given in various recent issues of *Fackföreningsrörelsen*, including Nos. 50–52, 1939, and Nos. 1, 2, 4, and 6, 1940.

[21] It will be recalled that similar devices for correcting wages in accordance with commodity price changes were used to some extent during the war of 1914–1918 (*supra*, pp. 125–126). However, these measures were not introduced until after the price level had been rising precipitously for some time and, even then, not until the violent protest from the worker side had practically forced the employers to make compensatory adjustment. There is little doubt that the principal aim of the S. F. T. U.–S. E. F. joint committee, in drawing up the "directive wage contract," was to prevent the occurrence of another such episode.

have been able to devise a "blanket" scheme for meeting this situation, and to secure for it the voluntary acceptance of all the constituent groups included within its purview, indicates that collective bargaining on an all-industry basis is no longer a mere experiment in Sweden but a usable and useful device for constructive policy and action in the field of labor relations.

Collective bargaining in Sweden has not yet attained a stage of development where all differences between employers and employees are adjustable through peaceful parleying and compromise. But it is apparent that the organized workers and managers are aware of the major obstacles barring the way to this goal, and are actively and coöperatively seeking the means of overcoming them. If these efforts could continue, without external interference, it is not inconceivable that Sweden might some day be entirely free from strikes and lockouts.

The catastrophic happenings in Europe during the past year, however, have rendered it impossible to make even a tentative prediction concerning the future of the Swedish bargaining system. At the present writing, the Swedes find themselves virtually hemmed in by a belligerent Germany, bent on national expansion through military conquest. While they have so far managed to preserve their political independence, there is no knowing how long they can continue to do so. If Germany should be victorious, it is not improbable that Sweden would be forced to accept political and economic domination, or even direct control, by the Nazi totalitarian regime. And if experience in Germany itself and in the other countries which the Nazis have "taken over" is any indication, this would very likely be followed by the liquidation of all worker organizations and the introduction of wage making by dictatorial decree.

However, such an eventuation might also bring an end to strikes and lockouts, for it would probably be accompanied by absolute prohibition of such measures. This state of affairs could not be brought about overnight, for the Swedish bargainers have been too long accustomed to "fighting it out among themselves" to submit readily to settlement by governmental edict. Yet considering the methods which dictators have at hand for overcoming such difficulties, it could undoubtedly be achieved in time.

Whether this route to industrial peace is in any sense a more desirable — or less desirable — one than that of collective bargaining within the framework of capitalistic democracy cannot, of course, be determined on any objective grounds. It is wholly a matter of one's own individual philosophy. The writer can only express it as his personal conviction that the method of voluntary dealings between free men is more likely to survive over the long pull.

BIBLIOGRAPHY

BIBLIOGRAPHY

BOOKS AND PAMPHLETS

BAGGE, GÖSTA, AND OTHERS, *Wages in Sweden, 1860–1930*, Stockholm, 1935.

CHILDS, MARQUIS W., *This Is Democracy: Collective Bargaining in Scandinavia*, New Haven, 1938.

COLE, MARGARET, AND SMITH, CHARLES (editors), *Democratic Sweden*, New York, 1939.

HALLENDORFF, CARL, *Svenska Arbetsgifvareföreningen, 1902–1927*, Stockholm, 1927.[1]

HANSSON, SIGFRID, *Den Svenska Fackföreningsrörelsen*, Stockholm, 1937 (fifth edition), and 1938 (sixth edition).

—— *Minnesskrift: Landsorganisationens Första Kvartsekel, 1898–1923*, Stockholm, 1923.[2]

—— *Svenskt Fackföreningsliv under Fem Decennier*, Stockholm, 1934.

—— *Svenska Träarbetareförbundets Historia*, Stockholm, 1925.[2]

KOOPERATIVA FÖRBUNDETS BOKFÖRLAG, *Nutida Svenskt Arbetsliv*, Stockholm, 1932.

LANDSORGANISATIONEN, *Fackföreningsrörelsen i Sverge, Norge, Danmark, Tyskland, England och Frankrike*, Stockholm, 1912.

LIND, ALBIN, *Solidarisk Lönepolitik*, Stockholm, 1938.

LINDAHL, ERIK, AND OTHERS, *National Income of Sweden, 1861–1930*, Stockholm, 1937.

LINDBOM, TAGE, *Den Svenska Fackföreningsrörelsens Uppkomst*, Stockholm, 1938.

—— *Tobaksarbetarnas Stockholmsavdelning*, Stockholm, 1934.[2]

LINDGREN, JOHN, *Det Socialdemokratiska Arbetarpartiets Uppkomst, 1881–1889*, Stockholm, 1927.

—— *Från Per Götrek till Per Albin*, Stockholm, 1937.

—— *Svenska Metallindustriarbetareförbundets Historia, 1888–1905*, Stockholm, 1938.[2]

[1] Employer association histories.

[2] Trade union histories.

MAGNUSSON, GERHARD, *Socialdemokratin i Sverige*, Stockholm, 1920.

MOLIN, A., *Svensk Arbetslagstiftning* (second edition), Stockholm, 1934.

MONTGOMERY, ARTHUR, *Industrialismens Genombrott i Sverige*, Stockholm, 1931.

NATIONAL INDUSTRIAL CONFERENCE BOARD, *Systems of Wage Payment*, New York, 1930.

OLIN, G., *Kollektivavtal i den Utländska Lagstiftningen*, Stockholm, 1911.

SCHMIDT, CARL CHRISTIAN, *1936 Års Lagstiftning om Förenings- och Förhandlingsrätt*, Stockholm, 1937.

SPÅNGBERG, VALPRED, *Från Arvid Posse till Per Albin Hansson*, Stockholm, 1936.

STYRMAN, GEORG, *Verkstadsföreningen*, Stockholm, 1937.[1]

SUNDHOLM, HERMAN, *Järnbruksförbundet*, Stockholm, 1931.[1]

SVERIGES INDUSTRIFÖRBUND, *Sveriges Industri*, Stockholm, 1936.

UNDÉN, ÖSTEN, *Från Arbetsdomstolens Praxis*, Uppsala, 1932.

VON SYDOW, HJALMAR, *Om den Svenska Arbetsgivareorganisationen, dess Verksamhet och Betydelse*, Stockholm, 1932.

WISTRAND, LODE, *Kollektivavtalslagen och Arbetsdomstolen*, Stockholm, 1936.

ARTICLES IN PERIODICALS

BOWER, ROY E. B., "Industrial Relations in Sweden," *Monthly Labor Review*, July 1937.

EKBLOM, OLLE, "Verordnungen zur Beilegung von Arbeitsstreitigkeiten in den Nordischen Ländern," *Schriften des Vereins für Sozialpolitik*, 1930, pp. 129–130.

ERICHSEN, EINAR, "Scandinavian Employers and Collective Agreements," *International Labor Review*, vol. 26 (1932).

INTERNATIONAL LABOR OFFICE, "Sandvik Steel Works," *I.L.O. Studies and Reports, Series A, No. 35* (1932).

OHLIN, BERTIL (editor), "Social Problems and Policies in Sweden," *The Annals of the American Academy of Political and Social Sciences*, May 1938.

[1] Employer association histories.

GOVERNMENT PUBLICATIONS [1]

Arbetsdomstolen, *Arbetsdomstolens Domar* (annual volumes, 1929–1936, inclusive).

—— *Sakregister till Arbetsdomstolens Domar*, 1929–1934 (one volume), 1935, 1936, 1937.

Kungliga Kommerskollegium, *Arbetsstatistik A:5* (*Kollektivavtal*), 1910.

—— *Arbetsstatistik E:1* (*Arbetsinställelser*, 1903–1907).

—— *Arbetsstatistik E:2* (*Arbetsinställelser*, 1908).

—— *Arbetsstatistik E:3* (*Arbetsinställelser*, 1909).

—— *Arbetsstatistik E:4* (*Arbetsinställelser*, 1910).

—— *Arbetsstatistik F:1* (*Kollektivavtal*, etc., 1908).

—— *Arbetsstatistik F:2* (*Kollektivavtal*, etc., 1909).

—— *Arbetsstatistik F:3* (*Kollektivavtal*, etc., 1910).

Kungliga Socialdepartmentet, *Arbetskonferensen i Stockholm* (1929).

Kungliga Socialstyrelsen, *Arbetsinställelser i Sverige* (annual statistical reports), 1911–1922, inclusive.

—— *Kollektivavtal i Sverige*, 1911–1922, inclusive.

—— *Statens Förlikningsmäns Verksamhet*, 1907–1922, inclusive.

—— *Arbetsinställelser och Kollektivavtal samt Förlikningsmännens Verksamhet*, 1923–1937, inclusive.

—— *Kollektivavtal i Sverige vid Årsskiftet 1920/21.*

—— *Lönestatistik Årsbok för Sverige*, 1936.

—— *Social Work and Legislation in Sweden*, 1938.

—— *Underdånigt Utlåtande med Förslag till Lag om Vissa Åtgärder till Främjande av Arbetsfred*, 1916.

Statens Offentliga Utredningar, 1923:29 (*Den Industriella Demokratins Problem*).

—— 1927:4 (*Utredningar till Belysande av Arbetsfredsfrågan*).

—— 1935:18 (*Betänkande med Förslag till Lag om Arbetsavtal*).

—— 1935:59 (*Betänkande med Förslag till Lag om Förenings- och Förhandlingsrätt*).

—— 1935:65 (*Betänkande om Folkförsörjning och Arbetsfred. Del I. Förslag*).

[1] Includes legislative documents, annual statistical publications of administrative bureaus, reports of special investigating commissions, etc.

—— 1935:66 (*Betänkande om Folkförsörjning och Arbetsfred. Del II. Specialutredningar*).

—— 1938:10 (*Byggnadsindustrin i Sverige*) Del I.

STATISTISKA CENTRALBYRÅN, *Statistisk Årsbok*, 1935, 1937.

Förliknings- och Skjiljenämndskomiténs Betänkande (1901).

Statens Järnvägars Författningssamling. Särtryck nr. 28 (1937).

Utkast till Lag om Kollektivavtal jämte Kortfattad Motivering (1927).

UNITED STATES DEPARTMENT OF LABOR, *Report of the Commission on Industrial Relations in Sweden*, U. S. Government Printing Office, Washington, 1938.

TRADE UNION PUBLICATIONS

LANDSORGANISATIONEN, *Beslut i Frågor Rörande Organisationsgränserna* (1936).

—— *Fackföreningsrörelsen* (weekly journal).

—— *Beslut i Industriförbundsfrågan* (1936).

—— *Protokoll vid Landsorganisationens Representantskapsmöte den 22 Mars, 1901.*

—— *Protokoll Förda vid Landsorganisationens Elfte Ordinarie Kongress* (1936).

—— *Sifferuppgifter och Grafiska Framställningar, 1888–1912.*

—— *Sifferuppgifter och Grafiska Framställningar, 1913–1930.*

—— *Utredning Angående Industriarbetareförbund* (1925).

—— *Landsorganisationens Verksamhetsberättelse*, for years 1918–1937, inclusive.

SVENSKA GROV- OCH FABRIKSARBETAREFÖRBUNDET, *Förbundskamraten* (quarterly journal).

SVENSKA METALLINDUSTRIARBETAREFÖRBUNDET, *Verksamhetsberättlese*, for years 1936 and 1937.

—— *Metall, 1888–1938* (1938).

EMPLOYER ASSOCIATION PUBLICATIONS

SVENSKA ARBETSGIVAREFÖRENINGEN, *Industria* (semi-monthly journal).

—— *Svenska Arbetsgivareföreningens Kalender*, for years 1936 and 1938.

—— *Styrelse- och Revisionsberättelse*, for years 1907–1937, inclusive.

COLLECTIVE AGREEMENTS

(This list includes only national and major regional agreements. Printed copies are obtainable from the headquarters of the signatory organizations, which are located in Stockholm except where otherwise noted.)

COLLECTIVE AGREEMENTS

Industry or Occupation	Signatory Organizations: Union	Signatory Organizations: Employers' Association
Agriculture	Svenska Lantarbetareförbundet	Svenska Lantarbetsgivarnes Centralförening
Automobile Repair Garages	Svenska Metallindustriarbetareförbundet	Bilverkstädernas Arbetsgivareförbund
Bakeries	Svenska Livsmedelsarbetareförbundet	Sveriges Bageriidkareförening
Bookbinding	Svenska Bokbindareförbundet	Sveriges Bokbinderi-idkares Arbetsgivareförbund
Building Construction	Svenska Murareförbundet Svenska Byggnadsträarbetareförbundet Svenska Grov- och Fabriksarbetareförbundet	Svenska Byggnadsindustriförbundet
Clothing (Ready-made)	Svenska Beklädnadsarbetareförbundet	Svenska Konfektionsindustriförbund
Confectionery	Svenska Livsmedelsarbetareförbundet	Sveriges Chockladindustriförbund
Construction Materials	Svenska Grov- och Fabriksarbetareförbundet	Byggnadsämnesförbundet
Custom Tailoring	Svenska Beklädnadsarbetareförbundet	Sveriges Skrädderiarbetsgivares Centralförening
Electrical Installation	Svenska Elektriska Arbetareförbundet	Elektriska Arbetsgivareföreningen
Flour Milling	Svenska Livsmedelsarbetareförbundet	Sveriges Kvarnyrkesförbund
Glassware — bottles	Svenska Grov- och Fabriksarbetareförbundet	Sveriges Buteljglasbruksförbund
Glassware — general	Svenska Grov- och Fabriksarbetareförbundet	Sveriges Småglasbruksförbund

Hotels and Restaurants	Sveriges Hotell- och Restaurangspersonalsförbund	Sveriges Arbetsgivareförening för Hotell och Restauranter Restauranternas Arbetsgivareförening
Iron and Steel	Svenska Metallindustriarbetareförbundet	Järnbruksförbundet
Iron Mining (mines owned by iron and steel producers)	Svenska Gruvindustriarbetareförbundet (Grängesberg)	Järnbruksförbundet
Iron Mining (middle Sweden — independent mines)	Svenska Gruvindustriarbetareförbundet	Mellansvenska Gruvförbundet
Iron Mining (northern Sweden)	Svenska Gruvindustriarbetareförbundet	Grängesbergskoncernens Gruvförbund
Leather Production (Tanning)	De Förenade Förbunden	Svenska Garveriidkareföreningen
Lithographing and Engraving	Svenska Litografförbundet	Svenska Litografiska Tryckeriägares Förbund
Logging	Svenska Skogs- och Flottningsarbetareförbundet (Gävle) Riksförbundet Landsbygdens Folk	Föreningen Skogsarbeten
Machinery	Svenska Metallindustriarbetareförbundet Svenska Gjutareförbundet	Sveriges Verkstadsförening
Municipal Works	Svenska Kommunalarbetareförbundet	Svenska Städernas Förhandlingsorganisation
Painting	Svenska Målareförbundet	Målarmästarnas Riksförbund
Paper Manufacturing	Svenska Pappersindustriarbetareförbundet	Sveriges Pappersbruksförbund
Pipe Fitting	Svenska Metallindustriarbetareförbundet	Rörledningsfirmornas Riksförbund
Printing — general	Svenska Typografförbundet	Sveriges Tryckeriers Arbetsgivareförbund
Printing — newspapers	Svenska Typografförbundet	Tidningarnas Arbetsgivareförening
Printing — Social-Democratic newspapers	Svenska Typografförbundet	Aktiebolaget Samorganisationen
Railways — privately owned	Svenska Järnvägsmannaförbundet Sveriges Lokomotivmannaförbund	Svenska Järnvägarnas Arbetsgivareförening

Collective Agreements (*Continued*)

Industry or Occupation	Signatory Organizations	
	Union	Employers' Association
Railways — state owned	Svenska Järnvägsmannaförbundet Sveriges Lokomotivmannaförbund	Kungliga Järnvägsstyrelsen
Road and Watercourse Construction	Svenska Väg- och Vattenbyggnadsarbetareförbundet	Kungliga Väg- och Vattenbyggnadsstyrelsen
Sawmills	Svenska Sågverksindustriarbetareförbundet	Sågverksförbundet
Sheet Metal Work	Svenska Bleck- och Plåtslagareförbundet	Sveriges Bleck- och Plåtslagaremästareförbund
Shoe Manufacturing	Svenska Sko- och Läderindustriarbetareförbundet	Svenska Skofabrikantföreningen
Slaughtering and Meat Packing	Svenska Livsmedelsarbetareförbundet	Almänna Arbetsgivareföreningen
Telegraph and Telephone	Telegraf- och Telefonmannaförbundet	Kungliga Telegrafverket
Textiles	Svenska Textilarbetareförbundet (Norrköping)	Sveriges Textilindustriförbund
Textiles (Loomfixers)	Svenska Vävlagareförbundet (Borås)	Sveriges Textilindustriförbund
Tobacco Products	Svenska Tobaksindustriarbetareförbundet	A.B. Tobaksmonopolet
Water Transportation (ocean)	Svenska Sjöfolksförbundet	Sveriges Redareförening
Wood Products (furniture, joinery, etc.)	Svenska Träindustriarbetareförbundet	Sveriges Träindustriförbund
Wood Pulp	Svenska Pappersindustriarbetareförbundet	Pappersmasseförbundet

INDEX

INDEX

Bei Fragen zur Produktsicherheit wenden Sie sich bitte an:
If you have any questions regarding product safety,
please contact:

Walter de Gruyter GmbH
Genthiner Straße 13
10785 Berlin
productsafety@degruyterbrill.com